WRITINGS ON INDIAN ANTHROPOLOGY AND ANTHROPOLOGISTS

About the Editors

Subir Biswas is the founder Head of the Department of Anthropology, West Bengal State University. He was also one of the founder faculty of the Department of Anthropology, North Bengal University. He has to his credit several research projects of UGC, ICSSR, CWS (NBU), UGC-IUC Associateship at IIAS, Shimla; and successfully guided 9 doctoral and 2 post-doctoral scholars. He has published ten edited books as well as several research articles. At present, he is the General Secretary of the Indian Anthropological Society.

Barun Mukhopadhyay currently is a retired Professor who was attached to the Biological Anthropology Unit, Indian Statistical Institute, Kolkata till October 2019. He remained engaged in research on demographic aspects and socio-cultural determinants of health and health care of the tribal populations of Sikkim-Darjeeling Himalaya since 1980s. His other major areas of research interest are: biocultural dimensions of ageing, ethno-biology, as well as bioethics and research ethics. He conducted several research projects on abovementioned topics and has many publications in international and national journals including edited volumes. Currently, he is serving as the Research Director of The Indian Anthropological Society.

Rajat Kanti Das, formerly Professor and U.G.C. Emeritus Fellow in the Department of Anthropology, Vidyasagar University, West Bengal, has a long experience of teaching and research in different capacities. He has a number of publications in the form of books, research papers and articles on various topics of anthropological significance. At present, he is the President of the Indian Anthropological Society and is the editor of the '*Journal of the Indian Anthropological Society*'.

WRITINGS ON INDIAN ANTHROPOLOGY AND ANTHROPOLOGISTS

Edited by

Subir Biswas
Barun Mukhopadhyay
Rajat Kanti Das

Celebrating 100 years of Teaching Anthropology in India
by
The Indian Anthropological Society
Kolkata

CONCEPT PUBLISHING COMPANY PVT. LTD.
NEW DELHI - 110 059

ISBN: 978-93-5594-517-4

First Published 2023

Published and Printed by

Concept
Since 1974

Concept Publishing Company Pvt. Ltd.
A/15-16, Commercial Block, Mohan Garden
New Delhi-110059 (India)
T : +91-11-41101460
E: publishing@conceptpub.com, W: www.conceptpub.com

Cataloging in Publication—Courtesy: D.K. Agencies (P) Ltd. <docinfo@dkagencies.com>

Writings on Indian anthropology and anthropologists / edited by Subir Biswas, Barun Mukhopadhyay, Rajat Kanti Das.
pages cm

"Celebrating 100 years of teaching anthropology in India by the Indian Anthropological Society, Kolkata."
Includes bibliographical references and index.
ISBN 9789355945174

1. Ethnology--India--History. 2. Anthropology--India--History. 3. Anthropologists--India. I. Biswas, Subir, 1974- editor. II. Mukhopadhyay, Barun, editor. III. Das, Rajat Kanti, 1942- editor. IV. Indian Anthropological Society.

LCC GN635.I4W75 2023 | DDC 305.800954 23

Preface

For the purpose of celebrating 100 years of teaching anthropology in India, the Council of the Indian Anthropological Society undertook a programme of organizing a series of Special Lectures in the cherished memory of a selected group of distinguished anthropologists of India who immensely contributed to the growth of Indian anthropology in three of its sub-disciplines over the last 10 decades.

A committee was constituted to take up the responsibility to select the number of distinguished anthropologists representing three major sub-disciplines of anthropology in a broader perspective in whose memory the lectures would be organized and also to select the corresponding speakers of such Special Lectures included in the series. The other aspect of committee's responsibility was to search for institutions who would serve as the collaborating partners of the Indian Anthropological Society in jointly organizing this prestigious Lecture Series. The Indian Anthropological Society emphasized on this kind of collaboration very dearly in order to be able to recognize the potentials and abilities of these institutions nurturing anthropology in terms of teaching and research since their inception.

It became a difficult task for the committee to choose the distinguished anthropologists in whose memory the lectures were going to be organized as well as to find the most suitable persons to deliver the lectures. A lot of deliberations were made and ultimately the committee decided that it would select those distinguished anthropologists of India who immensely contributed to teaching and research in anthropology and earned a name for themselves as human scientists. Furthermore, the committee considered that the anthropologist thus selected should be one for whom no memorial lecture was organized by the Indian Anthropological Society in the past. And, of course, the number of such lectures should be less than fifteen owing to time and other constraints. The committee decided to choose the group of speakers who either as doctoral students or as close associates or colleagues of the distinguished anthropologists or as independent researchers came in direct contact with them or came under their influence, gathered enough information or knowledge about them and their works thereby attaining a level of proficiency to speak about them. Needless to say, some arbitrariness might have arisen in the process of selection which can be ignored because all those distinguished anthropologists who have found a place in this volume are undoubtedly stalwarts in their respective fields who could make Indian Anthropology rich and vibrant. Finally, the committee decided to give full freedom to the speakers in formulating and organizing the theme or content of their lectures.

Thus, in all 14 special lectures were organized by the Indian Anthropological Society in collaboration with 14 different institutions engaged in either teaching and/or research in Anthropology, 13 of which were in West Bengal and 1 in Sikkim, during the period from August 2019-November 2021. It was due to COVID-19 pandemic that the duration of the Lecture series had to be extended till November 2021, when the lectures were organized virtually.

If we divide the distinguished anthropologists by their generally known sub-disciplinary specializations, we find that there are seven social-cultural anthropologists (S.C. Roy, B.K. Roy Burman, P.K. Bhowmik, L.P. Vidyarthi, B.N. Saraswati, B.N. Banerjee and G. Sarana); four biological anthropologists (D.P. Mukherjee, P.K. Ganguly, U. Deka and A. Basu) and three archaeological anthropologists (A.K. Ghosh, V.N. Mishra and D.K. Bhattacharya).

The distinguished anthropologists whose life and academic contributions are portrayed in this book, barring one, were all born in the pre-independent India, but they made their contributions in the independent India. So the story of Indian Anthropology is actually a story of Independent India. S.C. Roy, however, was an exception. He could leave behind a tradition of anthropology, which was started by him, to be followed by his successors in the post-independent era. That way, he is no less relevant in the making of contemporary anthropology.

The papers (11 in numbers) in this book written by serious anthropological scholars of today are rich in content and analysis, for which the Indian Anthropological Society remains indebted to them. They have made this programme of the Indian Anthropological Society a meaningful exercise and a purposeful venture pertaining to the celebration of 100 years of teaching anthropology in India aided by our colleagues of collaborating institutions and the publisher of this volume.

It is expected that this rich collection of papers should be of much help to all serious students of anthropology, providing them with enough motivating spirit to work towards the advancement of anthropology.

Subir Biswas
Barun Mukhopadhyay
Rajat Kanti Das

Contents

Preface v
List of Contributors ix
Introduction xi

1. Why North East India Holds a Special Place of Importance in Dr. B.K. Roy Burman's Line of Approach to Community Studies with Reference to Tribes? 1
   – *Rajat Kanti Das*

2. Walking with Professor Baidyanath Saraswati on the Road to Indian Civilization 14
   – *Gopal Krishna Chakraborty*

3. Professor Usha Deka: A Humanist to the Core 32
   – *Sarthak Sengupta*

4. Professor Prabodh Kumar Bhowmick: An Action-*cum*-Development Anthropologist of India 39
   – *Tilak Bagchi*

5. Lalita Prasad Vidyarthi: An Anthropologist with a Difference 55
   – *Jayanta Sarkar*

6. Pranab Ganguly: A Rare Kind of Anthropologist 69
   – *Abhijit Guha*

7. The Master Theoretician: Gopala Sarana and His Contributions to Anthropology 83
   – *Sumahan Bandyopadhyay*

8. Professor Deba Prasad Mukherjee and the Essence of Bio-cultural Approach in Anthropology in India 98
   – *Bidhan Kanti Das*

9. Remembering Sri Biswanath Banerjee and His Teaching of Anthropology: A Tribute 121
– *Sekh Rahim Mondal*

10. In the Memory of Professor Dibyendu Kanti Bhattacharya 135
– *Avick Biswas* and *Rupendra Kumar Chattopadhyay*

11. Professor Amitabha Basu, Indian Statistical Institute and Our Research 148
– *Susmita Mukhopadhyay*

Index 161

List of Contributors

Abhijit Guha, Former Senior Fellow, Indian Council of Social Science Research at the Institute of Development Studies Kolkata and former Professor, Department of Anthropology, Vidyasagar University, West Bengal, India. **Email:** abhijitguhavuanthro @rediffmail.com

Avick Biswas, Assistant Professor, Department of Anthropology, Vidyasagar University, **Email:** avickbiswas@gmail.com

Bidhan Kanti Das, Faculty of Anthropology, Institute of Development Studies Kolkata, **Email:** bidhand@gmail.com

Gopal Krishna Chakraborty, Former Professor of Anthropology, University of Calcutta, **Email:** g_k_c@rediffmail. com

Jayanta Sarkar, Former Director-in-Charge, Anthropological Survey of India, Government of India, **Email:** jsjayanta0@gmail.com

Rajat Kanti Das, Former Professor & U.G.C. Emeritus Fellow, Department of Anthropology, Vidyasagar University, West Bengal,
Email: rajat_p_das@yahoo.com

Rupendra Kumar Chattopadhyay, Former Vivekananda Chair Professor of Social Science, University of Calcutta, and Former Paresh Chandra Chatterjee Professor of History, Department of History, Presidency University, Kolkata, **Email:** rupendrachattopadhyay@gmail.com

Sarthak Sengupta, Former Professor of Anthropology, Dibrugarh University, Assam, **Email:** sarthak_sengupta @yahoo.co.in

Sekh Rahim Mondal, Former C.C. Sanyal Chair Professor of Anthropology and Sociology and Director, Centre for Himalayan Studies & Former Professor and Founder Head, Department of Anthropology, University of North Bengal, Dt. Darjeeling, West Bengal, **Email:** rahimanthnbu @yahoo.co.in

Sumahan Bandyopadhyay, Professor, Department of Anthropology, Vidyasagar University, **Email:** sumahan.b @rediffmail.com

Susmita Mukhopadhyay, Professor, Biological Anthropology Unit, Indian Statistical Institute, Kolkata, **Email:** susmi.mukho@gmail.com

Tilak Bagchi, Formerly of Anthropological Survey of India, Western Regional Centre, Udaipur; **Email:** tilak_bagchi @yahoo.com

Introduction

Formal anthropological education in India at the post-graduate level, though began in 1918, was first included in the curriculum of Ancient History and Culture of the University of Calcutta. A separate M.A./ M.Sc. course in Anthropology was introduced only in 2020. With the establishment of the post-graduate department of Anthropology of the University of Calcutta in 1921, the circle turned full. Since then, Indian Anthropology has not quite looked back, albeit temporary dislocations and dampening effects, and has grown enormously in terms of number of Institutions offering post-graduate and/or under-graduate courses in anthropology as well as providing greater opportunities for conducting anthropological research. Beginning from the colonial to the present times, the eclectic science of anthropology in India has reasonably maintained its steady progress throughout this country in spite of some inherent problems of definition and new found meanings of contemporary existence. At almost the same time, anthropology was introduced as an academic discipline, a need was felt for professional bodies to infuse a sense of professional approach. Probably, as a result of this realization, the first professional body of anthropologists of this country was formed in the name of Anthropological Club in 1921 and later on it was revived as a registered body, namely, 'The Indian Anthropological Society' in 1958 with the moral, academic and organizational inputs of a band of dedicated and resourceful anthropologists. Since the initial years of its emergence till today, Indian anthropology has been fortunate to have quite a large number of teachers and students within its fold who showed their worth in making Indian anthropology a very viable name in the global and the national scene. And thus in 2020, it could complete hundred glorious years to reach the centenary year of teaching anthropology in India. Needless to say, there is enough reason for celebration of this occasion which has tremendous historical significance and sentimental values for the professional anthropologists in India.

The present Council of the Indian Anthropological Society, like many other Institutions of the country, decided to celebrate the occasion by paying homage to a number of Indian anthropologists, who as teacher-researchers could put an indelible mark in the field of anthropology and whose significant contributions could motivate young scholars to grow and earn a name for themselves in the world of anthropology. It was decided to organize special lectures in memory of those personalities in collaboration with some Institutions of learning and research. In order to disseminate the rich historical information generated through these lectures delivered by experienced and senior scholars, the necessity of publishing them in a volume was simultaneously felt and fortunately it could materialize. The present volume is the outcome of that effort.

A synoptic note of the proceedings of the academic programmes undertaken by the Society that had culminated into the production of this volume is given below.

The Special Lecture Series began on 22 August, 2019 with a lecture in memory of Professor Bikram Kesari Roy Burman titled "Why North East India Holds a Special Place of Importance in Dr. B.K. Roy Burman's Line of Thinking about Community Studies with Reference to Tribes?" delivered by Professor Rajat Kanti Das at the Cultural Research Institute, Government of West Bengal, Kolkata. Professor Roy Burman, a prominent social anthropologist of India, commands a thorough knowledge both in theoretical and applied aspects of anthropology. One of his major concerns was to highlight the role of anthropology in social and developmental policy formulation for the tribal and local communities and in this endeavour North East India proved to be a happy haunting ground for him. Professor Das, who has enough knowledge and academic experience about India's North East, in his lecture very competently analysed the contributions of Professor Roy Burman in the light of tribes and other communities of North East India raising several development issues of considerable significance.

On 26 September, 2019, a lecture in memory of Professor Baidyanath Saraswati titled "Walking with Prof. Baidyanath Saraswati on the Road to Indian Civilization" was delivered by Professor Gopal Krishna Chakraborty, which was hosted by the Department of Anthropology, West Bengal State University. Professor Baidyanath Saraswati's contribution in social anthropology is well-known and his approach towards the study of Indian civilization is respectfully recognized. Professor Chakraborty, himself a social anthropologist of repute and a serious researcher on the study of Indian civilization, very skilfully and critically portrayed several dimensions pertaining to Professor Saraswati's study of Indian civilization.

On 5 November, 2019, a lecture in memory of Professor Usha Deka titled "Prof. Usha Deka: A Humanist to the Core" was delivered by Professor Sarthak Sengupta at Mrinalini Datta Mahavidyapith, Birati, Kolkata. Professor Usha Deka is recognized as one of the very reputed women anthropologists of India whose contribution in bio-anthropological studies of Eastern Indian tribal and local communities has widely been acknowledged. Professor Sengupta, a senior biological anthropologist of North East India and a close associate of Professor Deka, presented a very lucid picture of the life and works of Professor Deka.

On 29 November, 2019, a lecture in memory of Professor Prabodh Kumar Bhowmik titled "Professor Prabodh Kumar Bhowmik: An Action cum Development Anthropologist of India" was delivered by Dr. Tilak Bagchi, the collaborating Institution being Prabhat Kumar College, Contai, Purba Medinipur. Professor Prabodh Kumar Bhowmik contributed significantly in several fields of social anthropological research, but his particular interest was in pursuing action anthropology for deriving practical benefits to the marginalised groups. In this respect, his Lodha experiment is worth following. He was a popular teacher and an institution builder. Dr. Bagchi, a student of Professor Bhowmik and one who has contributed much in the field of social anthropology, elaborately discussed Professor Bhowmik's contributions in anthropology, both at the theoretical and applied level.

On 5 December, 2019, a lecture in memory of Professor Virendra Nath Mishra titled "Situating Professor V. N. Mishra in Indian Archaeology: A Historiographical Account" was delivered by Professor Kishore K. Basa. The event took place in collaboration with the Centre for Archaeological Studies and Training, Government of West Bengal, Kolkata. Professor V. N. Mishra's contribution in Indian archaeology has far-reaching implications and his research endeavours, especially on the Indus Valley civilization, have tremendous value. Professor Basa, being a renowned archaeologist and a leading palaeo-anthropologist of the present-day India, portrayed a brilliant exposition on Professor Mishra's academic contributions. Professor Basa's written contribution could have enriched the volume further. But due to his busy schedule he could not make it possible to contribute full length paper for the present volume.

On 22 January, 2020, a lecture in memory of Professor Lalita Prasad Vidyarthi titled "Lalita Prasad Vidyarthi: An Anthropologist with a Difference" was delivered by Dr. Jayanta Sarkar in the Department of Anthropology and Tribal Studies, Sidho-Kanho-Birsha University, Purulia. Professor Vidyarthi is well-known for his versatility and dynamism in anthropological research in India. He was instrumental in making Indian anthropology visible at the global level. Dr. Sarkar, himself a student of Professor Vidyarthi and a renowned anthropologist of this country, gave a vivid account of the academic life and organizational activities of Professor Vidyarthi, laying stress on his unique way of nurturing anthropology.

On 6 February, 2020, a lecture in memory of Professor Pranab Kumar Ganguly titled "Pranab Ganguly: A Rare Kind of Anthropologist" was delivered by Professor Abhijit Guha in the Department of Anthropology, Vidyasagar University, Paschim Medinipur. Professor Pranab Kumar Ganguly was a dedicated biological anthropologist, more so a bio-cultural anthropologist, whose contributions are significant enough. Professor Guha, who is a passionate researcher in the field of social historical anthropology and other fields of contemporary relevance and who was the younger colleague of Professor Ganguly, dwelt at length on Professor Ganguly's type of anthropology and gave his own justification for considering him as a rare kind of anthropologist.

On 15 February, 2020, a lecture in memory of Professor Gopala Sarana titled "The Master Theoretician: Gopala Sarana and His Contributions to Anthropology" was delivered by Professor Sumahan Bandyopadhyay in the Department of Anthropology, Acharya Prafulla Chandra College, New Barrackpore, Kolkata. Professor Sarana was an illustrious social anthropologist whose range of research spanning from theoretical constructs to methodological issues could generate much debate and discourse. His thorough understanding of the subject was an example for his contemporaries and students to emulate. Professor Bandyopadhyay, a bright scholar in social anthropology showing a dynamic line of thinking, could very well discuss the importance of Professor Sarana's contributions in Indian anthropology.

On 22 August, 2020, a lecture in memory of Professor Deba Prasad Mukherjee titled "Professor Deba Prasad Mukherjee and the Essence of Bio-cultural Approach to Anthropology in India" was delivered by Dr.Bidhan Kanti Das, which was organized by the Department of Anthropology, Dinabandhu Mahavidyalaya, Bongaon, North 24-Paraganas in the virtual mode. Professor Mukherjee was one of the best known biological anthropologists in India who had interest in all the domains of holistic anthropology. Human population genetics and bio-cultural anthropology were his very favourite fields of research. Dr. Das, who was a student of Professor Mukherjee, gave an elaborative account of research endeavours of Professor Mukherjee and went on to provide additional details of how Bio-cultural approach to anthropology became a passion for Professor Mukherjee.

On 4 February, 2021, a lecture in memory of Professor Biswanath Banerjee titled "Remembering Sri Biswanath Banerjee and His Teaching of Anthropology—A Tribute" was delivered by Professor Sekh Rahim Mondal, which was hosted by the Department of Anthropology, Ramsaday College, Amta, Howrah in the virtual mode. Professor Banerjee was a dedicated Indian anthropologist whose research endeavours revolved around rigorous fieldwork covering many socially relevant areas of social-cultural anthropology. His teaching and mentoring abilities could motivate many young students to become dedicated scholars. Incidentally, Professor Mondal himself was a student of Professor Banerjee, who has to his credit substantial contributions in the field of social-cultural anthropology and on social development issues, much of which is the result of Professor Banerjee's inspiration. While touching upon this point, Professor Mondal gave a vivid account of Professor Banerjee and his contributions to anthropological research following his own chosen path.

On 6 February, 2021, a lecture in memory of Rai Bahadur Sarat Chandra Roy titled "A special lecture in memory of Rai Bahadur S.C. Roy" was delivered by Dr. Gautam K. Bera; the event was organized by the Department of Anthropology, Haldia Government College in virtual mode. Rai Bahadur Roy was responsible for introducing meticulous ethnographic research on Indian tribes in anthropology and remained a legendary scholar in anthropology during the pre-independence period. Dr. Bera, who has researched intensively on Rai Bahadur Roy, quite elegantly narrated many aspects of life and academic achievements of Rai Bahadur Roy, regarded as the 'Father' of Indian ethnography. However, due to his busy schedule Dr. Bera could not contribute full length paper for the present volume.

On 12 March, 2021, a lecture entitled "In the Memory of Professor Dibyendu Kanti Bhattacharya" was delivered in virtual mode by Professor Rupendra Kumar Chattopadhyay, the collaborator of the event being the Department of Anthropology, University of North Bengal. Professor Bhattacharya was one of the very eminent archaeological anthropologists of India. His contributions to prehistoric archaeology of Europe and India are of immense significance. Professor Chattopadhyay, an archaeologist of repute who has contributed much in archaeological field of studies of Eastern India, very aptly discussed the academic achievements of Professor Bhattacharya and his contributions to the field of archaeological anthropology. Avick Biswas of Vidyasagar University joined as a co-author of the article to enrich the same by providing further inputs based on his personal interactions with Professor Bhattacharya as a student.

On 11 September, 2021, a lecture in memory of Professor Amitabha Basu titled "Professor Amitabha Basu, Indian Statistical Institute and Our

Research" was delivered by Professor Susmita Mukhopadhyay in virtual mode, the host being the Department of Anthropology, Visva-Bharati, Santiniketan. Professor Basu was an internationally reputed anthropologist who could think ahead of his time. Professor Basu believed in holistic anthropology and was intensely in search of finding social relevance of the academic endeavours pursued by anthropologists. He contributed enormously in bio-cultural anthropology with special emphasis on studies of human bio-cultural adaptation. Inspired by Professor Basu, Professor Mukhopadhyay has also contributed significantly by undertaking bio-cultural research among women in their life course. As a student of Professor Basu, she had the opportunity of directly coming in contact with Professor Basu and his many-sided personality. She discussed at length on Professor Basu's academic achievements, love and dedication for his place of work, i.e. ISI and the continuation of his research traditions through his students at ISI.

And finally, on 22 November, 2021, a lecture in memory of Professor Asok Kumar Ghosh titled "Prehistoric Research in Bengal: Recent Advances" was delivered by Dr. Bishnupriya Basak in virtual mode, which was organized by the Department of Anthropology, Sikkim University, Gangtok, Sikkim. Professor Ashok Kumar Ghosh earned enough reputation and international recognition as an archaeological anthropologist. He was instrumental in making the sub-discipline of prehistory popular in India. His primary focus of research centred around prehistoric archaeology of Singbhum area as well as other important domains of the sub-discipline. Dr. Basak has earned a name in contemporary studies of prehistoric archaeology through her extensive research in the prehistory of western upland in Bengal. She discussed about the research-based contributions of Professor Ghosh in a lucid manner. However, due to her other commitments she could not present the full-length paper for the volume.

Each speaker, to the best of his/her ability and exercising his/her own personal choice, tried to give a reasonably good account of the topic under discussion. Their deliberations dealt with the personality of the anthropologist in question, his/her competence in teaching and mentoring, institution building and other components of personal and professional life with special reference to the academic contributions made.

The chapters of this book are the written versions of the lectures given in course of the last two years or so.

We will be happy if the rich information contained in this volume provides help in broadening our understanding about anthropology in the Indian perspective and gives enough encouragement to the young generation of anthropologists to pursue the field of anthropological research with renewed vigour.

1

Why North East India Holds a Special Place of Importance in Dr. B.K. Roy Burman's Line of Approach to Community Studies with Reference to Tribes?

Rajat Kanti Das

Let me start with making a seemingly innocuous statement about Dr. B.K. Roy Burman. He was among those who thought and spoke about establishment of rights and responsibilities of the members of the community located in their self-created natural sphere. The reference is obviously to North East Indian tribes who hold a special place of importance in B.K. Roy Burman's line of thinking. There are unmistakable signs and points of reference when his humanistic vision could get a direction from his deep involvement with tribes of North East India as a moral entity. Tribe as a moral entity was not simply confined within the local limits but it had a global outreach. As he observed (1998 : 91),

> *Community as a moral entity was sovereign in its own sphere, trying to reach through free interaction unto the global community.*

So far as North East India is concerned, the differentiated existence of the community process and state process has always been at the centre of debates or regulated discussions. Roy Burman (1998:91) also made a special reference to the Report of the North-East Frontier (Assam) Tribal and Excluded Areas Subcommittee (Bordoloi Committee) of the Constituent Assembly. The Report submitted by the Bordoloi Committee highlights the fact that the differentiated existence of the community process and state process was a reality. Each had a clearly delineated sphere of its own which remained separate for a long time without impinging on one another. The emphasis of the Committee was actually on establishing two-way feedback mechanism involving the two processes. Obviously, such a system cannot continue for a long time and Roy Burman could also realise this. He could foresee that ultimately the state process would get the better of community process considerably reducing its capacity to function on its own terms. As a process, erosion of the community or autonomy of the community lies embedded in the very "concept, ideology and functioning of the state". We will return to this particular point of discussion later.

B.K. Roy Burman's concern about human welfare and development with social justice is reflected in his thoughts and actions, which may cover the following roles performed by him in various capacities:

(1) That of an anthropologist-*cum*-social scientist;
(2) That of an administrator who, though not formally trained, was having all the knowledge about government policies and their implications towards development of the underdeveloped in the form of tribes and other weaker sections of the society;
(3) That of an expert in North East Indian tribal affairs and development issues relating to tribes and other minority groups of the region; and
(4) As a Human Rights activist.

The image he still carries with him as an expert in North East Indian tribal affairs has been emboldened by the roles he could so successfully perform as an anthropologist-*cum*-social scientist, as an administrator not strictly guided by official line of approach but inculcating a spirit of social scientific tradition of liberalism, and of course, as an ardent follower of the principles of Human Rights.

Although I had a long relation with the North East India, which happens to be my place of origin and with which I have been connected in many ways, I could come in contact with Dr. B.K. Roy Burman only after my post graduation. My direct association with him grew after I had joined the Social Studies Section of the Assam Census in Shillong during mid-Nineteen Hundred Sixty's. I did not stay there for long, but I had the opportunity to meet him on a few occasions. Besides, I had direct access to some of his writings or written instructions because the Section with which I was associated was his brain child and in a way I was accountable to him. It was only after I had left Assam Census, I had more occasions to meet him personally. I still remember the occasion when in a meeting with him some time in 1966, the first thing he said to me, "Your report on the village South Salmara is ready for publication." South Salmara, a village in the Goalpara district of Assam on the border with the Mymensingh district of the present Bangladesh, was one of those villages selected for a detailed study under 'Village Studies' programme of the Census. Much later, when I met Abhijit Guha at Vidyasagar University as a colleague, in the very first meeting itself he said, "I could first know about you by reading your report on the Assam village in the National Library." During my one and half year's stay in Shillong I could complete reports on two villages, a report on the 'Bhutan Mela' held at close to the Bhutan border of the Darrang district of Assam and a report on housing patterns in the Brahmaputra and Barak valleys of Assam. I do not know what had happened with them? Of course, with the completion of Dr. Roy Burman's tenure as the Deputy Registrar General of the Census of India, the Social Studies Section itself stopped functioning. As I have already said, my relation with him continued to grow once my short stint with the Assam Census came to an end. After I had joined the Government D.M. College at Imphal, he once came to the Manipur Capital on some official work. It was winter and he was staying in the Dak Bungalow, which was close to my College. He sent information that I should meet him at the Dak Bungalow in the evening. I went to see him around six in the evening. After exchanging a few words, he gave me some blank sheets and asked me to take dictation. It continued for the next three to four hours. Imphal at that time was not quite safe for free movement at night, particularly in some areas, of which the College campus was one. The dimly-lit approach road to the College was the safe heavens for the rowdies. The prospect of facing them worried me a lot. By the grace of God nothing of that kind happened on that night and on the following night when I went to his place for the same purpose. But I could learn a lot from the prolonged sessions I had with him. Analysis of a table carrying demographic and social data is itself a process. At the first stage, features which are clearly visible or evident need to be identified and explained. After that, features which lie hidden or are mere possibilities are to be listed. Attempts will then be made to relate them with other features dealt with in other tables. Comparison should also be made with past records or figures to show decadal changes. Propositions, accordingly, may fall under two broad categories: (1) those which are immediately supported by first hand data, and (2) those in need of further concrete data in their support but may be put forward as likely correlates of or as contributing factors to the way social or social demographic process functions. Dr. Roy Burman had an extraordinary capacity to see beyond what was clearly visible. He could see multiple implications of data which change meaning depending on their association with other data from different contexts. One should be able to discern the contextual significance of data, which varies with time and place. Beyond data, researcher's capacity to make significant observations, to have perceptive understanding and analytical power matter a great deal in fixing areas of active social interaction with differentiated emphasis on inner values and practical implications or utilities, the latter being guided more by the exogenous factors and situational demands. Roy Burman's approaches display a combination of all of these.

While dealing with the question of correct and unbiased representation of the reality phenomenon at the socio-cultural level, his approach also displays some flexibility and not particularly rooted to a stereotypic frame of reference. I quote below a few sentences from his introductory note bearing the title 'North East India on the March Towards the 21st Century' in the book *North-East India: Ethno-Cultural Perspectives and Process* edited by A.K. Danda *et al.* (1998):

> *At the surface level, the deviation from the deeper structure of the social entities in the region may impress many as the overriding feature of the reality. But with a humanist plunge into the eye of the social hurricane which is sweeping the region, one can realise how unreal is the facade of reality that overwhelms one's perception.*

That was the time when ethnic violence was at its peak, which did have its impact on the concerned peoples destroying 'the institutional structure of harmonious moral space of living.' But he was not prepared to see the extreme form of ethnic violence as a deviation from the normative structure, which, in other words, means it was a form of structural transformation as a net effect of institutional control imposed from outside by the state. In this context, he even suggested that the 'institutional constraints and all other factors which hover like hanging dust and cover the region's authentic real self have to be removed fast, – very fast.' When structural constraints developed from within and institutional control imposed from outside come in direct clash with one another, the situation becomes volatile. Whether or not, the former is the direct result of the latter is debatable, but it is generally accepted that in the present situation structural mode of traditional control deters the process of liberation of the self as symbolised by the community. Ethnic expressions in that sense symbolise liberation of the community from the socially determined structural representations as prescribed by the colonial anthropologists and so faithfully followed by us for a long time without posing a serious question. From the individual perspective, the tormented self, not only loaded with the burden of structure but also crippled because of the pressures exerted by external forces including state, finds an opportunity to seek liberation through such actions. Liberation of the self and liberation of the community carry almost the same meaning in this case, though both are against larger national interest and therefore, become a problem for the state to tackle. From a different perspective, Roy Burman's humanistic concerns probably got the better of one's almost total, uncritical acceptance of tribal societies and their cultures in the form they have been presented by the structurally moulded anthropologists. In such descriptions, individuals in a tribal society remain totally subdued or hidden, institutionally controlled as they are in a socially bounded system. The authoritative control exercised by the traditional chief, accordingly, symbolised the status associated with the institution of chieftainship. The prestige of the community rested with him and it was he who represented the community. As an individual, he was of little consequence and therefore, had no standing in the community. Suppression of individual expressions may otherwise suggest that conflicts are in-built within the system represented by the structurally-bound society in the form it reveals itself.

B.K. Roy Burman has referred time and again about the Constitutional provisions safeguarding the interests of tribes and other weaker sections of the population. The subject has been critically discussed in some of his writings. The Constitution of India has provided for protection and promotion of social and economic interests of the communities notified as 'Scheduled Tribes'. But he had his doubts about how far the interests of the community could be protected under such provisions. His opinion that the rights of individuals within communities and the collective rights in over-all social-political milieu may not always coincide is significant enough. It is a pointer to a situation when community as a corporate body and individuals within it come into conflict with one another over the question of conferment of rights. The question of legality is involved with it because the community on its own is not legally empowered to accord rights to individuals over resources which were once community's sole property. When we speak of progressive integration of tribes into national communities, it implies collectivity reorientation. The substantive provisions enshrined in the Constitution in respect of indigenous and tribal peoples appear to be primarily individual-oriented. The point of consideration is, as has always been, by recognising individual rights to what extent it will be possible to keep the community structure in tact? Or has community as a group lost its credibility? Communities are now recognised in the way government recognises them. Roy Burman has even questioned the appropriateness of listing the Scheduled Tribes. He writes (1998),

> *Scheduled Tribes are recognised collectivities listed as such according to procedures laid down in the Constitution. There are many communities whose self-image is that of being tribals and/or who are recognised as tribals by their neighbours but who have not been listed as STs. On the other hand, there are communities who are not considered as tribals by their neighbours but who are in the list. For instance, the Swanglas who are Brahmans in Himachal Pradesh are treated as a Scheduled Tribe in the statute. In such context when the World Bank categorises all STs in India as indigenous it is nothing but uninformed interferences.*

The arbitrariness associated with listing of STs is even more glaring in North East India and Roy Burman was also quite aware of that. The listing, according to him, was far from perfect. Out of roughly 600 community names listed in the 1991 Census, many are sub-tribes or synonyms. Moreover, by simply listing communities as STs, the 'rights' question cannot be resolved automatically. What rights are related to communities and what are exclusively those of individuals depend on the state of social structure and cultural ecology of the collectivities and personal as well as family histories of individuals. Where do they converge? Roy Burman thinks there is 'an emerging sense of one-ness rooted in the feeling of being dispossessed from traditional command over respective life support systems and consequently collective marginalisation'(Roy Burman, 1998). Such a system may result in augmenting in-group feelings among the members of a community, which may even lead to ethnic separation and at times ethnic militancy. Roy Burman draws a distinction between inter-ethnic relations and ethnic movements and he thinks in the national context inter-ethnic relations play a significant role in enforcing desired roles of each ethnic group in the inter-ethnic milieu. It is but natural that the national government will look at tribes and other weaker sections of the society from its perspective. Accordingly, it keeps provisions for affirmative action for promotion of social and economic interests of the communities notified as STs under the Constitution. Roy Burman reminds us that there 'is a growing recognition of the rights of self-management of the communities and peoples in social, cultural, economic and political realms articulating with wider and wider social formations...' (op.cit.). The government also keeps Constitutional provisions for welfare and exercise of autonomy by tribal communities, e.g. Article 38 relating to the Directive Principles of State Policy requiring the state to secure a social order for the promotion of welfare of the people; Article 38(2) envisages welfare not only of individuals but also groups of people residing in different areas; Article 19 stipulating that all citizens have the right to freedom of speech and expression; the 73rd Amendment of the Constitution; the Fifth Schedule of the Constitution and the Sixth Schedule of the Constitution. Roy Burman's assessment about the Fifth Schedule is that in the matter of stimulating self-reliance and self-management of the tribals, the Fifth Schedule has been a non-starter. It is basically protective and paternalistic in its thrust, providing for surveillance by the Union Government of the administration of the area covered by the Schedule. The Governor is vested with the power to set aside or modify legislations enacted by the parliament or the state legislature. He is further vested with power of promulgating regulation for the peace and good governance of the scheduled areas. The good intentions are not always translated into action because of differences of opinion between the Governor and the State on such issues. In actual practice, it is the State Government which becomes the ultimate decision-making authority. The Governor rarely opposes welfare programmes undertaken in the name of STs or other disadvantaged sections of population. The Fifth Schedule provides for the establishment in each State having scheduled areas a Tribes Advisory Council consisting not more than twenty members, of whom three-fourths must be the representatives of the Scheduled Tribes in the Legislative Assembly of the concerned State. Other than those States having Scheduled Areas, it is difficult to find so many Scheduled Tribe members in the Legislative Assembly. Actually such States are not supposed to have a Tribes Advisory Council, but if the President of India so desires, Tribes Advisory Councils may also be established in the States with less Scheduled Area. Paragraph 4(2) of the Fifth Schedule stipulates that Tribes Advisory Council may advise on such matters pertaining to the welfare and advancement of the Scheduled States as may be referred to them by the Governor. On the whole, the Fifth Schedule, according to B.K. Roy Burman, envisages welfare as a protection of the interests of tribals under the 'benign umbrella' of the Union Government, which is what finally matters. Here, the interests of tribals are also set in tune with the programmes undertaken by the government.

Dr. Roy Burman examines the introduction of the Sixth Schedule in historical-ecological and geopolitical contexts. His stand that it was mainly through colonial political control attempts were first made to create sustained ties to unite North East India with the rest of the country without much of social and cultural interaction has a solid ground. Of course, the colonial political control did not have a smooth sailing. Very often, it had to take resort to application of physical force and even carry out full scale military campaign. Imposition of punitive measures for the raids carried out by the hill people was the common practice. Such raids were almost a regular feature throughout the nineteenth century and the first two or three decades of the twentieth century. The British Government particularly targeted the centre of socio-political control operating at the tribal level. The British administration introduced the Chin Hills Regulation, 1896 in some parts of North East India, according to which the authority and powers of the 'headman' or 'chief' were defined with reference to his relations with the officials of the British Government. The Regulation stated that the headman within the local limits of his jurisdiction in accordance with the local custom would have a general control over the clan or the village or both. This amounted to giving recognition to tribal customary practices. There were provisions by which the headman could collect customary dues from the villagers and impose punishments as authorised by the local customary rules. He was also allowed to try any person charged with a punishable offence subject to his general control under the Indian Penal Code as specified in the Regulation. Ultimately, he would be legally bound to the Indian legal system, which gave the administration the opportunity to directly interfere into tribal affairs. With the Independence of India in 1947, the Chin Hills Regulation,1896 was abolished and a new framework to administer the tribal areas in the region, now known as 'North East India', was put into effect in the form of the Sixth Schedule to the Constitution of India after its adoption in 1950. The Sixth Schedule provides for the formation of District Councils that are empowered to make laws with respect to establishment of village or town committees or councils and their powers or any matter relating to village and town administration like the appointment of or succession of chief and headman, defining customary rights. With the enactment of the Sixth Schedule to the Constitution (Amendment) Act, 1995, the District Councils, henceforth known as Autonomous Councils, were empowered to make laws on 15 additional subjects. Looking at tribal autonomy from the administrative point of view will help us to understand the gap between administrative action and people's aspiration level. This is in essence the position taken by Roy Burman in his assessment of the North Eastern tribal situation centring on the question of tribal autonomy.

The Sixth Schedule operating mostly in the tribal predominant areas of North East India is supposed to be guided by the ethos of self-management. Each tribal area covered by the Sixth Schedule has an Autonomous Council consisting of not more than thirty members including not more than four nominated members. The Council has legislative, executive and judicial powers but in actual field it is crippled by many restrictive conditions imposed by the state and national executive bodies. As a result, 'such Councils have to become political toys of the state and national level political elites.' Public discourses have long been started on the amendment of the Sixth Schedule initiated by the government in which political elites have their say. Roy Burman sums up the results in the following manner:

> *There is a school of thought that the amendment should pave the way for self-determination of the tribal collectivities; there is another school of thought that the amendment should enhance the participatory role of the citizens inhabiting the tribal areas.*

This brings in the question of citizenship rights and the full implications of it in respect of tribals. Now the citizenship issue has been a fiercely debated matter creating much ill feeling between the original settlers in the form of tribals and the later migrants who are mostly non-tribals. The Autonomous Councils are supposed to ensure the citizenship rights of the tribals in the face of relentless non-tribal pressure. The plain truth, however, is that the Autonomous Councils can hardly function on their own. Their jurisdiction is fixed by the Union Government, keeping national interest above giving any leeway to such regional bodies striving for autonomy. At the practical level, the Autonomous Councils do not enjoy financial independence. Constitutionally, they have been made to depend on respective state governments in matters of financial allotments greatly reducing and restricting their performances. A common complaint of the Autonomous Councils is the obstructive attitude of the respective state governments in the matter of release of fund. One of the sources of finance of A.D.C. is the share of royalty accruing each year from licences and leases given for the purpose of prospecting for or extraction of minerals, iron ores, petroleum products granted by the state government in respect of any area within an autonomous district. But here also state interferences or encroachment into tribal rights is no less evident. Actually, the Constitution confers very few developmental functions on A.D.C. Dr. Roy Burman thinks that "the Autonomous District Councils have been reduced today to be subordinate organs of the state rather than institutional structures for channelizing self-regulatory impulses of the communities, complementary to the institution of the state." In a tribal state, it creates a wedge between the state protagonists and a section of local elites pleading for full autonomy. And Roy Burman believes that the elites of the Sixth Schedule Areas have a bigger role to play in the functioning of Autonomous Councils. They should prepare themselves to provide meaningful, constructive leadership. My haunch is he has hinted at their capacity to think independently and give an independent direction to people's movements, which would not be in the best interest of the nation, that is, India. His message to them, though not loud and clear, is that they should join hands with the elites working at the national level. Many of the elites of the Sixth Schedule Areas have started doing that and one only expects that nationalistic forces would be gaining more and more ground with their participation. There are already indications to that effect as the national level political parties have made their presence increasingly felt in the region. But are we in a position to say that the gap between the elites working at the national level and elites representing the Scheduled Tribes has been bridged permanently? Probably, the time has not yet come to such a conclusion because we still find there is a division between the two groups over the question of national allegiance and type of autonomy. We may downplay such an occurrence and dismiss it outright on the ground that movements for greater autonomy are mere manifestations of parochial interests and ethnocentric tendencies and have no place in the national agenda. The national government, on its part, has been making every effort to win over the local elites ensuring their participation at the national level, which is a reflection of the integrationist approach of the government. Roy Burman pleads for adopting collectivity-oriented approach, which, according to him, is logically more correct. Such an approach would ensure greater participation of local elites. But in the face of multiple or multi-tier representation of tribals at the social and cultural level and at the political power structure, how far it will be possible for a tribe to retain its collective form or function as a closely-knit collectivity remains to be seen. This question was only indirectly raised by Roy Burman. Collective representation to him was a reflection of collective wisdom as displayed by tribes and indigenous groups. In our eagerness to impose our own wisdom on them we rarely attach importance on what is exclusively their strong point. Moreover, many of them have greater access to global panorama, which puts them in an advantageous position of thinking ahead of traditionalists working with limited ethnic option. At the basic level, the rights of the indigenous and tribal peoples are involved and as Roy Burman (2003) thinks, these need to be considered 'with the world economic system and ethnicity in various forms'. As 'the basic frame of social mobilisation', ethnicity is bound to play an important role in years to come. Consequently, ethnic groups based on language, culture, religion, shared history and a common way of life seem to be 'stable structures of mobilisation'. He, however, considers ethnicity to be a contributory factor in any discourse on indigenous and tribal peoples. For the peoples in question, ethnic group formation has a valid existence mainly for the reason that it strengthens their identity as a group and gives them a moral boost. Understanding ethnicity in the context of tribes and/or indigenous groups touches upon the conceptual validity of it. Ethnicity as a relational concept is manifested through a dialogue within or between communities, of which tribe or indigene could be an extreme form. This does not mean that such a dialogue takes place on equal terms. More often than not, it becomes an encounter between the powerful and powerless and between the dominators and dominated even in its implicit form. That indigenous or tribal peoples are minorities on whom rights may be conferred is decided by the powerful nations and it is they who have the sacred duty to maintain the 'world order'. Roy Burman has questioned whether such rights could be conferred 'without disturbing the established world order' or only 'to reinforce the world order'? Either way, it is suggestive of lack of freedom of such groups to decide their own course. Roy Burman in this case is more explicit and he says,

> *Raising these questions should not mean that recognition of indigenous and tribal rights is wrong, rather that, the denial of indigenous and tribal rights to many social entities by manipulating the term 'indigenous' and 'minority' is wrong* (Roy Burman, op. cit.).

Tribes of North East India are not outside this global agenda, though they are first and foremost nationals of the State, which sets its own terms for their integration. It may be worthwhile to examine the North East Indian tribal situation in the context of substantive provisions made at important international forum in respect of indigenous and tribal peoples. The ILO Convention 107 of 1957, 169 of 1989 and UNWGIP's Draft Declaration 1993 have come up for critical appraisal by Roy Burman. He observes that in ILO Conventions, the onus for implementing the provisions having emphasis on actions in respect of all factors which have hitherto prevented peoples of such a category to participate fully in the progress of national community rests with the respective member-states. Member-states are advised to practise non-discrimination in every walk of life, much of which still remains a wishful thinking. Regarding UNWGIP's Draft Declaration, Roy Burman holds the view that 'all the provisions relating to individual and collective rights and right of self-determination ... are in line with the humanistic ethos of the age' (Roy Burman, op. cit.). But simultaneously he has raised a valid point:

> *Certainly indigenous peoples [including tribes] have the right to maintain and strengthen distinct political, economic, social and cultural characteristics as well as their legal system, while retaining their rights to participate fully in the political, economic, social and cultural life of the country. But is non-participation in the political life of the state, for instance as envisaged in Article 4, a right or an erosion of right?*

Probably he himself did not expect a clear-cut answer, but it has to be admitted that rights defined on the basis of consensus of member-states must have legal sanction which such Conventions in their present form cannot enforce.

What distinguishes Dr. B.K. Roy Burman as an anthropologist? This much can be said about him that he did not uncritically follow the course of 'official anthropology', although he had enough scope to be the spokesperson of the official position by making compromises with his pro-people, humanistic concerns. The connotation 'official anthropology' must have been in use in common parlance, but I could come across it in one research article by Nicholas B. Dirks (1997), who had preferred to apply it to most of the colonial anthropologists in India. Even during post-colonial period there have been attempts to use anthropology for justifying an official position. That Dr. B.K. Roy Burman did not totally subscribe to the official line of approach was good for anthropology because he could leave a lasting impression in critical areas of social scientific studies, of which the tribal form of representation in North East India having multidimensional significance occupies a special place.

REFERENCES

Dirks, Nicholas B. 1997. "The Policing of Tradition: Colonialism and Anthropology in Southern India". In *Comparative Studies in Society and History.* Vol. 39, No. 1. Cambridge University Press: Cambridge.

Prasad, R.N. 1987. *Government and Politics in Mizoram 1947-1986.* Northern Book Centre: New Delhi.

Roy Burman, B.K. 1998. "Constitutional Framework for Tribal Autonomy with Special Reference to North-East India". In *North-East India: The Human Interface.* Edited by M.K. Raha and Alok Kumar Ghosh. Gyan Publishing House: Delhi.

Roy Burman, B.K. 1998. "North East India on the March Towards the 21st Century". In *North-East India: Ethno-Cultural Perspectives and Process.* Edited by Ajit K. Danda *et al.* The Indian Anthropological Society: Calcutta.

Roy Burman, B.K. 2003. "Indigenous and Tribal Peoples in World System Perspective". In *Studies of Tribes and Tribals,* Vol.1, No. 1. Kamala-Raj Enterprises: Delhi.

2

Walking with Professor Baidyanath Saraswati on the Road to Indian Civilization

Gopal Krishna Chakraborty

Invitation to Take a Walk

I was never acquainted with Prof. Baidyanath Saraswati personally though I heard a lot about his simple lifestyle, charming personality, dedication to fieldwork, and his wholehearted devotion to the anthropological study of Indian civilization from my teacher Late Prof. Biswanath Banerjee. India, particularly its religious ideas and traditions were subjects closest to Saraswati's heart. I had to go through his works on traditional Sanskrit scholars and ascetics of Kashi (also known as Varanasi/Benaras/Banaras) for I had almost the same scheme of research for my doctoral study on Indian civilization in different research settings of West Bengal. The present article is rooted to my study, personal experience, introspection, and understanding of anthropology of Indian civilization. Writing a critique of his study on Indian civilization by Baidyanath Saraswati is aimed at expressing my sincere gratitude to him who had loomed large in my journey to understanding a small part of Indian societies and cultures in time and space.

Down the Boulevard of History

For a considerable span of its history, India turned into an 'object' of intellectual curiosity of the colonial power which gradually took control of the different regions of the country though the land of fortune was known to foreign traders for several centuries. The treaty the European traders had with the sitting rulers of the Mughal Empire offered them the right of trading that gradually unseated the Mughal rulers and brought almost the entire region of the present-day India under their control. To the British colonial power, India was an uncharted territory. The knowledge about its people, way of life, thoughts and values were of utmost importance to it for the purpose of extending the British Empire in South-east Asia. The economic and political process of change witnessed multiple responses from the Western scholars, politicians, diplomats and royals. Liberals among them had 'discovered' the intellectual treasure of India, translated works from the Sanskrit and presented India as the 'other' to the 'enlightened' European 'self'. This way of looking into 'other' did not earn appreciation from the hardliners who had taken upon themselves the noble 'mission' of civilizing the Indian people and for that matter the entire non-European societies. The former group have helped us 'rediscover' our own 'self' as a civilization, while the latter introduced us to a 'civilized world' of the West. Civilizing the 'natives' by the West was carried out under 'modernization' – a term mostly used by the specialists in social sciences to mark the social process of abject submission by the Indians to the rulers of the mighty British Empire. Among the Sanskrit philosophers, historians, archaeologists and other experts, the 'friends of India' had a relatively easy access and uncritical acceptability. This group of urban literati were enthusiasts about the discourse on Indian civilization. To them, 'civilization' meant the hallmark of achievement by a society and such a meaning provided them with the necessary boost to oppose the 'civilizing mission' of the British Empire. The opposition was backed by a sense of identity and belongingness to India in the name of 'nationalism'. Indian anthropology was born in such an ambience when anthropologists were anxious to maintain their identity as Indian on the one hand, but on the other were dependent on the Western method of looking into what constitutes the society of the 'other'. In anthropology, civilizational study was developed as a methodology of studying complex societies of the old world by anthropologists belonging to the Chicago School under the leadership of Robert Redfield. In India, even before Redfield, an attempt was made in that direction independently by Nirmal Kumar Bose who was influenced by M.K. Gandhi's 'Swadeshi' movement, and which was followed by a host of Indian anthropologists influenced by him. Belonging to an intellectual climate of empiricism, Bose hardly made any attempt to theorize his observations on Indian complex societies though he was a follower of Franz Boas and was well acquainted with Alfred Kroeber, Robert Redfield and other scholars of the Chicago school (Bose, 1959). Bose's influence on Prof. Baidyanath Saraswati was immense and it was clearly visible in the latter's several works. After revisiting his favourite domains of 'categories' of 'tradition(s)', their 'continuity' and searching their 'identity' as well as interconnectedness in the context of Indian civilization one would be able to discern the whole depth of his anthropological understanding and a thorough knowledge about the thoughts and ideas that pervaded the anthropological discourses in India. It was more or less an accepted position that in anthropology the discourse on Indian civilization was created by the Western scholars which was later taken over by the Indian scholars.

A Life's Journey from Mithila to Varanasi via Gaya and Calcutta

Prof. Saraswati was born in a Brahman family of Mithila in Bihar province of India in 1932. When the teaching of anthropology under the auspices of the University of Calcutta commenced, he was a mere child of 12 years. He earned his M.A. in Anthropology and later in 1967-68 got his Ph.D. from Ranchi University for his thesis titled 'The Peasant Potters of North India'. An anthropologist with an illustrious career, he served many academic institutions of repute. Association with Anthropological Survey of India for nearly a decade drew him closer to Nirmal Kumar Bose. By participating in a Survey-sponsored research project on the material culture of India, he got an opportunity to have a glimpse of Indian civilization. Under this project, he was primarily engaged in studying pottery making techniques, one of the ancient material cultural traditions, practised in different regions of India. He did not remain in the Anthropological Survey of India for long and became Professor of North Eastern Hill University, Visva Bharati University for a brief period. As a Fellow of Indian Institute of Advanced Studies, Simla, he came closer to a host of luminaries in social sciences, which probably helped him to organize his ideas about what India could offer to the rest of the world from the treasures of its civilization. With all his expertise in anthropology, he opened an NGO in the name of 'N.K. Bose Memorial Foundation' in Varanasi (Benares) dedicated to the cause of children's education, and a centre for heritage research. Later, as UNESCO Professor in Indira Gandhi National Centre for Arts, New Delhi he could earn national and international recognition.

Saraswati was anxious to find the linkages, interrelations, and continuity among a bewildering variety of cultural practices followed by the people of India. This anxiousness probably had its origin in the findings of his previous studies on pottery making groups, their technology and social cultural practices. He found that though traditional technology and social practices among the potters of India were confined to five zones, the technology practised in all the zones had a common origin from the days of Indus valley civilization. In social practices, the marital network was confined within the respective zones, though other social practices including the ritual ones were similar. This research was part of a grand survey scheme of cultural traits undertaken by the Anthropological Survey of India under the leadership of N.K. Bose (1967). Regarding the findings of this grand survey, Bose opined that material cultural traits did not directly correspond to the local physical environment but were juxtaposed one upon another. This was because in ancient India populations along with cultural traits migrated from one region to another. Cultural historical character as revealed through studies encouraged Saraswati to identify it as a 'tradition' of the civilization process of India that withstood the wear and tear of historical upheavals. Was he in search of unearthing the 'essence' of Indian civilization as other American anthropologists did? He published a thin book titled "Kashi: Myth and Reality of a Classical Cultural Tradition" in 1975 that embodies his researches centred round cultural traditions of Varanasi. In that book, he discusses his empirical studies on the cultural traditions of Banaras and how the present populace of the city identified with the tradition of Banaras while the tradition itself had passed through historical upheavals. Re-reading of the book would enable one to know his ideas about anthropology of Indian civilization. The points that have emerged are discussed below.

Quiet Flows the Ganga

Banaras (Varanasi), one of the most ancient cities of the world, has always attracted pilgrims and the Sanskrit scholars, philosophers for its geographical location on the confluence of three ancient rivers of North India – the Ganga on the east and Varuna and Asi on the west. The last two rivers have been reduced to canals now and are choked with the city's waste. Being the most ancient city and frequently referred in the texts of major religious pantheons of India, it attracted people from all social spheres as well as political power groups. History has left an indelible mark in the physical existence of the city and at the same time shaped the social-cultural practices of the city's population. Under the influence of modernization, the city presents itself to the outsider as colourful but chaotic. While the social life of the populace continues to get choked in its innumerable alleys in the old part of the city, the new part with flashy high-rises on both sides of broad roads makes a total contrast. In short, the city is impervious but hospitable.

Varanasi is a place of anthropological wonders that attracted tourists, scholars from various disciplines particularly Sanskrit and Indology as well as anthropologists like Eck (1985), Parry (2011) from abroad. Saraswati's first visit to Kashi as a 'Buddhist neophyte'—a phrase he never elaborated – certainly refers to his attraction to the city as a place of religious significance to both the Buddhists (Sarnath, one of the most important pilgrimage centres in Buddhism, is only 12 kilometres away), and Hindus. In the historical period, the city acquired name and fame of both as a pilgrimage centre and a seat of Sanskrit teaching, learning, and cultivating of Sanskritic philosophy.

His fieldwork in Varanasi was built on his previous experience of undertaking fieldwork in other sacred place(s) and inspired him on giving a concrete shape to his anthropological experience and knowledge. As one of the ancient cities of the world, Varanasi has offered him an exciting anthropological vista of tradition coming in contact with modernization. He finds that the canonical Sanskrit term '*vidya*' (knowledge) is embodied in Indian cultural tradition and as per the Sanskrit texts they are of three types namely, '*para*' (transcendental), '*apara*' (metaphysical), and the other that belongs to outside the purview of the former two is '*laukik*' (related to mass, practical). On the basis of his experience in Banaras and elsewhere, he classifies Indian cultural tradition into three categories. They are, as per Saraswati's coinage, Transcendental Cultural Tradition (Trans-CT), Textual Cultural Tradition (TCT), and Oral Cultural Tradition (OCT) and all of them are inevitably connected to the religious activities of the city's population and pilgrimage. On another occasion, he provides alternative terms borrowed from the Sanskrit for the same three traditions. These are, '*naivritik*' culture for Transcendental cultural Tradition; '*sastriya*' culture for Textual Cultural Tradition; and, '*laukik*' for the Oral Cultural Tradition (1970a, pp. 47-51). Both *para* and *apara vidya*, Saraswati envisages, are associated with the 'texts' composed in Sanskrit and their preservation through teaching and learning. In Transcendental Cultural Tradition, the practice may differ according to religious groups devoted to the expounding philosophy of realizing the ultimate principle of the universe. Practice of the Textual Cultural Tradition and its preservation and communication are confined within the Brahmins. This tradition is sourced in the Veda,Vedic rituals, metaphysical doctrines and the various schools of philosophy. These two modes of tradition depend upon the 'texts' and scholar specialists for their communication through generations. Unlike these two traditions, *laukik* Cultural Tradition is preserved by the non-Brahmins and communicated orally across generations. *Laukik* tradition is confined within a region rendering it characteristically most diverse, while Textual and Transcendental Cultural Traditions are pan-Indian and universal (Saraswati, 1975b; also 1970b, 1975a).

However, the readers of Saraswati are mostly kept at bay regarding the kind of theoretical approach(es) he has taken up for his studies of Indian cultural traditions. In any case, those studies reflect that he is out and out an empiricist, always trying to find out and present what is novel in its finding. At an early stage of his career, he got in touch with Prof. L.P. Vidyarthi who was Professor of Anthropology in Ranchi University. Incidentally, Vidyarthi did his Ph.D. under the supervision of Robert Redfield and McKim Marriott in 1956. In 1950s and 1960s, the Chicago school of anthropology in civilizational studies exercised a considerable influence on Indian anthropology covering the whole gamut of Indian societies, particularly sacred complexes to theorise Redfield's concepts of Little and Great Traditions. Saraswati remains silent about his indebtedness to the Chicago school so far as the methodology of his studies is concerned. But we have reasons to believe that his interest, particularly in sacred complexes developed under the influence of the Chicago school through Vidyarthi. Later, his interest in the study of Indian civilization was guided by N.K. Bose which he acknowledged in his book "Contribution to the Understanding of Indian Civilization" (1970a, p. ix). To deal with the modernization of the age-old cultural traditions, as Singer did in his study of Madras (today's Chennai) city (1972), Saraswati has probed into the identity of '*banarasi*' culture alongside the previously mentioned cultural traditions. He has undertaken a novel seminar on "Social Cultural Profile of Kashi" in 1973 and invited participants from every walk of life starting from local academics privately researching on different aspects of Banaras to the NGOs and common people. The participants expressed different views regarding what they understood as '*banarasi*' (what is exclusively of Banaras). Instead of attributing a definite boundary to what is called '*banarasi*', Saraswati to his surprise finds Banaras projected as the 'city of cultural pluralism' along with traditional cultural practices (1975b, pp. 48-55). Contrary to our belief of Kashi as a seat of orthodox religious practices, cultural pluralism of Kashi is definitely a revelation. But, is it not a fact that Redfield and Singer had already discussed the 'cultural role of city' particularly the multifarious roles of a city of orthogenetic transformation in 1954? Banaras is also a city of orthogenetic transformation from the civilizational perspective. May be Saraswati expected that in the seminar all the participants would subscribe to his view on the three traditions. But certainly he was out of his wits as he laments, "For, *banarasi* culture is free from the ubiquitous 'other worldly' elements, and it emphasizes on the cultivation of excellence in this 'worldly' life. . . . The 'reality culture' of Kashi also overlooks many of the traditional social values which are bred in the bones of narrow sectarianism, and presents a certain style of life which is abhorrent to both orthodox Hindus and Moslems" (1975b, pp. 52-53). If it is so, his classification of Indian traditions into three spatial (if not hierarchical) categories is automatically reduced into a 'myth'. The 'reality' is that the *Banarasi* culture has been evolved in historical phases that Banaras as a city has passed through. This qualifying term is used by the long-term settlers of Banaras to distinguish themselves from the relatively new settlers. The in-built subtle tension in the term might have escaped his attention which could very well be a contribution of modernization of Banaras like many other cities of India. His idea of '*Banarasi* culture' is somewhat queer. He presents a diagram showing the 'structural relationships' of important categories of 'cultural life in Kashi' (1975b, pp. 52-55) that includes two major religious communities of Hindu and Moslem. An interested reader may go through it in the page 54 of his text under re-reading. To the Hindus, Kashi is a sacred place with the temple of Vishwanath (Shiva) at the centre. But such sacred shrine is not available for the Moslem. Since two communities are participating to 'cultural life in Kashi' though they have separate culture complex, they are, as expected, somewhere bound to overlap. This overlapping zone he identifies as '*banarasi* culture' and characterize it as free from influence of any religious tradition. He says, "It must be clearly stated that the *banarasi* culture is not a true synthesis of Hindu and Moslem elements like Sufism or Kabir panth . . . but a particular style of life which is cultivated independent of ecclesiastical authority" (1975b, p. 55). He claims that if one does not go deep into the 'cultural life of Kashi' he is bound to fail to understand the 'effluent *banarasi* culture'. His queer description actually restores the concept of 'sacred secular continuum' that he describes in the previous chapter (1975b, pp. 41-47). We should not have any reason to be unhappy. But the question is how many Kashi and its traditions we have at the end of the book! One is Hindu Kashi, second one is Moslem Kashi, and the third one *banarasi* Kashi. All of his categories of tradition have been attributed to the Hindu or at best may include the textual tradition of the Moslem. The Moslem's Transcendental Cultural Tradition and Oral Cultural Tradition are missing from his account of 'cultural life in Kashi'. But he agrees that the Moslems are integral part of it. He does not have any more category of 'tradition' for that Kashi, which is practising *banarasi* culture. An uneasy feeling may overpower us to thinking of a culture that is not backed by any tradition, He is, in fact, re-establishing the anthropological myth that the tradition is immutable and handed down to the generations without any change therein. What is changeable is not tradition but may be termed as culture. The reality is that tradition is invariably connected to the history of a community living in a particular territory. It is the people's way of interpreting their past to legitimize their present.

Mythologising the Reality

Saraswati's treatment of myth and mythology in the context of '*Banarasi* culture' may invite some discussion. Any attempt to mythologise the 'Reality Myth' – a term owing its origin to Greek 'mythos' – may generate a few questions, particularly when it is compared with the 'logos'. While the former is associated with the irrational phenomenon like religion, the latter as an approach is considered to be rational and logical that is involved with the Greek philosophy. The emergence of modern science and scientific orientation of mind as a result of 'enlightenment' inherited the Greek rationality dismissing religion as full of irrational myths. The capacity of myth-making is not confined to the archaic societies alone. Modern societies are also involved in creating myths continuously around the consumable goods and items under the influence of capitalistic economy. Anthropologists are also myth makers through their approach of studying the unknown or little known cultures. Anthropologists and ethnographers by way of studying the small communities around the world are also creating myths about their 'object' of study who, incidentally, are also 'thinking subjects' in their own rights. One of the most circulated anthropological myths is about the timelessness of pre-modern small communities. When the complex societies are put under the anthropological scanner, they are studied with the methodological assumption currently in use for the study of pre-modern small-scale societies. Timelessness (i.e. immunity from change) of that dimension should have put anthropological studies in the arena of 'science' rather than in 'history'. Anthropological studies since the very beginning have been suffering from this dilemma. The attributed character of 'immune to change' of small communities became the 'tradition' of the pre-industrial complex societies as in India. Where should one place the tradition-loving, myth-making communities of Banaras? Baidyanath Saraswati remained true to anthropology, but he carefully avoided entering into the tricky and problematic areas of anthropology.

Saraswati presents a chronology of major historical events that range from 1000 B.C. coinciding with the travels of Jain *Tirthankara* (prophet) and continue till the country's independence (1975b, pp. 5-9). Apart from indicating that the city of Banaras is an ancient one, the chronology bears little historical significance. He might have assumed that what he envisages as 'tradition' remained the same throughout the history of Banaras. If it is so, it means that he equates tradition with the 'essence' of Indian civilization. But some questions need to be answered. Outwardly, how the life of Banaras population churned out during the first half of the twentieth century at the time of freedom struggle which lead to conflict among the different groups over the practice of Hinduism has been depicted with master strokes of field data. But he remains silent why such conflict arises if tradition is really immutable. He has depicted 'How Kashi Modernizes its Tradition' through the establishment of government run schools, colleges, and Sanskrit university. How this very process of modernization has been interacting with the long established way of life having multi-community representation is more important a question than describing it as 'sacred secular continuum' or as a symbolic expression of 'Nilakantha syndrome' (1975b, p. 66). Nilakantha (blue throat) is a name attributed to the God Shiva who held the poison churned out during gods' endeavour to acquire '*amrita*' (nectar). Shiva held the poison in his throat without swallowing it to save the entire universe from being poisoned.

The debate over the encounter between tradition and modernity in fact covers all of the disciplines of social science. It has been questioned whether the modern can be taken as opposite to traditional.

> *The assumption that modernity and tradition are radically contradictory rests on a misdiagnosis of tradition as it is found in traditional societies, a misunderstanding of modernity as it is found in modern societies, a misapprehension of the relation between them (Rudolph and Rudolph, 1987, p. 3). Elsewhere, the same authors have written, "But we are now beginning to recognise that earlier interpretations based on sacred texts took too literally their description of social organization and assumed too readily the social validity of their legitimizing values. These texts of Brahmanic ideology in fact masked considerable mobility and social change. Conquest and novel economic opportunities often enabled alien or subordinate peoples or castes to establish themselves within the traditional system. These groups were provided with names, symbols, genealogies, and ritual rank appropriate to their newly won power and status. By the time British ethnographers got*

> *to work, these events and processes had disappeared from view; castes who might have established themselves in the fifteenth or seventeenth century were presented in terms of Vedic social structure, with the clear implication that they had been in place since time immemorial" (Rudolph and Rudolph, 1987, p. 5).*

The cultural practices or the ways of life of the ascetics of Kashi of what Saraswati calls transcendental cultural tradition is never a uniform or universal practice. However, his book (co-authored by Surajit Sinha) "*Ascetics of Kashi*" (1978) does not discuss the existing variations among the different schools of ascetics except saying that they belong to Hinduism. We have no information about the ascetic organization(s) of the Moslems who form other major religious group of Banaras excepting a passing statement that '*Banarasi*' culture is not a synthetic culture like those of Sufism and Kabirpanth, though the religious organizations of Buddhism and Jainism have come under reference. Saraswati provides unique observation regarding their organizations. He introduces the concept of 'cultivation of excellence' practised by the ascetics in terms of the knowledge of the Sanskrit texts. Ascetics enter into the organizations cutting across the geographical and linguistic boundary. In the organization, a kind of hierarchy is practised which is similar to the practice of social world. Here, the hierarchy is determined by one's advancement in the course of meditative practices and knowledge acquired in Sanskrit philosophical texts. Lack of ethnographic details has prompted Saraswati to assume that all the organizations of the ascetics are similar. In effect, Saraswati has considered those ascetic organizations which are basically pan-Indian and has elaborate structure to maintain and exercise control over their members. There are also ascetics whose organizations are small and do not have significant impact upon the general population. Variations among the different sects and organizations make it difficult to arrive at any generalization about the ascetic organizations. But it is true that a kind of hierarchy is present in all of them and that is determined in terms of excellence in transcendental knowledge. Actually, the knowledge of Sanskrit texts and philosophy is not necessarily a part of transcendental tradition. Following the observation of Saraswati, it may be argued that it is possible for the neonates to come from any social background and therefore, they may not necessarily be from Brahmin families equipped with the requisite knowledge of Sanskritic texts (1970a, pp. 38-42). But the details about how many ascetic organizations are not following the transcendental life as prescribed in the Sanskritic texts are not provided. Saraswati's observation (1978, pp. 89-90) on Textual Cultural Tradition occupying the central place in Kashi's sacred tradition, Oral Cultural Tradition at its margin and Transcendental Cultural Tradition at the peripheral position is somewhat difficult to accept uncritically. If the Transcendental Cultural Tradition exercises its supreme authority for which the Textual Cultural Tradition accepts the Oral Cultural Tradition, then Transcendental Cultural Tradition should be considered as the supreme authority. Again, when the ultimate aim of Textual Cultural Tradition is to logically establish the '*Brahman*' (The Ultimate) and experience the supreme bliss, then Transcendental Cultural Tradition is a way to achieve it and should have been placed at the centre of Indian Cultural Tradition. On a previous occasion Saraswati explains *grihi* (householder)'s association with the ascetic orders stating that the householders look forward to the ascetics in search of ideals (value) of life. Such values (meaning) as per his understanding are the creation of the ascetics or at best of the Texts (1970a, p. 35). This statement not only denies the creative power of the householders but also their involvement in religious activities. Such ambiguities are bound to take place if the categories are conceived from the perspective of 'sacred – secular continuum'. Separation of sacred from secular and an imaginary continuum between them overlooks the overlapping areas of cultural practices. The three traditions categorized by Saraswati do not reflect the continuum. For, the sacred aspects are so inextricably connected to the daily lives of the practitioners of traditions that treating different traditions as separate categories, even for analysis, becomes a meaningless exercise. Therefore, the material prosperity and changing way of life cannot be termed 'syndrome' and certainly not a suitable situation for the metaphorical use of '*Nilakantha syndrome*'.

The Road Leads to Nowhere

Genealogy of ideas those motivated and nutured us to observe the external world, are quite complex and had been nourished by the knowledge cultivated in various streams. Empiricism, the philosophy behind the natural science, believes in the existence of an external world that can be studied by the observer by making classifications of different events, facts, relations, and systems. It is believed that the personal opinions of the observers-*cum*-scientists and their systems in which they belong do not interfere into their enterprise. Thus, the researchers out there to create the categories are assumed to be 'pure' and bear the essences of the phenomena embedded into those categories. But purities assigned to such categories are questionable and as such there is enough scope to question the real intention of the researchers.

Categorization or classification, we all know, is basic to scientific study that Max Müller (1823-1900) championed in India. As Inden observes, "Müller was an empiricist who combined empiricism with strong dose of religious idealism" (Inden, 1990, pp. 13-14). He further writes, "Classification, Max Müller informed us, is where true science begins. The principle of classification used by those who have adhered to the representational theory of knowledge is more often than not taxonomic, placing phenomena into hierarchically ordered, mutually exclusive classes, each of which had its defining attributes or essences. The reason for this, of course, is that taxonomies 'mirrored' the systems of objects supposed to exist 'out there'. Again and again, scholars and officials have used taxonomies for classifying the 'Others'. Inevitably, the analyst has represented (*sic*!) the highest type or society of most advance stage, more as a justification for his position of hegemony (Inden, 1990, p. 16). Indian anthropology is yet to get rid of the crude empiricism based representational knowledge that we had learnt from our colonial masters. Therefore, Saraswati did not restrain himself to describing the tradition of Banaras but went further to classifying the tradition itself into three categories and placing the textual cultural tradition practised by the *brahman* Sanskrit scholars at the centre and the rest two corroborating it. Along with the three traditions, Saraswati wanted to explore the *Banarasi* culture, i.e. the identity of the inhabitants of Banaras. But the scenario of Banaras was no less perplexing because it was inhabited by the people of all religious faiths found in India. While the Hindu dominated in number, the Muslims' presence in the city was a foregone conclusion since the city was under the Mughal rulers for a considerable period of time.

In anthropological parlance, tradition is a familiar concept that we use both in the studies of small-scale societies, large-scale complex societies in India and elsewhere as well as the entire gamut of Indian civilization. The term quite often means the set of social rules and customs, ideas and values practised by an ethnic group from time immemorial that has been handed down to generations without any change. This idea has been challenged by several authorities. For our present purpose citing a couple of them would help to undo the misconception. Lele opines that tradition is 'world-views and beliefs' of a community whose reinterpretation and transformation into a new system develop new institutional order (Lele, 1981, p. 1). Ethnic groups generally use the same to legitimize their action and practices in reference to the past. Traditions are sometimes invented, claims Hobsbawm. 'Invented tradition' ..."include both 'traditions' actually invented, constructed and formally instituted and those emerging in a less easily traceable manner within a brief and dateable period"

(Hobsbawm, 2000, p. 1). He further says, "Invented tradition is taken to mean a set of practices, normally governed by overtly or tacitly accepted rules and of a ritual or symbolic nature, which seek to inculcate certain values and norms of behaviour by repetition, which automatically implies continuity with the past. In fact, they normally try to establish a continuity with a suitable historic past" (Hobsbawm, 2000, p. 1). Traditions are not customs though both are sometimes used interchangeably. So writes Hobsbawm, "Custom cannot afford to be invariant, because even in 'traditional' societies life is not so. Customary or common law still shows the combination of flexibility in substance and formal adherence to precedent... The decline of 'custom'[results in] inevitable changes in the 'tradition' with which it is habitually intertwined" (Hobsbawm, 2000, pp. 2-3).

Tradition(s) is (are) invented as there are historical necessity to connect with and modify the 'old' traditions. If the 'old' traditions continue, there is hardly any need to invent. Traditions are invented and connected to the old one in such a way it looks as if the old traditions are continuing. The purpose of inventing traditions is to formalize and ritualize the gap between two historical periods. One among three types of overlapping invented traditions during the periods after industrial revolution as per Hobsbawm's general observation provides a case for India. It refers to "those establishing or legitimizing institutions, status or relationships of authority,...." (Hobsbawm, 2000, p. 9), which in other words means modernizing the India's old institutions. The British felt a need to reorient the authoritative structure following what is called the Brahmanic authoritative structure (Textual Cultural Tradition as per Saraswati) and gradually replaced the brahman pundits from the helm of traditional affair. Regarding differences between the old and the invented inventions, Hobsbawm further writes, "The former were specific and strongly binding social practices, the latter tended to be quite unspecific and vague as to the nature of values, rights and obligations of the group membership they inculcate" (Hobsbawm, 2000, p. 10). Contrary to our common belief, tradition is not monolithic, immovable cultural system. It responds to the historical conditions as depicted by the historians and anthropologists like Bernard S. Cohn and Ronald Inden.

Incoherence between the old and invented traditions is evident in cultural practices of the 19th century India. "In the first half of the nineteenth century", argues Cohn (2000), "... there was an incompleteness and contradiction in the cultural-symbolic Constitution of India." Then he quotes Inden, "A cultural symbolic constitution embraces such things as classificatory schema, assumption about how things are, cosmologies, worldviews, ethical systems, legal codes, definitions of governmental units and social groups, ideologies, religious doctrines, myths, rituals, procedures and rules of etiquette" (Ronald Inden, 1976, "Cultural Symbolic Constitution of India", mimeographed). Cohn continues, "The elements within cultural-symbolic constitution are not a mere assemblage of items or things, but are ordered into a pattern, which asserts the relationship of the elements to each other and constructs their value" (Cohn, 2000, p. 173). Saraswati has touched upon the colonial history of Banaras but maintained an honourable distance from analysing how it affected Textual and/or Oral Cultural Tradition(s) of Banaras. Interestingly, Singer in his Madras study (1972) has described that while the Sanskritic great tradition of Hinduism (Saraswati's Textual Cultural Tradition) is passing through a phase of modernization, it is transforming itself in order to accommodate elements of the Western culture.

A swiping account of Cohn regarding the changing educational scenario of Banaras during the colonial period would focus on the intention of the colonial power. He writes, "The Sanskrit College in Banaras had a similar history. The college owed its inception to the initiative of Jonathan Duncan, a Resident of Banaras. He recommended that surplus revenue, expected to accrue to the Company from the Permanent Settlement of the Banaras zamindari, be applied to the establishment of a Hindoo college .... for the preservation and cultivation of Laws, Literature and Religion of that nation, at this centre of their faith. Such an institution, Duncan felt, "would endear our government to the Native Hindoos" (Cohn, 1997, pp. 47-48). The intention of the colonial power was clear. Its aim was to establish the British political authority replacing the traditional authority in the garb of reviving the traditional. Cohn further writes, "The history of the British experiments with the Calcutta Madrassa and the Sanskrit College in Banaras are symbolic of wider issues entailed in the establishing of educational institutions under the colonial state. The British conceived of education as taking place in institutions, meaning buildings with physically divided spaces marking of one class of students from another, as well as teachers from students. . . . a British metalogic of regularity, uniformity, and above all fiscal responsibility could not help but participate in the erosion and transformation of what the British wanted to preserve, that is, Hindu and Muslim learning" (Cohn, 1997, pp. 47-48). Sanskrit college was set up in 1791 and since then many Western scholars of Sanskrit like William Jones, Wilkins, John Gilchrist, H.T. Colebrooke, W. A. Brooke, Colonel Wilford,

Demetrius Galanos, H.H. Wilson, Edward Fell, J.R. Ballantyne, Fitzedward Hall visited Benaras in order to be acquainted with the works written in Sanskrit. Apart from the mentioned ones in Sanskrit, there was no dearth of scholars in Arabic, Persian, Hindi, Bengali, Marathi, Gujarati, Tamil and Telugu (Swami Medhasananda, 2002, pp. 523-555). So, the textual tradition mentioned by Saraswati provides partial picture of the cultivation of textual tradition of Benaras. "Local pundits had certain common characteristics, including deep religious faith in Vishwanatha, Annapurna, and the Ganga, imparting free education, efficiency in disputation (*shastrarthas*), dedication to the study of scriptures, perfection in pronunciation, and above all leading a life of plain living and high thinking" (Swami Medhasananda, 2002, p. 483). Many of the monks were also great Sanskrit scholars though their specialization was in metaphysical religious texts. In effect, what we find is that there is no distinct boundary between the Textual Cultural Tradition and Transcendental Cultural Tradition. As far as Saraswati's categories are concerned, there are grey areas that do not imbibe characters of any of the categories.

Why such confusions occur in understanding and making generalizations about our country's enormous diversity of societies or cultures? Perhaps the confusion exists in our anthropological approaches of understanding the reality. Dipankar Gupta asserts that our approaches of studying culture(s) are taking two different directions. "The first" of two approaches, "denies the communicative and solidarity aspects of culture and emphasizes instead the contradictions and class antagonisms that are sought to be hidden, or veiled by cultural bravura. The other stream of scholarship highlights membership, solidarity, and bonding but does not pay enough attention to the issue of cultural conflict, dissensions, and struggles over legitimisation. The need to overcome this divide becomes all the more palpable once the nation-state is featured as an important anthropological phenomenon. Small scale societies are bound by what is called tradition" (Gupta, 2000, p. 10). We sometimes fail to accept that culture is only created and re-created by its practitioners. "Culture is primarily practice", writes Gupta in order to recognize the role of anthropologists in the study of nation-state. And he values such a practice "... in the pursuit of a 'good life'. The good life is not conceived individualistically or solipsistically. When the conception of good life is accessed through root metaphors it involves interaction with other people. . . . A multivocal regnant set of meanings of root metaphors allows us a perspective on culture that is neither individualistic nor consensual. The multiple saliences in the regnant set of meanings arise from varying locations of actors and groups in society" (Gupta, 2000, p. 18). We have to rethink about the unilinear understanding of India as an eternal, hierarchical, and changeless traditional entity. Side by side, it has also to be acknowledged that our history lies embedded in our tradition.

REFERENCES

Bose, N.K. 1959. "Comparative Study of Civilization". *Man in India*, 39(3).

Bose, N.K. (Ed.) 1967. *Peasant Life in India: A Study in Indian Unity in Diversity*. Memoir No. 8. Calcutta: Anthropological Survey of India.

Cohn, B.S. 1997. *Colonialism and its Forms of Knowledge: The British in India*. New Delhi: Oxford University Press.

Cohn, B.S. 2000. "Representing Authority in Victorian India". In Hobsbawm and Ranger (eds.) *The Invention of Tradition*. Cambridge: Cambridge University Press.

Eck, Diana L. 1985. *Darsan: Seeing the Divine Image in India*. 2nd Edition. Pennsylvania: Anima Books.

Gupta, Dipankar. 2000. *Culture, Space and the Nation State*. New Delhi, Thousand Oaks, London: Sage Publications.

Hobsbawm, Eric & Ranger, Terence (Eds.) 2000. *The Invention of Tradition*. Cambridge: Cambridge University Press.

Inden, Ronald. 1990. *Imagining India*. Oxford and Cambridge: Basil and Blackwell.

Lele, Jayant 1981. "The Bhakti Movement in India". In Jayant Lele (Ed.) *Tradition and Modernity in Bhakti Movement;* pp. 1-6. Leiden: E.J. Brill.

Parry, Jonathan. 2011. *Death in Banaras*. First South Asian edition in 1994. New Delhi: Cambridge University Press India Pvt. Ltd.

Redfield, R. and M. Singer. 1956. "Cultural Role of Cities". *Man in India*, 36(3).

Rudolph, L.I. & Rudolph S.H. 1987. *The Modernity of Tradition*. Hyderabad: Orient Longman Limited. First published in 1967.

Sharma, Vijay Prakash. 2013. "Baidhyanath Saraswati (Obituary)". *Journal of Indian Anthropological Society*, 48:3:307-308.

Singer, M. 1972. *When a Great Tradition Modernizes*. Delhi, Bombay, Bangalore etc., Vikash Publishing House Pvt. Ltd.

Swami Medhasananda. 2002. *Varanasi at the Crossroads: A Panoramic View of Early Modern Varanasi and the Story of its Transition*. Kolkata: Ramakrishna Mission Institute of Culture.

Works of Baidyanath Saraswati (The incomplete list does not include reports, miscellaneous writings etc. However, it includes those works referred in the text).

Monographs

1965a. "A Resume on the Seminar on Social and Cultural Profile of Kashi". *Man in India*, 53:1.

1965b. "The Holy Circuit of Nimsar". *Journal of Social Research*, 8(2).

1966. *Pottery Making Techniques in India* (with N. K. Behura). Memoir No. 13. Calcutta: Anthropological Survey of India.

1970a. *Contributions to the Study of Indian Civilization*. Dharwar: Karnatak University.

1970b. "Traditional Modes of Learning in Indian Civilization". *Journal of Indian Anthropological Society*, 5(1-2):153-69.

1974. "Studying Sacred Complex of Kashi" In *Symposium on the Sacred Complex in India*. Ed. by L.P. Vidyarthi and M. Jha.

1975a. "Study of Specialists in Traditional Learning: The Pundits of Kashi". *Journal of Indian Anthropological Society*, 10(2):103-16.

1975b. *Kashi: Myth and Reality of a Classical Cultural Tradition*. Simla: Institute of Advanced Study.

1976. "Experiments in Anthropological Methods", *Man in India*, 56(4).

1977. *Ritual Tradition in the Crucible of Time*. Simla: Indian Institute of Advanced Study.

1978a. "Sacred Complexes in Indian Cultural Traditions". *Eastern Anthropologist*, 31(1):81-92.

1978b. *Ascetics of Kashi: An Anthropological Exploration*. Varanasi: N.K. Bose Memorial Foundation [with Surajit Sinha].

1979. *The Sacred Complex of Kashi: A Microcosm of Indian Civilization* (with Makhan Jha and L.P. Vidyarthi). New Delhi: Concept Publishing Company.

1984. *Spectrum of the Sacred: Essays on Religious Traditions of India*. Delhi: Concept Publishing Company.

2000. *Bhog-Moksa Sambhava: Kasi ka Samajika-Sanskritika Svarupa* (in Hindi): New Delhi: D.K. Printworld (P) Ltd.

2004a. *The Eternal Hinduism*. New Delhi: D.K. Printworld (P) Ltd.

2004b. *Culture and Cosmos: The Cosmic Anthropological Principles*. New Delhi: Aryan Books International.

2005a. *Mrityu ki Dastak: Prachin Sastra evam Aadhunik Gyan* (with Ramlakhan Mauriya) (in Hindi). New Delhi: D.K. Printworld (P) Ltd.

2005b. *Voice of Death: Traditional Thought and Modern Science*. New Delhi: D.K. Printworld (P) Ltd.

2006. *Voice of Life: Traditional Thought and Modern Science*. New Delhi: D.K. Printworld (P) Ltd.

2007. *Voice of Senses: Traditional Thought and Modern Science*. New Delhi: D.K. Printworld (P) Ltd. & N.K. Memorial Foundation.

2009a. *Voice of God: Traditional Thought and Modern Science*. New Delhi: D.K. Printworld (P) Ltd. & N.K. Memorial Foundation.

2009b. *Sasvata Jiwan: Prachin Sastra evam Aadhunik Gyan*. New Delhi: D.K. Printworld (P) Ltd.

Edited Books

1991. *Tribal Thought and Cutlure: Essays in Honour of Shri Surajit Chandra Sinha*. New Delhi: Concept Publishing Company Pvt. Ltd.

1995a. *Computerizing Cultures*. New Delhi: Indira Gandhi National Center for

Arts.

1995b. *Cross-Cultural Lifestyle Studies*. New Delhi: Indira Gandhi National Center for Arts.

1995c. *Primal Elements: The Oral Tradition*. New Delhi: Indira Gandhi National Center for Arts.

1996. *Interface of Cultural Identity Development.* New Delhi: Indira Gandhi National Center for Arts & D.K. Printworld Pvt. Ltd.

1997. *Integration of Endogenous Cultural Dimension into Development*. New Delhi: Indira Gandhi National Center for Arts.

1998a. *The Cultural Dimension of Education*. New Delhi: Indira Gandhi National Center for Arts & D.K. Printworld Pvt. Ltd.

1998b. *The Cultural Dimension of Ecology*. New Delhi: Indira Gandhi National Center for Arts & D.K. Printworld Pvt. Ltd.

1998a. *Lifestyle and Ecology*. New Delhi: Indira Gandhi National Center for Arts & D.K. Printworld Pvt. Ltd.

1999a. *Cosmology of the Sacred World: The Vision of the Cosmos of Different Peoples of the World.* Co-edited by Yolotl Gonzales Torres. New Delhi: Decent Books.

1999b. *Culture of Peace: Experience and Experiment*. New Delhi: D.K. Printworld Pvt. Ltd.

2001a. *The Nature of Man and Culture: Alternative Paradigms in Anthropology*. New Delhi: Indira Gandhi National Center for Arts & Aryan Books International.

2001b. *The Nature of Living Tradition: Distinctive Features of Indian Parampara*. New Delhi: Indira Gandhi National Center for Arts & D.K. Printworld Pvt. Ltd.

2009. *Pilgrimage: Sacred Landscapes and Self-organized Complexity*. Co-edited by John McKim Malville. New Delhi: Indira Gandhi National Center for Arts & D.K. Printworld Pvt. Ltd.

Other Work

1997. "Foreword". In D.K. Samanta *Sacred Complex of Ujjain*. New Delhi: D.K. Printworld (P) Ltd.

3

Professor Usha Deka

A Humanist to the Core

Sarthak Sengupta

I

Writing about Professor Usha Deka for me has been more an act of expressing my deep emotional attachment to her as well as paying veneration to one of the most renowned anthropologists of our country, whom I knew since my student days at Gauhati University where I was pursuing my Ph.D. degree. I fondly called her Usha *Baideu*.

Prof. Usha Deka was born on 16th October, 1931. She hailed from an elite family and her father Late Holiram Deka was the Hon'ble Chief Justice (1960-1961) of Gauhati High Court, Assam. She was the second of the fourteen children born to Mr. Holiram Deka and Mrs. Vidyabati Deka. Her childhood and school days were, however, spent in Calcutta. She passed her matriculation from St. Margarate School, Calcutta (1946); Intermediate (1948), and Graduation (1950) from Cotton College, Guwahati with core subjects Mathematics and Physics. She had a brilliant academic career. After graduation, Prof. Deka did her Post Graduation from the University of Calcutta (1952) and was awarded the University Gold Medal as the topper, besides being awarded by one more medal by the University for standing first among the women candidates of the University. Although she received training and had the opportunity to enrich her knowledge base because of her exposure to the teachings of some legendary figures of Indian anthropology like Prof. K.P. Chattopadhyay, Prof. T.C. Roy Choudhury, Prof. T.C. Das, Prof. D. Sen, Prof. N.K. Bose, it was the great physical anthropologist of our country Dr. Sasanka Sekhar Sarkar who had influenced her most. Dr. Sarkar could also appreciate her talent and research potentialities.

Her background in mathematics at the undergraduate level came to her advantage later in her professional career and enabled her to delve deep into the subject of quantitative human genetics with confidence. During that time in India, there was hardly anyone among anthropologists who could be comparable with her stature, particularly in the field of population genetics and bio-statistics.

After obtaining M.Sc. degree in Anthropology, she carried out research works at the Directorate of Research, NEFA (now Arunachal Pradesh) as an Assistant Research Officer and had the opportunity of working with the famous anthropologist Dr. Verrier Elwin from 1952 to 1954. In 1954, she married another renowned anthropologist Prof. L.K. Mahapatra and started her teaching career as a Lecturer in the Department of Anthropology, Lucknow University (1954-1956). This was immediately followed by her entry into the Department of Anthropology of Gauhati University in 1956, where she got the opportunity to work with Prof. M.C. Goswami, Prof. B.M. Das. Almost at the same time she was awarded the Alexander von Humboldt Senior Fellowship in West Germany (1956-1960). Subsequently, she earned her Doctorate in Science (Dr. rer. nat.) in 1960 from the Christian Albrecht's University, Kiel, Germany under the supervision of Dr. J. Schaeuble for her work on the finger and palmar dermatoglyphics of criminals (*Studies an Handabrucken Von Verbrechern Aus Deutschland*).

After her return to India from West Germany she rejoined the Department of Anthropology, Gauhati University and remained attached with it for a brief spell (till May 1964). She then moved out of Gauhati and joined the Department of Anthropology, Utkal University, Vani Vihar, Bhubaneswar as Reader in the year 1964. When she joined, the Department was only six years old. She served a relatively new Department in different capacities and was ultimately elevated to the post of Professor in 1985. Ultimately, she superannuated from the same Department as a Professor of Physical Anthropology in 1991. As an anthropologist of international repute, Prof. Deka held several distinguished positions in India like the Vice President of the Indian Anthropology Association, New Delhi, Member of the State Advisory Board of Orissa State Museum, Bhubaneswar, to name only a few. She was also offered visiting positions by many established Universities of India.

Prof. Deka was an excellent and loving teacher, but her sharp and open criticism, strong will, straightforwardness and uncompromising attitude towards dishonest activities earned her many critics. She appeared to be rigid and at times harsh externally but was soft and affectionate at heart. In the working place, she was a very strict disciplinarian, punctual, sincere, and honest. But her life as such was full of trials, tribulations and challenges. She had to cross many hurdles in life, yet she had displayed enough courage and strength to bear the pains of lonely life silently, circumvent all odds with dignity, alacrity, and mental power without succumbing to them. It was only expected that as a scientist she would lay stress on scientific rigour, but seen from the perspective of human values and ideas one is prone to believe that her approach was, if anything, humanistic.

II

The research areas covered by Prof. Deka are in the field of population genetics, demography, anthropometry, dermatoglyphics, somatic growth, and maturity (through both cross-sectional and longitudinal methods), micro-evolutionary dynamics in numerically small population groups from a diverse and wide variety of populations of Orissa, Assam, and Meghalaya. The results of the studies conducted by her have been disseminated through publications in peer-reviewed journals, edited volumes, books, reports, lectures and proceedings of several technical seminars. It is worth mentioning here that before the research initiatives undertaken by Prof. Deka, hardly any systematic genetic data were available to understand the nature of biological diversity amongst population groups of Orissa.

In order to establish a viable population genetical laboratory at the Department of Anthropology, Utkal University, Professor Deka initiated systematic bio-anthropological investigations along with her Post Graduate students, encouraging them to collect data on ABO blood groups, PTC taste sensitivity, screening of red-green colour blindness. She even made them utilize the vacations for the purpose when they visited their countryside homes. These efforts resulted in amassing data on various genetic traits on a wide variety of hitherto lesser-known population groups of Orissa.

During her tenure as a faculty member of the Department of Anthropology, Utkal University, Prof. Usha Deka completed two major research projects with the financial assistance from the University Grants Commission, New Delhi. These are:

(i) Anthropometric Study of the Malva (Pentiya) of Koraput district, Orissa; and
(ii) Anthropometric studies of Kansaris of Orissa.

Prof. Deka was strictly against producing frivolous or popular type research writings. During her tenure at Gauhati University, she got published a few research articles with Prof. B.M. Das on a least studied caste of Assam 'Suri', who now identify themselves as 'Baishya'.To understand her area of research interest, one should be acquainted with the research works which she carried out with the active participation of her students. Her thought-provoking research article on 'Fertility and reproductive wastage' was published in *Tribal Demography of India* (edited by R.N. Pati and L. Jagatdeb) in 1991. One more article having a similar title (with P. Patojoshi) was also published in the *Bulletin of the Department of Anthropology, Dibrugarh University* in 1978.

Prof. Deka has mentored around ten Ph.Ds. and all these doctoral dissertations were highly praised in the academic world. Many of her students have been highly placed in reputed academic institutions. Apart from Utkal University, Vani Vihar, Prof. Deka was also the recognized Ph.D. Research Guide of Sambalpur and Berhampur University.

Among her Ph.D. students, Dr. S.K. Ghosh Maulik (1977) worked on *Demogenetic Study of a Population: The Siyalgirs*, a numerically small rural community of Orissa. Dr. P.N. Sahu (1978) studied another numerically small genetic isolate in the fringe areas of Bhubaneswar, Orissa. Both the populations were little over one thousand numerically with a very low admixture rate. The studies reveal that the survival strategy of both the populations is regulated by varied occupational activities, social systems and cultural practices.

P.K. Patojoshi (1977) studied the *Somatic and Genetic Variation among the Gadabas of Orissa*. The study was mainly confined to two linguistically distinct sub-groups – Mundari speaking *Gutab* and Dravidian speaking *Ollar*, besides one more sub-group called *Sena* was also included. The study indicates very limited genetic variation within the *Gutab*, an example of a convergent type of micro-evolution, as they are confined to a small territory.

Dr. S. Patel (1980) studied the process of adaptation of Tibetan migrants rehabilitated in the Chandragiri hills of south Orissa. How these high-altitude Tibetans could adapt themselves biologically and culturally was thoroughly investigated by the researcher. The study reveals that cultural adaptation is relatively quicker than biological adaptive changes.

Dr. J. Kanungo (1982) conducted a meticulous study on the *Fertility Variation among the Oriya Castes in Urban Communities* – a departure from the communities usually selected by anthropologists.

Dr. G. Nayak (1983) studied the *Racial Affinities of the Khonds of Orissa*. Khonds of Orissa are sub-divided into three sub-groups and her study, though indicative of the existence of mutual segregation, also confirms that the segregation is not of a very diverse nature that could create significant differences in morphological and genetic characteristics.

Prof. P. K. Das (1983) made a sincere effort to understand the nature and extent of genetic segregation and relative divergence between the Mundari-speaking tribal populations of Koraput and Ganjam Districts of Orissa revealing differences in language, as could be understood from the linguistic classification of Norman Zide. The study supports the linguistic dendrogram of Norman Zide and confirms that language acts as a potent factor in the origin of genetic diversity.

Variation of Menarche of Oriya Women and its various correlations with socio-economic and other relevant factors were systematically analysed and assessed by Dr. B. Patnaik (1987).

From the above description it is clear that Prof. Deka made her Ph.D. students work on topics which have not only relevance in the field of Biological Anthropology but have far-reaching implications in expanding its domain of active research. Besides, the practice of consanguinity/ inbreeding in the perspective of social and cultural tradition and its impact also attracted her attention. Such practices as could be found in two cities of Orissa and among a traditional community of south Orissa were thoroughly investigated by her.

Growth was another area which came to her consideration. In India till then the pattern of body growth was mainly assessed through the cross-sectional method. It was Dr. B. Rath (1976) who studied the growth of Oriya children through the longitudinal method. One more study on this less-trodden area was taken up by Dr. S. Nanda (1993; *Study on Secular Growth Trend in Orissa*), who also ventured to conduct a growth study among the rural people following a time-consuming longitudinal method.

Prof. Deka also took interest in some other areas of anthropology. Incidentally, she collected a large number of prehistoric lithic implements from open sites in different parts of Orissa. Some of these lithic artifacts were later properly analyzed and reported by some of her competent colleagues.

She was elected as Recorder of Anthropology and Archaeology Section of Indian Science Congress Association held at Kharagpur (1970), and in 1980 she was elected President of the Anthropology and Archaeology Section of the Indian Science Congress in its 67th Session at Jadavpur, West Bengal. She delivered an illuminating speech on 'Taxonomic Relationship among the Hindu Population of Orissa'. In 1985 she became the Vice-President of the Indian Anthropology Association, New Delhi.

III

Although Prof. Deka remained away from her home state of Assam for a prolonged period due to her professional obligations, she was very much concerned about the 'Assam Movement' during the seventies of the last century. She studied the movement in great detail and authored a small treatise 'Background of Assam Movement' in 1981 which was co-authored by Mr. Devajyoti Deka and published by Bani Prakash, Guwahati, Assam. The book discusses in details how the discontent and a sense of deprivation brewing in Assamese hearts for a long time gradually culminated in starting the movement. She opines that 'discontent and deprivation' have become a part of the Assamese psyche and are hard to remove. After all, these are factors derived from a long-time Assamese experience. Here she speaks more like a social analyst. It is rather unfortunate that during her professional career Prof. Deka did not receive due recognition of her merit and innovative spirit from her peers. She, however, deserves to find a place of recognition in the history of Indian anthropology.

IV

Prof. Usha Deka is no more with us. She passed away on 17th June, 2014 afternoon at the age of 83 years. With her demise, the Anthropology fraternity in India in general and Assam in particular have become poorer. Her demise created a void in the field of Biological Anthropology in India and perhaps a promising phase of Biological Anthropology initiated by Professor Usha Deka came to an end. Biological anthropologists of India, however, owe a great deal to her.

Some of her research publications are:

i. 'Fingerprint of the Suri' (jointly with B.M. Das), *Journal of Gauhati University,* 9: 121-126, 1958.
ii. 'Physical Characters of the Suri of Assam'(Jointly with B.M.Das), *Journal of Gauhati University,* 11, 2:87-98, 1960.
iii. 'Growth during Adolescence among Oriya Boys and Girls'. *Journal of Indian Anthropological Society,* 4: 141-146.1969.
iv. 'Study of Fertility in a Tribe of North East India'. *Journal of Social Research,* 1, 12: 74-82. 1970.
v. 'PTC Taste Threshold in Some Castes of Orissa', *Adibasi,* 11, 3:7-13. 1969-1970.
vi. 'Palmar Dermatoglyphics of the Mundas of Orissa', (jointly with P. Behera), *Man in India*, 50, 2:54-59, 1970.

vii. 'Fertility in Some Groups of Orissa'. *Man in Society,* 51-62. 1972.
viii. 'Earlobe Variation in Various Populations of Assam' (jointly with P.B. Das), *Man in India,* 33: 256-261.
ix. 'Genetic Survey of the Gadabas of Orissa', (jointly with P. Patojoshi), *Man in India.* 55, 3. 1975.
x. 'Growth and Economic Condition of Oriya Urban Children' (jointly with B. Rath), *Bulletin of the Department of Anthropology, Dibrugarh University,* 6: 181-192, 1977.
xi. 'Fertility and Pregnancy Wastage' (jointly with P. Patojoshi), *Bulletin of the Department of Anthropology, Dibrugarh University,* 6: 192-199, 1977.
xii. 'Background of Assam Movement' (jointly with Mr. Devajyoti Deka), Bani Prakash, Guwahati, Assam, 1981.
xiii. 'Fertility and Reproductive Wastage', in R.N. Pati and L. Jagatdeb (Eds): *Tribal Demography of India,* Ashish Publication House, New Delhi, 1991.

Acknowledgements

I am thankful and indebted to Dr. Premananda Bharati, former Professor, Indian Statistical Institute, Kolkata for his sincere academic help in preparing this write-up.

4

Professor Prabodh Kumar Bhowmick: An Action-*cum*-Development Anthropologist of India

Tilak Bagchi

A Brief Life Sketch

Professor Prabodh Kumar Bhowmick, popularly known as P.K. Bhowmick (commonly addressed as *Mej Da, Baba* or *Jyatha Babu* by the Lodhas and other downtrodden people of the Bidisha Ashram founded by Professor Bhowmick), was born on 6th September, 1926 (19th *Bhadra*, 1333 B.S.) in Amdabad, a remote village of Nandigram Police Station of the then undivided Midnapore district (now in Purba Medinipur of West Bengal). He was the third child among five brothers and three sisters of Jogendranath Bhowmick and Sarnomoyee Bhowmick. All his brothers were well placed in their respective academic fields. Professor Bhowmick has two daughters and two sons. The promising career of the younger daughter came to an abrupt end when she met with a fatal accident. The elder daughter and two sons were well known in the academic and corporate (ONGC) world. Now it has been left to them to carry forward the good works of Professor P.K. Bhowmick.

P.K. Bhowmick got school education from Kalagachhiya High School (now renamed as Kalagachhiya Jagadish Vidyapith), established as early as in 1921. During non-co-operation movement launched by Mahatma Gandhi, 11 schools of the then undivided Bengal were recognized as National Schools primarily due to the initiative of two great national leaders, viz., Desh Bandhu Chittaranjan Das and Deshapran Birendranath Sasmal. Kalagachhiya High School was one of such National Schools. Several great personalities including Deshapran Birendranath Sasmal and renowned Chemist and founder of 'Bengal Chemical' Acharya Prafulla Chandra Roy visited the school and germinated the spirit of patriotism in the mind of young Prabodh. He also came in contact with several nationalist teachers like Jagadish Maity, the then Head Master Nikunja Bihari Maity as well as Paresh Nath Maity and Girish Maity, the reputed Assistant Teachers of the School of that time. Their teaching and inspiration accelerated the spirit of nationalism and patriotism in young Prabodh. As a result, he became an out and out nationalist and used to put on *Khadi* cloths right from young age. He was imprisoned and kept in the jail under Contai police station of the then undivided Medinipur district when he was a student of class Nine after joining in the Quit India Movement and participating in picketing at Contai. He was in jail for about two and half years. After his release he was readmitted in class IX and passed Matriculation examination with distinction (Letter Marks) in several subjects including Sanskrit. His family members insisted on his taking admission in the Medical College to become a Doctor. Young Bhowmick was not at all interested to join the Medical College. His elder brother brought him to Bangabasi College and got him admitted in the I.Sc. course. At the B.Sc. level he took Anthropology as a major subject of study. It is not out of context to state here that in those days Bangabasi College was the only college which offered Anthropology at the undergraduate level. During his college days, Bhowmick was highly influenced by the mode of teaching of Professor Satkari Mitra, the then Head of the Department of Anthropology and maternal nephew of Swami Vivekananda, the spiritual soul of India.

His college friends and batch mates were Bikram Keshori Roy Burman, former Deputy Registrar General of India (Social Studies), Hirendra Kumar Rakshit, former Director of the Anthropological Survey of India, M.R. Chakraborty, who proved to be an eminent Anthropologist later, D.P. Mukherjee, former Professor of Anthropology, Calcutta University and founder of Department of Anthropology, S.V. University and former acting Director of the Anthropological Survey of India, Pranab Kumar Ganguly, founder Head of Anthropology, Vidyasagar University among others.

He passed B.Sc. with Anthropology Honours and M.Sc. with specialization in Social Cultural Anthropology from the University of Calcutta in 1951. His teachers were T.C. Das, K.P. Chattopadhyay, T.C. Roychaudhury, S.S. Sarkar, M.N. Basu, Dharani Sen and others. Immediately after passing M.Sc. in Anthropology, Bhowmick joined Bangabasi College as a Lecturer in Anthropology in 1952. He subsequently joined the University of Calcutta as a Lecturer in Anthropology in 1960 and was superannuated from the same on the 30th

September, 1994 as a Professor of Anthropology. During his long teaching career he became Head of the Department of Anthropology, Dean of the Faculty of Science, and Member of the Senate and Syndicate of the University. Prof. Bhowmick met with a road accident at College Street, Kolkata and after suffering a fortnight or so he died on 5th September, 2003.

The Doctoral Work

Professor Bhowmick obtained his Ph.D. and D.Sc. Degrees in Anthropology from the University of Calcutta. His anthropological insight developed further when he had the privilege of being supervised by Professor Nirmal Kumar Bose, an architect of Indian Anthropology. Incidentally, Professor Bose was the Bengali Interpreter-*cum*-private secretary of Mahatma Gandhi during his stay in Bengal during mid-1940s, was the Director of the Anthropological Survey of India (1959-1964, Commissioner for the National Commission of Scheduled Tribe (1967-1997) and President of the Asiatic Society (1972).

Gandhian approach of Nirmal Kumar Bose influenced Bhowmick even in his research work. After coming in direct contact with the deprived and disadvantaged group of people in the field, he probably realized that simply to have empathy on such people was not enough; speedy action programmes were needed not only to ameliorate their sufferings but also to help them stand on their feet. He started his Ph.D. work in 1952 and was awarded the degree in 1961 for his doctoral work "The Lodhas of West Bengal : A Socio Economic Study", which was published in 1963 from Punthi Pustak, Kolkata. In his Ph.D. dissertation, Professor Bhowmick observed that in earlier times also Lodhas were not a purely hunting gathering group. As per 1901 Census Report they migrated from Madhya Pradesh as an agricultural community. However, in 1931 Census Report, they were shown to have indulged in criminal activities. In his study, Bhowmick covered the whole range of social, political, economic and recreational activities of the Lodhas. It was shown by him how different rituals or life cycle events from birth to death along with the participation of their kin members produced a feeling of commonness as reflected in the acts of sharing and reciprocity. A sense of belongingness to community's affairs strengthened the roots of tribal identity as cognized by the Lodhas. According to his observation, Lodhas take pride in declaring themselves as Savara, which help them identifying with the greater Mundari group of people. Professor Bhowmick's work revealed that earlier Lodhas must have enjoyed freedom of the forest life and were used to it, but in Midnapore during the British Colonial rule they were deprived of that freedom. They had to enter into certain economic relationships with their neighbouring agricultural caste communities, the results of which were not always favourable to them. A wrong notion was created and they were branded as a criminal tribe.

Abject poverty and social neglect were the root cause of their alleged criminality in the sense it was used. There can be nothing in the original culture to which they belong, which would have led them into this unhappy state of existence. Professor Bhowmick also observed that territorial displacement and destabilising effects of a new setting coupled with not so friendly attitude of communities all around had serious implications on the old pattern of socio-economic life of the Lodhas, which was by and large pivoted around hunting, gathering, fishing and fowling and it ultimately disturbed the equilibrium of the whole society. Probably under such circumstances pilfering, petty thefts, lifting of articles from the house of the neighbours and clandestine sale of jungle produces were first resorted to on individual basis more out of desperation. The individual practices gradually crystallized into a group activity. Together with poverty, unfriendly attitude of the neighbours and stoic apathy of the ruling class and Government was responsible for their getting involved in criminal activities which became an enigma to them. As a result, the Lodhas were branded as a 'Criminal Tribe' by the then British Government which remained effective till the revocation of Criminal Tribe Act in 1952. Professor Bhowmick on the basis of his study of 31 Lodha villages distributed in seven police stations of Midnapore Sadar (now in Paschim Medinipur District and Jhargram Sub Division, now in Jhargram District) concluded that criminality could not be a regular profession of any human society. He also argued that if criminality was their culture bound profession then there must be a psycho-social and ritualistic expression showing their link with criminality or criminal bent of mind, which the Lodha society and culture do not in any way suggest.

Apart from academic discourses, Professor Bhowmick has worked hard to rehabilitate the Lodhas in the midst of economically more advanced neighbouring communities. He has tried hard to dispel all kinds of misunderstandings or misapprehensions about them harboured by the neighbouring communities so that Lodhas could participate in development programmes on equal terms. From the academic point of view, his study of the Lodha is an excellent piece of ethnographic work. He has tried to present a comprehensive and coherent picture of the Lodha community interlacing all aspects of culture. His life-long work on the Lodhas has earned him the name 'Lodha Bhowmick' or 'Messaiha of the Lodha'.

Professor Bhowmick was also awarded the D.Sc. degree in 1967 by the University of Calcutta for his monumental work "Socio-Cultural Profile of Frontier Bengal" which was published in 1976 from Punthi Pustak, Calcutta. On the basis of his study of the then undivided Bengal and its adjacent areas of Orissa (now spelt as Odisha) and Bihar (now Jharkhand), which formed the frontier or border Bengal, he tried to show that diversified communities, each with its own tradition-bound lifestyle, could clearly reveal themselves during the period of his study (in the mid -1950s and early 1960s of the last century) giving vent to the exposition of different types of understanding about them. All these have been discussed under socio-cultural profile in the frontier region of Bengal. On the basis of micro study of diversified ethnic groups, Prof. Bhowmick tried to establish different life-ways and worldviews of the people of frontier Bengal. His primary objective of study was to show that they all contributed to a holistic socio-cultural pattern which could be attributed to the whole region encompassing the western border of the Greater Bengal. As stated earlier, the specific geographical terrain which Professor Bhowmick had selected for his study was the frontier boundary of the then undivided Midnapore District that was contiguous with the Districts of Balasore and Mayurbhanj of Odisha, with its northward boundary spreading along the Districts of undivided Singbhum and Dhanbad of Bihar (now Jharkhand). This particular tract was also associated with Purulia, Bankura and Birbhum districts of West Bengal, both of which had almost similar social composition and geographical congruity as observed by Professor Bhowmick. He also observed that this particular land was having a distinctive cultural background, a cumulative representation of a number of sub-cultures with criss-crossed or extended political boundary. This typical geographical region, since the beginning of history witnessed arrival of several kings, rulers and political agencies, but none could bring any significant change in the local cultural tradition because of the integrity, radicalism and spirituality displayed by the concerned groups of people. Bhowmick preferred to call this territory a frontier region denoting a specific terrain, which like any other region had witnessed several socio-political and culture-specific events prompted by migration, conquest and aggression of alien forces. It cannot be denied that the historicity of this region was built around people's experiences of colonial rule imparted by the British, the Portuguese and the French. This influence is still visible in some form or the other in the rural life of the people of contemporary times. Furthermore, arrival of the Pathans and the Mughals and their political activities had left deeper imprints on them.

From the remote past, the region was the home of tribal groups like Santal, Lodha, Munda, Mahali, Kora and others. Besides, there were small and isolated aboriginal derivatives like the Chirmar, Kakmara, the snake charming community Savara. This region was also the melting pot of Odishan and Rarh Bengali cultures. It was representative of a synthesis of cultural features characterized by the traditions and life ways of the people. Prof. Bhowmick strongly believed that in spite of several push and pull factors operative at the level of traditional cultures, the region was abound with tribal ways of life reflecting their perceptions and thought processes. Specific tribal orientation pattern was so strong and deep rooted in the region that it could not be displaced by the powerful Brahminical tradition. In his D.Sc. dissertation, Professor Bhowmick tried to show how the traditional tribal based indigenous cultures reacted with different facets of Brahminic, Islamic and Colonial thoughts and ideas in an attempt to bring about concrete reorientation of their thinking process.

Seminal Contributions to Anthropology

Professor Bhowmick was a prolific writer both in English and Bengali. He wrote sixteen books and more than two hundred research papers in both English and Bengali. The books written by him are:

1. The Lodhas of West Bengal: A Socio-Economic Study
2. Four Midnapore Villages
3. Occupational Mobility and Caste Structure in Bengal
4. Socio-Cultural Profile of Frontier Bengal
5. Occultism in Fringe Bengal
6. Some Aspects of Indian Anthropology
7. The Chenchus of the Forest and Plateaux : The Hunting Gathering Tribe in Transition
8. Applied, Action and Development Anthropology
9. Primitive Tribal Groups in Eastern India
10. Tribal Literacy in West Bengal
11. Rethinking Tribal Culture in India
12. Caste in Border Bengal
13. Customary Law of Austric Speaking Tribe
14. Bangalar Lok Utsab (in Bengali)
15. Medinipur Kahini, later reprinted as Amader Medinipur (in Bengali)
16. Lok Samaj o Sanskriti (in Bengali)

Professor Bhowmick in his studies could throw some light on the question of cultural integration in the midst of forced isolation or segregation. Though he had studied several tribes of West Bengal, Odisha, Jharkhand and Andhra Pradesh, he carried a special interest in the Particularly Vulnerable Tribal Groups like Lodha, Kheria, Birhor and Toto of West Bengal as well as the Chenchus of Andhra Pradesh in the context of their spontaneous or forced assimilation with the greater Hindu civilization. Besides, his study touched upon such aspects as population pattern and population dynamics, occultism, customary law of the tribal population, rural social system, religious centres and various festivals related to diversified folk life. The significance of cultural traits in the socio-political life of the people also attracted his attention. His broad objective was to see the social system in the rural context in terms of established or stereotypic notions and ideas. It may be possible to work out a link between micro-sociological formations with macro-sociological considerations which were particularly discernible in the way villages, households and temple organizations functioned. He even studied various fairs and festivals from insider's point of view. May be his ethnography did not follow a specific direction, but it could produce significant results.

Professor Bhowmick founded *Man and Life*, a journal devoted to study the Science of Man covering all its aspects and from 1976 till 2003, he was the Editor of it. He also organized several national and international seminars at Bidisa since 1974 as the key Organizer-*cum*-Seminar Director. He participated in several national and international seminars in India and abroad. Notable among them were the National Conference on De-notified Tribal Communities in 1963, the International Congress of Anthropology and Ethnological Sciences where he had chaired one session of Applied Anthropology in Amsterdam, Holand. Due to the effort of Professor Bhowmick and his close friend Ranjit Gupta, I.P. (retd.), the former Inspector General and Head of West Bengal Police, the Lodhas were included as a Primitive Tribal Group (now renamed as Particularly Vulnerable Tribal Group) and the tortures the Lodhas were subjected to in different police out-posts were withdrawn. Professor Bhowmick was the founder Chairman of the Syllabus Committee in Anthropology in Vidyasagar University where because of his initiative a non-traditional subject like Anthropology was introduced at the post-graduate level in 1980. He was also the President of the Indian Anthropological Society, Kolkata and Anthropological Secretary of the Asiatic Society, Kolkata for some time.

Bidisa – The Dream Project of Prof. Bhowmick

Professor Bhowmick started his research among the Lodhas since 1952 and as a sequel to that he established "*Samaj Sevak Sangha*" at Bidisa in 1955. Bidisa meaning 'what diffuses light' was set up in a presently depopulated village Bagavera meaning 'a path of the tiger'. It suggests co-existence of forest dwelling and a plains village located in Midnapore Sadar Sub-Division. The village was near to the Odisha Trunk Road and a kilometre away from Narayangarh Railway Station. Professor Bhowmick started living in the village along with a group of Lodha Savaras and other tribal groups to develop a social laboratory-*cum*-action anthropological research centre. For social work he developed "*Samaj Sevak Sangha*", while for applied and action anthropological research work, he founded "The Institute of Social Research and Applied Anthropology". Bidisa has been identified as a role model for applied and action anthropological research in India and he tried to develop Bidisa following the global perspective of applied and action anthropology. A lower primary school was established at Bidisa particularly for the Lodhas and other downtrodden sections of people which was upgraded to upper primary school in 1968. The school was further upgraded to government-aided High School after his death in 2007 and was renamed as "Daharpur Professor Prabodh Kr. Bhowmick Vidyalaya". An Ashram Hostel was established in mid-1960s to provide food and lodging to the Lodha children thereby catering to their basic needs. Ashram hostel in West Bengal was the brain child of Professor Bhowmick which was later taken as a model Ashram hostel by the Government of West Bengal. In this regard he observed (2003) that the Ashram hostel for boys in the form of an institutional complex was first organized when the Lodha children experienced dissociation from their parents and the consequent detachment from their long practiced questionable habits which mark their re-socialization and enculturation into a new social milieu. In the year 1968, a riot took place between the Lodha and the Santal tribal communities, after which a second hostel with 20 capacity was set up to provide free boarding and lodging to the riot victim Lodha boys. Later on, another hostel for 20 girls was established. Subsequently, it dawned on him that the Lodhas should be provided with vocational training to make them self-reliant. Professor Bhowmick observed that the expanding institutional complex at Bidisa would not only provide vocational training to the drop-outs but also reorganize the life of the tribal and lower caste boys and girls through various productive activities related to agriculture, fishery, bee keeping, dairy farming, carpentry, tailoring and weaving. In 1977, he set up a printing press at Bidisa. From this press books of several luminaries of anthropology including Professor Nirmal Kumar Bose, Professor Baidyanath Saraswati, Professor Sachchidananda, Professor R.S. Mann, Professor Vinay Kumar Srivastava, Professor N.K. Behura were printed and published.

Bidisa can also boast of a rock garden and artificial park decorated with archaeological findings and old sculptures of Rarh Bengal, a huge tank with an island that attracts birds during winter season and a deer park, a seminar hall in the name of Professor N.K. Bose. Large rooms in brick built houses as well as cottages were constructed for the guests and participants who might come to Bidisa for attending seminars and conferences, training courses and field based activities. Bidisa has also a library rich with rare anthropological and sociological books and dissertations. He also set up an open air stage in the name of his beloved departed younger daughter Sarita Bhowmick known as "*Sarita Mancha*". One "*Rarh Sanskriti Sangrahalaya*" and an open air ethno-archaeological museum were added in 1990 with the help of two Directors of Indian Museum Dr. R.C. Sharma and Dr. S.S. Biswas, both of whom later became the Director Generals of National Museum of New Delhi. The museum was inaugurated by Professor K.L. Chopra, the then Director of Indian Institute of Technology of Kharagpur. This museum exhibits preserved material cultural objects and objects related to art and craft of the local people including tribes as well as archaeological relics like a Shiva Linga of Makrana Stone, an old stone image of Jain Tirthankar Lord Risabh Nath. In addition, he also developed "*Kultikri Kiarchand Sanskriti Smarak*" and a "*Guha*", an artificial rock shelter at Bidisa. In this way, Professor Bhowmick developed Bidisa, a lone model organization of applied and action anthropology for which he will be ever remembered. Vidyarthi (1979) once observed that Professor Bhowmick was the only anthropologist in India who represented the fourth category of applied and action anthropology for his Bidisa experiment. The comment was probably made in the context of the Fourth World composition.

Professor Bhowmick's Major Contributions in Indian Anthropology

Professor P.K. Bhowmick made several significant and important contributions to Indian anthropology as one of the important exponents of Indian anthropology (Bhowmick *et al.*, 2021). Though his contributions have already been discussed elsewhere, an attempt has been made here to highlight some of his major contributions.

His Ph.D. work on the Lodha is not only an excellent piece of ethnographic work, it also made him one of the pioneer post-colonial ethnographers who could deal with a tribe once branded as a Criminal Tribe by the colonial British ruler and was recognised as a de-notified tribe after repelling of the Criminal Tribes Act in 1952. He in his descriptive ethnography not only focused on the stigma of criminality once imposed on them, but with the help of records of the British Colonial Government, he also made an attempt to highlight the root cause and genesis of it. According to him, the British Government once thought that caste system or occupational guild system was perhaps responsible for the creation of the maxim 'once a criminal always a criminal' implying that people whose ancestors took the crime as a means of livelihood must always remain a criminal (Bhowmick, 1963). He proved in his Bidisa experiment that the British notion did not hold good, but it still was deep rooted in the minds of many neighbouring communities even today. Professor Bhowmick in his ethnographic work focused on how the stigma of criminality created a rift between them and neighbouring caste communities. While evaluating the contributions of Bhowmick for the welfare of the Lodha, Prof. Vijoy S. Sahay (2003) described Prof. Bhowmick as a 'Messiah of the Lodhas'. Later on, several welfare measures have been initiated by the Central and State Governments and NGOs for the overall development of the Lodhas, which ultimately paved the way for their inclusion in the list of Particularly Vulnerable Tribal Group (PVTG). More than half a century after the publication of his work on the Lodhas, the Anthropological Survey of India has launched a massive national project on the anthropological study of de-notified communities of India and here Prof. Bhowmick has to be considered as a pioneer among post-colonial anthropologists for his important study of one of the de-notified communities of India, namely, the Lodhas bearing the stigma of criminality levelled on them by the colonial British Rulers.

Another of his most significant ethnographic work is on the "Chenchus of the Forest and Plateaux" published in 1992. After the work of Haimendorf (1943) during colonial era on the Chenchus, the work of Bhowmick on the forest and pleateau of Nallamalai hills of the then Andhra Pradesh is worth mentioning. Bhowmick's work focused mainly on the changing position and impact of the development programmes on the Chenchus living in the then undivided Andhra Pradesh. His detailed ethnographic work is also a sort of restudy of the work of Haimendorf to an extent where he has focused on many changes in the life of the Chenchus after the treatise of Haimendorf.

Bhowmick and his associates studied a good number of small and marginal communities including semi-nomadic communities and aboriginal derivatives like the Kakmaras, Bagals, Suklis, which had also added a new chapter in the anthropological literature and ethnography on small, marginal and semi-nomadic communities.

Bhowmick's work on occultism published in 1978 focused on many elements of magic, religion, spirits, ghosts and other supernatural powers that influence human societies of border Bengal (Rarh Bengal) in many ways and at the same time conjointly or individually exercise control over societies of that region.

His D.Sc. work on the "Social-Cultural Profile on the Frontier Bengal" (1976) has highlighted the operational process of radicalism and de-Brahminization, definitely a new concept in Indian anthropology during that time. His understanding of culture, society and behavioural patterns of different ethnic groups or communities has also been highlighted in the said study.

Bhowmick's work on four Midnapur villages, viz., Daharpur, a multi-ethnic village; Kasba-Narayangarh, a Muslim dominated village; Mirpur; a Christian, especially a Portugese Christian village; Bejda, a tribal Christian converted village; and, his own restudy on Daharpur exemplifies a synchronic and diachronic study in anthropological parlance (Bagchi, 2021). His village study could add a new dimension in village studies and restudies carried out by a group of anthropologists under the influence of American School of Anthropology from 1950 onwards and a large number of monographs published by the Office of the Registrar General of India with the methodology adopted by its Social Studies Division under the guidance of Shri Ashok Mitra, ICS, the then Registrar General of India and Prof. B.K. Roy Burman, Deputy Registrar General, Social Studies Division of the Office of the Registrar General India.

Bhowmick's Bidisa Project symbolises an application of clinical or experimental methods of action anthropology initiated by Sol Tax (1964). Vidyarthi (1968) in this context remarked that Bhowmick has been successful in combining the two processes of providing help and initiating learning process among an ex-criminal tribe, i.e., the Lodhas of West Bengal.

It has always been his endeavour to try to focus on cultures of different societies and interrelation between them as manifested in a micro level situation. At the same time, he tried to extend the horizon of Anthropology not only as a science of man but as a science for the service of mankind. It has made him a true action-*cum*-development anthropologist in India other than being an excellent ethnographer.

Contributions Beyond Anthropology

Professor Bhowmick along with his friend Professor Anil Gayen played a key role in the establishment of Vidyasagar University in Midnapore. He was also instrumental in the establishment of many colleges in rural Bengal which include Pathankhali College, Bajkul College, Nandigram College and Belda College. His active association with the West Bengal Council of Child Welfare, the organization dedicated to the development of downtrodden and orphan children was no less significant. He was also the *Editor* of *Sisu Kalyan*, the Bengali journal of the Council for several years. Professor Bhowmick with the help of the Council established '*Balwadi*' (Pre-primary) schools in Fulgeriya and Kalagachhiya villages of Narayangarh police station of Paschim Medinipur, West Bengal; Dhansol village of Baripada forest range of Mayurbhanj District of Orissa. A *Balwadi* school was set up by him in the Churachandpur District of Manipur with the active cooperation of his student Dr. T.S. Gangte. His association with several learned societies like "*Janasiksha Prochar Kendra*", National Science Society as President is worth mentioning. As a member of the visiting team of the West Bengal Higher Secondary Council he played a decisive role in introducing plus two (standard XI & XII) in several schools of rural Bengal.

Professor Bhowmick had shown particular interest in studying folklore and the regional history of Rarh Bengal. In this connection, he regularly organized seminars on the regional history and folklore and held "*Nabanna*" and "*Polly Punorgathon Utsav*" (post-harvest and rural reconstruction festival) at Bidisa during the months of September and December respectively.These were attempts for the revival of folk tradition of the region on the one hand and dissemination of rich cultural heritage of the region to the local people on the other. Professor Bhowmick wrote several books and articles on the folklore and regional history of the marginal communities like Kakmara, Christians of Mirpur. The list of regional folk-based rituals and festivals attracting his attention includes "*Gajan*", "*Tusu*", "*Bhadu*" and "*Jhumur*" and other folk songs of the western part of border Bengal. His paper on 'Poresh Patidar's life and creative activity of a scroll painter' deserves special mention.

International Exposure

Professor Bhowmick did not have the opportunity to make any international level collaboration. However, he visited Amsterdam to participate in a session of Applied Anthropology in the International

Congress of Anthropological Ethnological Sciences. He also participated in several international seminars and conferences at United Kingdom, Italy, West Germany, Holland, and Bangladesh. Scholars from Bangladesh and Nepal carried out Ph.D. works under his supervision. Anthropologists and other social scientists from Russia, United States of America, Japan, Holland, West Germany, Nepal, United Kingdom and Bangladesh visited Bidisa to be acquainted with the activities of his social laboratory at Bidisa or to participate in the Seminars held there. In recognition of his contributions, even Bill Clinton, the former President of the U.S.A., sent his best wishes to him.

Post-retirement Activities and Supervision of Ph.D. Works

After retirement Professor Bhowmick remained actively busy with development of Bidisa, teaching assignments as a Guest Faculty in several universities and IIT, Kharagpur as well as writing books and papers. About sixty researchers have carried out research works under his supervision for the award of Ph.D. He had supervised Ph.D. students on a good number of topics covering diverse areas. About fifteen scholars carried out their research works for Ph.D. degree on ethnographic account of the Mahali, Savara, Bagal, and Bauri of West Bengal, Dimasa Kachhari of Assam, Gadaba of Andhra Pradesh, Maring and Kuki of Manipur, Khond of Odisha, Bhoksa of unidivided Uttar Pradesh, Nicobarese of Car Nicober, Rout of Chhattisgarh, Dhimal of Nepal. Notable scholars who had carried out research in this line includes Professor Rajat Kanti Das of Vidyasagar University, Dr. Shyamal Kanti Sengupta of University of Calcutta, Dr. Dipali Ghosh Danda of the Anthropological Survey of India, Professor Rishikesh Rengmi of Tribhuvan University of Nepal, Dr. Niranjan Kumar Ghatak, former Director of the Ministry of Tribal Affairs, Government of India, Dr. T.S. Gangte, former Director of Education, Government of Manipur, and Dr. A.V. Subba Rao of Vijaywada Government College of Andhra Pradesh.

More than a dozen researchers earned their Ph.D. for carrying out research on religion, religiosity, religious complex and pilgrim sites like Tarakeshwar, Holy Godavari river, concept of food, disease, method of treatment and their nexus with the religion, magic, witchcraft, death rites, agricultural rituals and related topics which may broadly be included under the canopy of magic, religion and medical anthropology. Eminent scholars who have done research on these topics include Professor Swapan Kr. Bhattacharya of the Department of Sociology, University of Calcutta, Professor Debasis Debnath of Dr. B.R. Ambedkar University of

Social Sciences, Indore, Professor Pabitra Kumar Gupta, former acting Vice-Chancellor and Registrar of Bidhan Chandra Krishi Viswavidyalaya, Nadia, Professor Prafulla Chakraborty of Sociological Research unit of Indian Statistical Institute, Dr. Arun Kumar Chatterjee, former Chairperson of Indian National Chapter of International Council of Museums. About four researchers including Dr. S. Chakraborty of Bangabasi College, Dr.Chittarnajan Bandyopadhyay, former President of West Bengal Board of Secondary Education, Dr. Narayan Chandra Maity, former Principal of Mahishadal Girls' College carried out their research on joint family system, rural indebtedness, caste panchayat, rural administration which may be put under the broad category of rural social institution and administration.

About five researchers conducted research works under his supervision on the topics like methodology of development, anthropology in action in tribal area, constraints of development which may be put under the category of development, action and applied anthropology. Renowned scholars who had carried out research for their Ph.D. degree were Dr. Subir Kumar Biswas, IAS (Retd.), former Chairman of Uttar Pradesh Public Service Commission, D.R. Pratap, former Director of Tribal Research Institute, Andhra Pradesh, Dr. Dibakar Basak, former Joint Director of Scheduled Caste and Scheduled Tribe, Lucknow. About ten researchers carried out their research on ethnic interaction and cultural transformation. Notable among them are Professor Hasan Ali of Dhaka University, Sujit Som, former Joint Director of the Indira Gandhi Rashtriya Manav Sangrahalaya, Bhopal and some others. They worked on strategies of survival among the Oraon, displaced/migrated Santals of Bangladesh, biological and cultural adaptation of the refugees of Little Andaman, life in Sundarban, survival of Hindu rituals, pavement dwellers of Calcutta, social mobility, facets of historical anthropology and such other topics. About ten researchers carried out their research works on rural and urban problems and related issues like tribal food and nutrition, fertility and mortality, working women, urbanization and urban social situation, child labour, Naxalite movement, socio-psycho-economic problems of hospital patients, cycle-rickshaw pullers and the like. Names of some of the scholars who had carried out their research works for Ph.D. degree in those areas are Professor Bela Bhattacharya of Vidyasagar University, Dr. Krishna Mandal of the All India Institute of Hygiene and Public Health, Kolkata, Suraj Bandyopadhyay of the Indian Statistical Institute. The present author has carried out research for his Ph.D. degree under his guidance on food and nutritional aspects of the five tribal communities of West Bengal covering ethnographic, biological, ecological, economic, socio-cultural and developmental aspects related to food and nutrition. That Professor Bhowmick could supervise on a wide range of topics related to anthropology and allied disciplines in connection with Ph.D. works of his students speaks of his profound knowledge and resourcefulness.

Acknowledgements

The author is thankful to Dr. Monoranjan Bhowmick, Dr. Pradip K. Bhowmick, Dr. Dipak Adak and Sri Dibyajyoti Ganguly for their help and providing required information.

REFERENCES

References and Some of the Significant Writings on Professor Prabodh Kumar Bhowmick

Bagchi, T. 2021. "Role of Professor P.K.Bhowmick in the Field of Village Studies" in: *Professor P.K.Bhowmick, a Legendary Leader in Indian Anthropology*. Edited by P.K. Bhowmick, S. Manna, P.C. Kumar, New Delhi: Abhijit Publications, pp. 228-242.

Bhowmick, A. 2004. "Sriman Prabodh Kumar: Srmitir Aloy". In *Odhyapak Prabodh Kumar Bhowmick, Karmajiban O Darshan*. Edited by Pranab Roy; Bidisha; Samaj Sevak Sangha and ISRAA; pp. 44-46 (in Bengali).

Bhowmick, M. 2019. *Chirabhaswar Jnantapas Prabodh Kumar Bhowmick*; Bidisha, Narayangarh; Samaj Sevak Sangha (mimeograph in Bengali).

Bhowmick, P.K. 1963. *The Lodhas of West Bengal : A Socio-economic Study;* Calcutta; Punthi Pustak.

Bhowmick, P.K. 1976. *Socio-cultural Profile of Frontier Bengal*; Calcutta; Punthi Pustak.

Bhowmick, P.K. 1978. *Occultism in Fringe Bengal*. Calcutta, Subarnarekha.

Bhowmick, P.K. 1989. *Bidisha: An Introduction* (leaflate); Bidisha; Institute of Social Research and Applied Anthropology.

Bhowmick, P.K. 1992. *Chenchus of the Forest and Plateaux*. Calcutta Institute of Social Research and Applied Anthropology.

Chakraborty, B. 2019. *Amar Anubhabe Dr. Prabodh Kumar Bhowmick O Bidisha*; Sundarnagar, Purba Medinipur; Baneswar Chakraborty (Publisher).

Deb, P.K. 2006. "About Prof. P.K. Bhowmick". In *Exploration in Anthropology: P.K. Bhowmick and His Collaborative Research Work*. Edited by S.K. Pramanik and S. Manna; Bidisha; ISRAA; pp. i-ii.

Debnath, D. 2012. "Bhowmick's Thoughts and Action". In *World of Development Anthropology and Society: Issues and Applications*. Edited by Indu Talwar; New Delhi; Northern Book Centre; pp. 33-42.

Dustcher, I. 2006. "Foreword". In *Exploration in Anthropology: P.K. Bhowmick and His Collaborative Research Work*. Edited by S.K. Pramanik and S. Manna;

Bidisha; ISRAA; pp. iii-vi.

Haimendorf, F.C.V. 1943. *The Chenchus, Jungle Folk of the Deccan.* London, McMillan.

Koley, S. 2019. "P.K. Bhowmick". In *Anthropologist.* Edited by S.K. Koley *et al.* New Delhi; Maya Publication.

Pramanik, S.K. and Samita Manna. 2006. In *Exploration in Anthropology: P.K. Bhowmick and His Collaborative Research Work.* Edited by S.K. Pramanik and S. Manna; Bidisha; ISRAA; pp. vii-xi.

Sahay, V.S. 2003. "Dramatis Personae of Indian Anthropology: Messiah of the Lodhas". *The Oriental Anthropologists*; 3 (2): 184-199.

Sarkar, R.M. 2006. "Professor P.K. Bhowmick – The Field of Anthropologist Oriented with Indigenous Vision". In *Exploration in Anthropology: P.K. Bhowmick and His Collaborative Research Work.* Edited by S.K. Pramanik and S. Manna; Bidisha; ISRAA; pp. 41-62.

Tax, Sol. 1964. "Anthropological Tradition". In: *Horizons of Anthropology.* Edited by Leslie G. Freeman. Chicago, Aldine Publishing Company.

Vidhyarthi, L.P. 1968. *Applied Anthropology in India*, Allahabad, Kitab Mahal.

5

Lalita Prasad Vidyarthi

An Anthropologist with a Difference

Jayanta Sarkar

The year 1920 is the landmark in the history of development of teaching the discipline of Anthropology in India. The year saw establishment of a full-fledged Department of Anthropology for Post Graduate studies in Calcutta University. Prior to this, in 1919 Anthropology as a subject was introduced in the newly established Department of Sociology of Bombay University, which actually marks the beginning of teaching Anthropology in India.

In course of its journey of long 100 years up to 2020, the discipline of Anthropology in India has been enriched by several scholars, both from abroad and from our own country. Academic contributions of these scholars, who include both trained anthropologists and non-anthropologists, have appeared prominently in many professionally recognized writings and government reports.

At this stage, as a professional anthropologist when I look back and try to evaluate contributions of my teacher Professor Lalita Prasad Vidyarthi, I find that a fairly detailed account on his contributions to Indian anthropology is available in a publication of Mohan K. Gautam and Ajit K. Singh (Gautam & Singh, 1983). Upadhyay and Pandey have also discussed at length about the academic contribution of Vidyarthi in a volume "History of Anthropological Thought" (Upadhyay & Pandey, 1993). Vidyarthi's classification of tribes of Bihar from the consideration of ecology, economy, level of socio-cultural integration and the sequence of changes, with certain modifications, as well as his works on *Cultural Linguistic Regions of Bihar* (Vidyarthi, 1964:1) and Phases of *Development of Anthropology in India* (Vidyarthi, 1978:176) are well known in the anthropological world.

Review of his major publications, therefore, would be a repetition only. I, being a student of this great scholar, would rather try to see him as a teacher who made concerted efforts untiringly to groom his students and also towards expansion of the discipline in India. In doing so, I shall make relevant references to his works at appropriate places.

Initiation into Anthropology

Exactly after 33 years of establishment of the Department of Anthropology in Calcutta University, Lalita Prasad Vidyarthi passed out Master of Arts in Anthropology in 1953 from the newly created Post Graduate Department of Anthropology of Lucknow University. In the same year, he joined Ranchi College, then under Bihar University, as a lecturer in Anthropology. This was the phase in the history of development of Anthropology, which was later categorized by Vidyarthi as the Analytical Phase (1978, Vol. 1).

This was the period when a galaxy of Indian anthropologists like Nirmal Kumar Bose, Shyama Charan Dube, Surajit Chandra Sinha, Mysore Narasimhachar Srinivas dominated the stage, who had been involved in anthropological research in a big way spanning across different parts of India, largely under the influence of the theories developed by the British and American Anthropologists. Vidyarthi was also no exception to this. As a matter of fact, as a research fellow working for the Doctoral degree in Chicago University during 1957-58, he was greatly influenced by the anthropological theories of Robert Redfield and Milton Singer. On his return to India in 1958, he once again joined as a lecturer in the Department of Anthropology at Ranchi, which happened to be his original place of teaching Anthropology.

Ranchi has the distinction of being the place of work of Rai Bahadur Sarat Chandra Roy, known as Father of Indian Ethnology turned Anthropology. Roy's monumental works must have inspired Vidyarthi to initiate anthropological studies among the tribes of Chotanagpur all through his life which unfortunately was not long enough. Within 32 years of passing the Master's degree, his untimely death came on the First December 1985, putting an end to his tireless contributions to the development of Anthropology in India.

During these 32 years of his academic career, with his unique dynamic approach to the issues of anthropological interest relating to the people of India as looked at from diverse perspectives, Vidyarthi could carve out a special place for himself in the world of Anthropology in general and Indian Anthropology in particular.

Vidyarthi in 1960s

When I enrolled myself as a Post Graduate student in Anthropology in 1964, Vidyarthi's two pioneering academic works, "Sacred Complex of Hindu Gaya" (1961) and "The Maler: Nature-Man-Spirit Complex" were already published within a span of 10 years from his obtaining the Master's degree. He was then a young man of 30 years only. The concepts developed in the studies of these two areas almost instantly received wide acclaim from the anthropologists of the country as well as other parts of the globe.

It may be said without much hesitation that his concepts proved to be very useful for their application in the Indian situation, particularly in understanding the structure of Hindu civilization. With the publication of these two pioneering works,Vidyarthi could establish himself as a theoretically oriented anthropologist who could make significant contributions to the development of anthropology in India. These two publications had instantly helped him crossing the academic field limited to the region and in the process creating an impact on the anthropologists of our country and also of the world at the academic level.

His high scholastic position hardly got reflected in his teaching style. Like me, I am sure most of my classmates never felt that we were being taught by such an erudite scholar speaking from a position which was beyond our reach. I am one of those lucky students of Vidyarthi who had received his intellectual guidance not only during the preparation of doctoral dissertation but also throughout my professional career as and when I required it most.

In the beginning of my student life, it was not very much clear to me why Vidyarthi had opted for studying a non-tribal population and not a tribe or at least a rural people, which was the usual practice those days. Studying non-tribal people was a departure from the general trend in Anthropology prevailing at that time. It was much later, in course of his many deliberations on understanding the Indian civilization, that the reason became clear to us. Vidyarthi, as an undergraduate student of Geography in Patna University, studied the city of Gaya in 1948 which happened to be a place of work of his father. Since his boyhood he had been acquainted with many special activities of the people of this old city. After getting admitted in Anthropology, he decided to undertake an anthropological study in his known world, which he probably thought to be more rewarding and revealing.

Opting for an almost new area of research in the Indian context not only became a turning point in his academic career, it also opened a new dimension for Indian anthropology in the study of Indian civilization.

Understanding Indian Civilization

As an academician Vidyarthi was keen to look into the multiple dimensions of Indian civilization. In this exercise, the "Sacred Complex of Hindu Gaya" (Vidyarthi, 1961) proved to be an important analytical approach in the study of Indian civilization that encompasses interaction and integration of Great Hindu tradition with a countless number of local-based Little traditions. In this work Vidyarthi also tested concepts like Cultural Performances, Cultural Centres, Cultural Specialists and Cultural Media developed by Milton Singer and then developed three distinct original concepts, namely Sacred Geography, a set of Sacred Performances and crops of Sacred Specialists. These three concepts together were conceived collectively as "Sacred Complex" that proved to be a very effective and powerful tool in the study of Indian religion and also Indian civilization (Vidyarthi, 1961: xviii). While introducing the subject matter of the book, Vidyarthi made "a promise to investigate some other sacred complexes chosen from other region of India, with a view to examining the significance of the conclusions arrived at by this study regarding the problems and methods for the understanding of a sacred complex as a part of the larger civilization framework (*ibid.,* xxii-xxiii).

He could keep his promise by way of guiding and supervising a number of Doctoral students who extensively used the concept of "Sacred Complex" in their studies in Varanasi, Janakpur, Deoghar, Rajgir, Puri, Rameswaram, Dwarika, Prayag and a few others, which could contribute significantly to our understanding of Indian civilization in its composite form.

The other pioneering study in respect of understanding the relation of an ethnic group with the immediate ecology was accomplished among the Mal Paharias of Rajmahal Hills in Bihar. This study on "The Maler: A Study on Nature-Man-Spirit Complex", as Vidyarthi has mentioned, had no direct link with the propositions made by Fred Eggans and Julian Steward but in many respects it could stake a claim for finding a place in the field of ecological anthropology. This concept remained an effective tool in the study of tribal societies in the hills and forests. Unlike other approaches gaining currency in ecological anthropology, Vidyarthi's approach was more intensive and incisive, its purpose being to unfold the interaction of a tribe with their immediate surrounding ecology over a prolonged period of time taking individual life span in its focus. As a result, the interaction pattern of the Maler tribe covered individuals who, in course of their lifelong interaction with the forests and hills, had revealed a socialization process in personality formation and also relation with many spirits symbolizing nature-super nature connection. The use of long biographies in writing such a monograph, as pointed out by Vidyarthi, was a new experiment in Indian ethnography (Vidyarthi, 1978:175). The study of "Sacred Complex of Hindu Gaya" in fact, symbolized his effort to understand the orthogenetic growth of traditional urban pilgrimage centre and its cultural significance in the development of Indian civilization.

Unlike many Indian anthropologists of post-1950s, who were mainly involved in research towards formulating anthropological theories, Vidyarthi's focus of research was both theoretical and applied in nature. In this respect, his contributions to the growth and development of anthropological research in India differ from others. They are unique in their own right.

Understanding the Processes of Urbanization and Industrialization

A dynamic researcher like Vidyarthi could not confine himself within a limited range of academic activities while studying the Indian civilization and culture. He was eager to expand his areas of research activities towards understanding the changing socio-cultural situations in the upcoming urban and industrial centres of India. In order to reveal the multiple impact of urbanization and industrialization on the life and culture of the people of a particular region he did not follow the established ethnographic approach suited to study a single group as rigorously as possible. Instead, the focus of his study was to explore the nature of interactions of two distinct cultures, the folk and tribal or tribal or non-tribal and the processes of cultural transformation as unveiled by him at the Hatia Industrial Complex in Ranchi.

During the middle of 20th century, Ranchi started growing as an industrial centre with the establishment of Heavy Engineering Corporation at Hatia. This was also responsible for introducing several hitherto unknown factors of change in the life of the people of the area including Ranchi town. Industrialization in Chotanagpur was not a new phenomenon. This plateau was already known for its rich minerals like iron ores and coal. The likely impact of the upcoming heavy industrial complex on the existing human cultures did not escape the attention of Vidyarthi. The heterogenic growth of the newly developed urban and industrial centres leading to cultural adjustment and cultural change came to his notice as Ranchi, the town where he was settled in those days, was experiencing the direct effects of rapid urbanization and industrialization once it got started in Hatia.

Vidyarthi's interest was to know the ever-changing human situations in the Indian landscape which could be categorized into two major types. To him, the processes of urbanization and industrialization were responsible for quick and rapid transformation of the human society and were, therefore, likely to generate several processes of adjustment among the people so impacted. A situation like that demands the attention of anthropologists for a detailed understanding of the underlying processes of human adaptation.The nature and pattern of such changing processes functionally operative in rural areas always remained an area of his particular research interest.

Under his stewardship, a branch of Industrial Anthropology grew and developed in the Chotanagpur centring round the Department of Anthropology of Ranchi University. A series of Doctoral dissertations in Anthropology particularly focused on evaluating the impact of industrialization, the main impetus coming from Vidyarthi. The trend was initiated by him and two such studies at Patratu in Hazaribagh, Bokaro Industrial Complex, Coal Mines were first completed under his supervision (Singh, 1986: 63-80).

Action and Applied Anthropology: Welfare and Development

In the middle of 1950s, Vidyarthi established an Action Research Unit in the Department of Anthropology which undertook research in Chotanagpur region. On his return from Chicago, where he had some exposures to the Linguistic Anthropology, he introduced a course in Linguistic Anthropology at the Master's level, which was first of its kind to be introduced by any Indian university.

Vidyarthi from the very early phase of his academic career believed that in a country like India, where majority of the people represented socially as well as academically weaker sections, anthropologists cannot remain satisfied with making theoretical contributions only. He was a vigorous campaigner for involvement of the anthropologists in helping in the welfare and development of the weaker sections.

Early in 1966 he felt the importance of Action Anthropology and wrote "a challenge has been also posed to Indian social scientists to act as social doctors to help the administration at various levels in diagnosing social ills, in prescribing the appropriate remedies, and then for smoothing the course of change from traditional to transitional, and from transitional to "reorganizational" phases of our society, which has fast accelerated under the impact of modern forces" (Vidyarthi, 1966:144).

Vidyarthi was of the view that in the Indian situation purely academic works in anthropology, no matter how important those are, can be of little help to the people of weaker sections in elevating their standard of living at the biological and cultural levels. That could be possible only when the scientific knowledge of anthropologists was profitably used by the policy makers and by those who are in administration. This would also enhance the relevance of the discipline of Anthropology in a country like India.

With this view, Vidyarthi used to interact with administrators in the capacity of Member and Chairman of many high-power committees set up by the Government of India and some of its States. One such committee was the Task Force on the Development of Tribal Areas of Planning Commission, Government of India, set up in 1972 with Vidyarthi as its Chairman. The Committee opined:

> *One of the important factors for the lack of impact so far was that the development of Scheduled Tribes and Tribal areas had been looked upon as a problem of 'Welfare' as distinguished from 'Development'* (Bhowmick, 1986: 62).

Taking into account, the recommendations of the Task Force and other previous such committees during the Fifth Five Year Plan, an altogether new approach was adopted towards tribal development. This was termed as 'Tribal Sub-Plan'. It envisaged the total development of the tribal areas and provided the necessary mechanism for integrating the developmental activities of the government and the semi-government organizations by giving finance through the Integrated Tribal Development Project (ITDP). The Sub-Plan was aimed at narrowing the gap between the levels of development of tribal and other areas, and to improve the quality of life of the tribal communities in general.

Needless to say, this was a great achievement for the anthropologists to underline the importance of the discipline of Anthropology towards formulating development of weaker sections of the people overshadowing the top-level administrators who give the impression that they only matter in implementing all policies and programmes of the Government.

In the context of Vidyarthi's contribution towards development of Action and Applied Anthropology in India, Gautam (1984) remarked:

Action and Applied Anthropology's five categories as proposed by Vidyarthi can be of utmost use not only to the administration, but also to the private and public sectors in development processes of any Third World country. It will provide the willingness to work with a joint team of anthropologists and administrators (Gautam, 1973).

In Search of Indianness

In course of his study in Gaya, Vidyarthi had to consult ancient scriptures, sacred texts along with other records and therefore must have realized the importance of India's ancient scriptures in studying Indian Civilization. This has been reflected in his later thinking. On the occasion of All India Conference on Social Science and its Application held in Patna on 4-6th February, 1965, Vidyarthi emphasized that along with the writings of great thinkers, ancient scriptures like the Vedas, the Upanishadas, the Smritis, and the Epics are full of social facts and should be used in the study of cultural process and civilizational history of India (Vidyarthi, 1966a). Subsequently in his Presidential addresses delivered in the Anthropology and Archaeology Section of the 55th Indian Science Congress at Varanasi (Vidyarthi, 1968), he underlined the need of an integrated effort from various disciplines for a proper understanding of man and society. His main stress was on 'Indianness' as a distinct cultural milieu as well as an attitude oriented value system of the Indians. Later on, he further elaborated this in 1978. As the President of the Xth International Congress of Anthropological and Ethnological Science held in India, he once again reminded the anthropologists that "India's ancient scriptures like the Vedas, the Upanishads, the Smritis, the Puranas and the other great epics provide a sensitive insight into the social realities. Therefore, the Indianness in social science has to emerge with a proper appraisal of the ancient texts, whose influences on the behavioural pattern of our country men cannot be neglected." Also, "these ancient scriptures reflect the wisdom and provide guidelines for shaping the socio-cultural life in India. The patterns of nature-man relationship, man to man relationship and man-spirit relationships are explained in great depth."

According to him, ideas of Indian thinkers as reflected in ancient scriptures were full of social facts and so those could be fully explored in our understanding of cultural process and civilization history of India. He writes, "This Indianness in the field of social sciences refers to our distinct cultural milieu and value attitude system as well as ideas of Indian thinkers reflected in ancient scriptures, which are full of social facts and which should be used in the understanding of cultural process and civilization history of India (Vidyarthi, 1978). Vidyarthi was in favour of such an approach as he thought "many European–American anthropological thoughts are inapplicable to understand Indian society and 'Indianness'."

Grooming the Students

Every year, the Final year Master Degree students of Anthropology in Ranchi University had to undertake six weeks fieldwork staying at the place of field investigation along with one teacher of the department as the supervisor. Vidyarthi, along with his couple of research scholars used to visit the area, in spite of his several academic engagements, to have an on the spot assessment of the progress of work of each student, staying back for a couple of days in the camp along with the students. He was a hard taskmaster, if I can use the term to highlight his way of guiding students in the field.

Let me cite an example. It was in the winter of either 1981 or 1982 when Vidyarthi paid a visit to Jagdalpur in Bastar District of the present Chhattisgarh where I was working in the Office of the Anthropological Survey of India. A batch of Master Degree Final Year students were camping at that time at Narayanpur area for their fieldwork under the supervision of Professor K.N. Sahay. On his arrival at Jagdalpur in the evening, after covering a long distance of about 300 km by road from Raipur in public transport, he asked me to pick him up in the next morning for proceeding to the industrial belt of Bailadila, again a distance of about 350 km in a hilly terrain. As mentioned earlier, he had already developed a special field of Industrial Anthropology in the Department of Anthropology during that time. Since my subject matter of Doctoral dissertation under his supervision was also on the impact of industrialization, he asked me to have a fresh look on the issues developed by me in a different context. After visiting a few villages of the Dandami Maria tribe feeling the impact of activities of iron ore mines, and talking with some of the representatives of the tribe, we could return to Jagdalpur in the night. By that time he was ready chalking out the next day's travel programme. As per his wish, it was decided to proceed to Narayanpur early morning so that we could reach the village before noon and could see how the students were interacting with the villagers in the field. Vidyarthi on reaching the village did not relax, moved with the fieldworkers untiringly till evening punctuated by a very short break for lunch. The students were camping in two rooms of a Muria mud house along with Prof. Sahay. As usual, the mud floor was covered with hay and straw to give effect of a mattress. The villagers provided another adjacent similar room to Vidyarthi. Before and after having a common dinner with all of us in the evening, he sat with all the students and enquired about their experiences at the first instance, examined a few field notebooks and then advised each of them as per their issues of enquiry. However, before doing so in every case he sought the opinion of Prof. Sahay. This was his third day of travel. Next day early in the morning he knocked at my door and called me out for having a round in the village. I knew he was an early riser but never knew that even after three days of continuous travel in a hilly region he could remain so energetic as to explore a new field situation with everlasting curiosity. This apparently a usual and routine responsibility of a teacher had, in fact, an immense psychological boosting for the students.

Even otherwise, Vidyarthi would always advice and encourage his students, specially the research students to publish their research findings so that they could make their way to the arena of academicians.

Expansion of the Discipline

Expansion of the discipline of anthropology in the country was a passion to Vidyarthi. When he joined Ranchi College in 1953 and then again in 1958 as Head of the Department, after a break of two years during 1957-58, there was no other college in Bihar offering anthropology course to the students. With the aim to have trained students from different parts of the region, Vidyarthi took extra initiative in introducing the discipline of Anthropology in a number of degree colleges. Being the Head of the Post Graduate Department of Anthropology and because of his natural capacity of impressing others with solid arguments, he was successful in his effort. The discipline of Anthropology was introduced in a number of colleges in Chotanagpur. He always emphasized upon the need of teaching anthropology as an integrated discipline. As a matter of fact, once he had expressed his reservations to me when two departments of Sociology and Social Anthropology were opened, one each at the Northeastern Hill University at Shillong, Meghalaya and North Bengal University in Siliguri, West Bengal. In later years, the two departments were restructured as Departments of Anthropology in line with Vidyarthi's thinking.

Seminars and Conferences

Vidyarthi was of the opinion that the discipline can get enriched through the exchange of ideas and views of the professional anthropologists, but the views and ideas of the scholars of other disciplines in several spheres of human development were no less important in enriching anthropological thoughts.With such a view he used to organize regularly national and international seminars and made it almost mandatory, specially for the research scholars, to actively participate in those by way of contributing research papers for presentation before eminent anthropologists for discussion. Besides, in order to develop student's academic skill by interacting with others, during his tenure a weekly seminar used to be held in the Department where the faculty members, research scholars and also the students, who had already completed fieldwork for their dissertations had to present their findings. Occasionally, eminent anthropologists of the country visiting the Department used to deliver lectures, which were definitely an added input. Needless to say, such an exercise not only helped the students in gaining confidence, it also proved to be extremely rewarding for many students in their professional career.

Department of Anthropology and Vidyarthi: Inseparable

The Department of Anthropology in Ranchi was established on 05.07.1953 under the then Bihar University of Bihar State. Sachchidananda and L.P. Vidyarthi joined the Department as founder Head and founder teacher respectively. Vidyarthi left the Department for a period of two years for completing his Doctoral Dissertation under Professor Robert Redfield in Chicago University. On his return to India, Vidyarthi again joined his old Department, this time as its Head. Since then, the Department became a vibrant centre of teaching and research. Under his dynamic leadership and openness in accepting new areas of teaching and research, the status of the Department was raised to a level of any major department of anthropology in the country. To its credit, courses in Tribal Welfare and Tribal Development, Linguistic Anthropology were introduced in the curriculum.

Besides regular teaching, the Faculty members were allowed to undertake individual research projects of contemporary relevance. Sponsored research projects of the University Grants Commission or Governments, individual research projects of the Doctoral Fellows were also run from this Department. "*The Journal of Social Research*" started publishing under the editorship of Prof. Vidyarthi that had widened the scope for the researchers in the Department in disseminating their research findings. Frequent visits of eminent scholars of our country and also from abroad to the Department for academic interactions made the Department an important centre of postgraduate study and research in Anthropology in the country.

In the year 1975, the Department of Anthropology, Ranchi University was recognized by the University Grants Commission as the Centre of Excellence in Anthropological Studies. The Department further raised its status by becoming the "Centre of Advance Studies in Anthropology", the first of its kind in India in 1985.

President of the IUAES

As a result of his untiring efforts to make the Indian Anthropology known to the academics of the world, he was elected the President of International Union of Anthropological and Ethnological Sciences (IUAES), continually from 1973 to 1978. In his report of the Indian delegation to the Permanent Council of the IUAES, at the meeting in Rome May 3-5, 1976, Vidyarthi stated:

> *The Xth International Congress of Anthropological and Ethnological Science will be held in the Third World Country—India—and this is evidently a recognition of India's valuable contribution to global anthropology. Further, "The Xth World Congress, to be held in India in December 10-21, 1978, will provide a strong base and a broad-based platform for the development of anthropology in India and the Third World in particular and the world in general. To meet the challenges in any developing nation, the strategy must be interdisciplinary and cross-cultural; isolation will bring gradual decay and extinction"* (Vidyarthi, 1976).

Vidyarthi became the President of the International Congress of Anthropological and Ethnological Sciences (ICAES) in 1978.

At the end, I must say that like any other academician all works of Vidyarthi's were not beyond any criticism. But what makes him different from other anthropologists of his time is besides being a very good teacher and resourceful theoretician he had in him the rare qualities of a good administrator and also of a successful organizer. Combination of all these made it possible for him to receive the "distinguishable service award" conferred jointly by the Association for Anthropological Diplomacy, Politics and Society, and Association of Third World Anthropology in the year 1983. He was the first person from a developing country to receive such an honour. His multidimensional academic works make him as one of the top anthropologists of the world.

Vidyarthi's untimely death created a huge vacuum in the Department of Anthropology, Ranchi University, from where he could continue his multidimensional academic activities and almost single handedly elevated its status as an advanced centre of anthropological learning. An equally irreparable vacuum occurred in the field of Indian Anthropology which was in need of leadership of an able academician with a vision and with exemplary administrative and organizational abilities as could be found in Professor Lilita Prasad Vidyarthi.

REFERENCES

Bhowmick, P.K. 1986. "Reports on Scheduled Tribes: An Appraisal", In *Tribal Development and its Administration* (2nd edition), Edited by L.P. Vidyarthi, pp. 47-63, New Delhi, Concept Publishing Company.

Gautam, M.K. 1973. "Reciprocity of Information". *Man,* 8:4.

Gautam, M.K. & Ajit K. Singh (Ed) 1985. *Contribution to the Development of Anthropology.* New Delhi, Concept Publishing Company.

Singh, Ajit. K. 1985. "L.P. Vidyarthi: A Dynamic Anthropologist", In *Contribution to the Development of Anthropology,* (Ed.), New Delhi, Concept Publishing Company, pp. 63-80.

Upadhyay, V.S. and Gaya Pandey. 1993. *History of Anthropological Thought,* New Delhi, Concept Publishing Company.

Vidyarthi, L.P. 1961. *The Sacred Complex in Hindu Gaya*, New York, Asia Publishing House, reprinted in 1978 by Concept Publishing Company.

Vidyarthi, L.P. 1963. *The Maler: Nature-Man-Spirit Complex in a Hill Tribe of Bihar*, Calcutta, Bookland Private Limited.

Vidyarthi, L.P. 1964. "Cultural Linguistic Region of Bihar: A Methodological Approach", In *Culture Contours of Tribal Bihar*, Calcutta, Punthi Pustak.

Vidyarthi, L.P. 1966. "Studies on Social Change in Tribal India: A Methodological Review", *Journal of Ranchi University,* Vol. III.

Vidyarthi, L P. 1966a. *Social Science in India: A Social Anthropological Approach: Some Observations.* Pennsylvania University, Accessed on 1st March, 2016 from < *SSI. sagepub.com*>

Vidyarthi, L.P. 1968. "Presidential Address to the Anthropology and Archaeology Section". *Journal of Social Research,* under the title "Culture Change in the Tribes of Modern India".

Vidyarthi, L.P. 1976. "Report to the Permanent Council of IUAES, at the meeting in Rome", May 3-5, 1976. *Current Anthropology,* 17(3): 543-548.

Vidyarthi, L.P. 1978. "Presidential Address to the Xth ICAES, New Delhi", In *Ideas and Trends in World Anthropology.* Edited by Charles Frantz, New Delhi: Concept Publishing Company, 1981.

Vidyarthi, L.P. 1978. *Rise of Anthropology in India: A Social Science Orientation,* Vol. 1, New Delhi, Concept Publishing Company.

6
Pranab Ganguly
A Rare Kind of Anthropologist

Abhijit Guha

Introduction

Pranab Kumar Ganguly[1] was not known to be a leading bio-cultural anthropologist of India. But apart from his contributions in the specialized field of Biological Anthropology, Ganguly made important contributions in the fields of social demography, ethno-history, material culture, language, religion and political system. Moreover, he also contributed significantly on some policy issues of the Onges of Little Andaman, which had far-reaching implications.

I begin with Pranab Ganguly's contributions on material culture, religion, life-cycle rites, political organisation and ethno-history. Under this background, I would prefer to begin with Ganguly's contributions (some of them were written jointly with another meticulous anthropologist, Anadi Pal who was also a known Physical anthropologist) on various topics of socio-cultural anthropology apart from his contributions in the typical fields of Biological Anthropology like anthropometry, dermatoglyphics, human genetics and dental anthropology (Ganguly, 1960; Ganguly & Pal, 1961, 1963b & 1974; Ganguly & Mukherjee, 1964; Dutta & Ganguly, 1965; Ganguly, 1973a, 1976, 1978 & 1979; Chaudhuri & Ganguly, 1983). I have consciously chosen this route just to show how difficult it is to categorize an anthropologist like Pranab Ganguly within the limits of one of the subfields of anthropology. I strongly believe that it would be sheer injustice to classify Ganguly as a 'Physical or Biological Anthropologist'. Unfortunately, his solid papers in prestigious national and international peer-reviewed journals on religion, material culture, life-cycle rites and judicial system of the tribes in Andaman and Nicobar Islands during 1961-63 did not receive the attention they deserved from the social and cultural anthropologists in India.

One of his early papers on the religious beliefs among the Onges of Little Andaman should have received better treatment. The said paper entitled 'Religious beliefs of the Negritos of Little Andaman' was published in *The Eastern Anthropologist* in 1961. In this pioneering study Ganguly described the cognition of the Onges about their supernatural world in vivid details.[2] The ethnography emerged out of Ganguly's painstaking fieldwork during 1953-57 when he stayed among the hunting-gathering tribe for about eight months in total, learned their language without an interpreter and observed the everyday life of this little community.[3] This short paper of only six pages on a difficult subject is remarkable for its clarity and coverage of ethnographic details through which the author finally reached a conclusion of wider significance. Let me quote:

> *In the first place, though the Onge are one of the most primitive tribes of the world, the universe conceived by them is far from simple. It is indeed a remarkable creation of the unsophisticated Onge mind. The supernatural beings living in the different planes or layers of the Onge universe are, strictly speaking, neither divine nor immaterial. They eat, drink, marry, multiply and die just like human beings....I did not find among the Onge any belief concerning a superior spirit or High God* (Ganguly, 1961a: 247-48).

With Bimal Chandra Roy as the first author Ganguly wrote another ethnographic paper in *Folklore* in 1961 on the life-cycle customs and ceremonies of the Onges. The meticulous details of the paper in course of recording the Onge beliefs around birth, marriage and death were simply wonderful, but at the same time the authors also acknowledged their failure in recording the chants which were recited during the male initiation rites of the community (Roy & Ganguly 1961: 370).

The next social anthropological paper of Ganguly which I would take up was an account on the material culture of the Jarawa of Great Andaman published jointly with Anadi Pal in the prestigious journal *Ethnos* of the Ethnographical Museum of Sweden in 1962. This study was done by Ganguly and Pal on the basis of observations and measurements made on a collection of Jarawa implements and weapons given by the Andaman and Nicobar Police Department to the researchers of the Anthropological

Survey of India for meticulous study. This 15 page article contains a detailed morphological description with measurements and diagrams of bows, arrows, bark armour, basket, bamboo vessel, bucket and resin torch. In addition, we could find in this article how the Jarawas used the spine of the tail of Sting-Ray (a cartilaginous fish related to sharks) to injure their enemies. The most interesting part of the article is the brief theoretical exercise attempted by the authors in the concluding section. I quote from the paper:

> *Some anthropologists and linguists accept it as an axiom that language is the most stable part of culture that "linguistic changes do not proceed at the same rate as most cultural changes, which are on the whole far more rapid". But here we find that the differences between the Onge and Jarawa in respect of material culture are few and unimportant whereas linguistic differences between them are so great that the language of one is incomprehensible to the other. As we do not have adequate data on the culture history of Andaman Islanders, we are unable to offer any satisfactory explanation on the matter. It is, however, quite obvious that after the separation of the Onge from the Jarawa, which took place long ago, their languages underwent many changes in course of time, but their technologies changed very slowly, partly due to the lack of the pressure of social needs and partly due to the limitations imposed by the physical environment* (Ganguly & Pal, 1962:97).

In a footnote to the above paragraph, the authors of the article referenced page 26 from the selected writings of Edward Sapir edited by D.G. Mandelbaum which was published in 1949. Suffice it is to say that through his empirical data Ganguly had challenged the then established idea on the relationship between language and culture propounded by Edward Sapir in Cultural Anthropology.

Ganguly's other two articles on Car-Nicobarese oil press and Onge harpoon and spear (written jointly with A.Pal) also deserve attention from social anthropologists, particularly to those interested in the study of material culture. It must be emphasized here that these were the results of his painstaking fieldwork. The articles were published in *Anthropos* in 1961 and 1963 respectively. Both the articles revealed Ganguly's interest areas in clear terms. He never forgot to mention the measurements while drawing the implements and describing almost graphically the method of their uses. In the article on Onge harpoon and spear, the authors did not hesitate to refute A.R. Radcliffe-Brown's assumption on the non-existence of harpoon and spear among the tribes of Little Andaman which included the Onge (Ganguly & Pal, 1963a : 557-560). The article on indigenous oil press is a beautiful example of simple description of material culture with photographs and diagrams, which are now-a-days almost non-existent in the writings of social anthropologists (Ganguly, 1961b: 934-935).

After material culture, I shall briefly describe Ganguly's excursion in the area of political system encountered by him in one of the remote areas of Andaman Island. In 1960, Ganguly and Pal did their fieldwork in Chowra Island which was situated about 48 miles south of Car Nicobar. The fieldwork was conducted for three weeks to collect demographic and physical anthropological data but Ganguly's interest in social anthropology led him to gather useful information on the 'judicial organization' of the Chowra Islanders. The result of this social anthropological inquiry was published in an article in 1961 in *Folklore* under the title 'Some aspects of the judicial system in Chowra Island'. In this paper, Ganguly and Pal first described the basic structure of governance in the island which was characterized by a territorial subdivision combined with ranked headmen and a supra-village chief. The chief and the 15 village headmen constituted a council (*kanyu-u*) which was the central authority in the island and the government administration of the Andaman and Nicobar also recognized the position of the chief and the village headmen and the government did not also intervene into the working of this tribal institution except in extreme cases of homicide. The most interesting aspect of this paper is the concrete case studies which were narrated in vivid details. The following observations of the authors deserve special attention:

> *From the cases which were brought for trial to kanyu-u during the last few years several are presented.... It is hoped that these concrete cases will represent the methods of administering justice in Chowra more clearly than what general statements can do* (Ganguly & Pal, 1960:155).

In the rest of the paper we find detailed cases under (a) drunkenness and assault upon wife, (b) sexual offence, (c) theft, (d) dispute about the ownership of land, and (e) homicide. If one reads the cases one will find the same remarkable clarity and logical consistency with which Ganguly described the religious life and the material culture of the Onge and the

Jarawa of Andaman Islands. This paper on the judicial system, however, ended with a longer conclusion in which Ganguly and Pal noted the democratic way of dealing with allegations and disputes; although the chief of the island is the highest authority, he cannot decide a case without discussing the matter in the council. Furthermore, we learn from this important ethnographic account that in this patrilineal society of Chowra with the feature of primogeniture women were not admitted to become the head of the village or the chief of the island, but women were never punished. Even in cases of adultery, it was usually the male who was held responsible (*Ibid.*, 160).

Last in this series of social anthropological papers, I pick up a unique contribution of Ganguly on the ethno-history of the Nicobar islanders. In this long paper published in an off-beat journal (*Journal of the Gujarat Research Society*), Ganguly laboriously searched for the ethnic history of the different population groups inhabiting the Nicobar islands, which included the Shom-Pens.Unlike any typical social anthropologist Ganguly searched the ethnic origin of the Nicobarese from a bio-cultural perspective.[4] In the process, he collected anthropometric and serological data as well as detailed information on demography, history, subsistence activities, social organization and environment from all possible sources. Finally, with the help of the aforesaid data, Ganguly postulated a sequence of migrations in the Nicobar Islands in a holistic framework (Ganguly, 1973: 234-270).

Policy Issues Around the Onge

Ganguly's interest in the study of the Onges of Little Andaman took its final shape during the mid-seventies when he published a full-length paper entitled 'The Negritos of Little Andaman Island: a primitive people facing extinction', which was published in the *Indian Museum Bulletin* in 1975. This paper can be regarded as one of the finest works on policy anthropology. The paper covered almost every aspect of this small island tribe in the context of the global debate on the position of the anthropologists regarding the study of endangered and disappearing populations.[5] Ganguly made his position clear after narrating the differences between two schools of thought on the task of the anthropologists. He quoted Sol Tax's (1971) editorial of *Current Anthropology* in which Tax observed a 'split' among the anthropologists on what should constitute the urgent task before them after the 8th International Congress of Anthropological and Ethnological Sciences held in 1968. Should the anthropologists give priority to study the last speaker of a disappearing community to build up their theory or should they accept change as an obvious outcome and invest their time towards their development? Pranab Ganguly while studying the Onges clearly underlined his position in the following manner:

> *The author feels that the two approaches are not mutually exclusive, but are complimentary to each other. The study of vanishing tribes does not prevent anthropologists from being interested in urgent problems of development and change in large societies; both types of research may be carried on simultaneously* (Ganguly, 1975:8).

I shall now describe how Ganguly made an attempt to combine the aforementioned approaches in his own way in the long article on Onge. Apart from the detailed and meticulous ethnography written in the classical Malinowskian style which also included the physical anthropology and demographic contours of the tribe, Ganguly described the society and culture of the Onges like a professional social anthropologist. He described the material culture, subsistence activities, kinship, marriage, family, rites of passage, political organization and the religion in a systematic and comprehensive manner.[6] The most important part of the paper however is the section on the policy aspects revolving around the major problem faced by the Onges in the form of their decreasing numbers. Ganguly investigated the problem of the depopulation of the Onges from a demographic perspective by carefully taking into consideration the three contesting hypotheses, which were (i) economic exploitation, (ii) assassination of the natives by the colonists, and (iii) introduction of new diseases against which the natives had no immunity. Ganguly was probably the first anthropologist who studied the Onges for a long period of time from a biosocial perspective and differed with the aforementioned hypotheses. The disagreement was based on his own observations and reading of the history of Little Andaman and he did not hesitate to state his policy recommendations towards the betterment of the tribe in clear terms. In Ganguly's words:

> *Ameliorative measures such as establishment of coconut plantations, introduction of horticulture, distribution of iron implements and other useful articles, carrying out routine health surveys and giving medical relief, etc., though very useful and commendable, cannot prevent the decline of Onge population. These do not even touch the fringe of the real*

> *problem. Systematic investigations into the causes of Onge infertility and proper remedial measures against them are now urgently required* (Ganguly, 1975:25-26).

Finally, Ganguly proposed that as a long-term measure the Onges should be relocated in the Rutland Island 31 miles north of Little Andaman where they once lived but left the place to get away from an epidemic several decades ago. The island was capable of supporting the Onge population with their traditional mode of subsistence and Ganguly suggested that they should be allowed to live there without any outside interference because it would be increasingly difficult for them to survive in Little Andaman owing to 'the rising demands of officials and workers for pork, fish, honey, fruits, etc.', the staple food of the Onges (*Ibid.*).

The Story of Human Adaptation

If we look at the works of Pranab Ganguly in a chronological order we find that during 1960-66 he contributed in physical and social-cultural anthropology by using the methods of anthropometry, ethnography and linguistics with equal competence and his interest towards the formulation of policies was no less visible in his later work on Onge, which has been described in the previous sub-section. During the mid-seventies,Ganguly turned his attention towards macro-level data on large samples and he also organized his thoughts around the bigger problems of human adaptation and evolution in an ecosystem framework, although he was not a dogmatic supporter of maintenance of stability.[7] In this context, one particular research work of Ganguly, and this was his most remarkable one, was on the gradual decline in average height (negative secular trend) about some tribal and caste populations in India.With Anadi Pal, Ganguly first wrote a short paper in a volume published by the University of Calcutta in 1974. In this paper, the authors presented figures on the average height of 20 population groups (caste and tribes) measured by different authorities in an interval of at least 25 years and concluded that unlike many Western and Asian countries, the studied Indian populations had become shorter since the late 19th and early 20th century (Ganguly & Pal, 1974: 42-48). It was a remarkable finding. Ganguly pursued the work and made it global by publishing under his single authorship a whole chapter in a book edited by the famous anthropologist William Stini in World Anthropology series volume by Mouton in 1979. Ganguly began this chapter by challenging the then scholarship in biological anthropology, which presumed that the progressive increase in stature was a universal phenomenon as it happened in many technologically advanced Western and non-Western countries. In this chapter, he demonstrated with the help of simple anthropometric data that in India three groups out of every four have become shorter in varying degrees in course of one or two generations and it was not due to malnutrition or inbreeding but probably caused by a relaxation of natural selection against undersized individuals (Ganguly, 1979: 315-337). Sadly enough, such interest areas are fast losing our concerted attention.

In another pioneering study for which he had won the prestigious Bertillon Medal of France (in 1973) on the variation in physique in North India in relation to urbanization and economic status, Ganguly was able to show with the help of carefully controlled experimental design (rare in Indian physical anthropology), the relationship between various somatometric measurements and observations (e.g., height, weight and skin colour) and some socio-economic parameters.[8] For example, he found that among the Brahmin and Muslim populations of western Uttar Pradesh in North India, the well-to-do men are significantly taller and heavier and have absolutely broader hips and shoulders than the poor. The increases in different measurements observed in the well-to-do clearly reflected a general enlargement in the size of the body. In the circumferential measurements of limbs and torso, the differences between the economic classes were particularly pronounced. The well-to-do men had significantly larger heads, larger in both length and breadth dimensions than the poor (Ganguly, 1974a: 3-43).

The last remarkable work of Ganguly, which I propose to discuss was a theoretical paper entitled 'The problem of human adaptation: an overview' published in *Man in India* in 1977.[9] In this brilliant article, Ganguly viewed the major human problems of the modern world (e.g. malnutrition and inequality) from the perspective of adaptation. For him adaptation should be considered in its broadest sense in the context of society and culture.Under a section in this paper entitled 'Socio-economic Milieu' Ganguly after reviewing the literature exhaustively including his own study on the Brahman and Muslim groups of western Uttar Pradesh commented:

> *From the foregoing discussion it should be evident that the socio-economic status effect manifests itself at every stage of life from birth to adulthood. The upper class children have significantly bigger bodies than the lower class children, and this difference persists to a remarkable degree in the*

> *final adult size. It may be argued that the genetic potential for growth of the Indian children, who suffer under the constraints of adverse socio-economic environment remains to some extent unrealized* (Ganguly, 1977:10).[10]

But how does the poor really adapt to this adverse socio-economic deprivation? Ganguly's answer to this basic question can be found in the next section of the article titled 'Nutritional Stress':

> *Adaption to malnutrition during critical stages of growth is likely to induce permanent reduction of body size which in turn will reduce the energy needs of the body. People having small body size will survive more easily on low calorie diets and they will have some adaptive advantage in areas where scarcity conditions prevail* (*Ibid.*, pp. 10-11).

At this juncture one may ask a very legitimate question, which is 'Did Ganguly view poverty as an outcome of adaptation only?' I would say, 'Yes, Ganguly looked at the unconscious strategies of survival of the poor but he also viewed the extremes of this adaptation'. Let us move with him further in course of this paper:

> *It may be mentioned here that the survival of a population through diminution of body size and reduction of energy requirements is possible if only the nutritional deficiencies remain within tolerable limits. When the stress of malnutrition becomes very acute, the adaptive advantage of size reduction loses much of its significance and the population is threatened with the danger of extinction* (*Ibid.*, p.14).[11]

Ganguly's paper on adaptation is a complete bio-cultural exercise on macro-level policy issues and I regard his Indian Science Congress address of 1977 as the true successor of the lectures delivered by his teachers Tarak Chandra Das in 1941 and Sasanka Sekhar Sarkar in 1951 at the Congress.This is because like his predecessors Pranab Ganguly also dealt with the major national problems and the role of anthropology and anthropologists in providing some solutions to these problems.[12]

Geographical location, contact situation and demographic characteristics with respect to known anthropological references like tribe, caste drew his attention for some time. For example, western Midnapore settlements had closeness with the tribal areas of the district than the eastern towns which had more caste populations and this was also reflected in the demographic data. He even joked with us by saying 'you social anthropologists often forget to mention the most fundamental and objective criterion of a tribe, which is nothing but their balanced sex-ratio!' In the contemporary situation such a balance cannot always be maintained and this probably necessitates change in our approach to tribe as an ideal category.

Conclusion

Pranab Ganguly as a professional anthropologist belonged to post-colonial India who practiced intensive fieldwork and published in physical and socio-cultural anthropology with equal competence – a rare quality which has almost vanished or lost importance among the succeeding generations of anthropologists in India. Ganguly, however, was not a run-of-the-mill empirical anthropologist. His remarkable works on the progressive decline of stature among sixty endogamous population groups and the relationship of somatic variability with economic condition and urbanization demonstrated his ability to interpret huge mass of empirical data in a theoretical framework, which was basically bio-cultural in nature. Finally, it should be emphasized that Pranab Ganguly was not an ivory tower scholar, who only gathered knowledge but made sincere attempts to apply his findings in formulating policies for the welfare and betterment of the underprivileged sections of the Indian population, starting from the endangered Onges of Little Andaman to the vast majority of the undersized and malnourished people of independent India.

Acknowledgements

I owe my debts to my senior student Ms Subhra Bhattacharya of the Anthropological Survey of India (AnSI) for sending me important articles of Professor Ganguly from the Central Library of the Institute. I would like to express my thanks to Ramu Ram and his staff at the Central Library of AnSI for their assistance in procuring materials for the paper. I also thank my Ph.D. student Ayan Bandopadhyay for preparing the nice power point slides for the lecture. Last but not the least, I am indebted to my wife Priti for patiently listening to my day-to-day progress at the time of writing the paper.

NOTES

1. Pranab Kumar Ganguly (1929-2014) was an outstanding anthropologist of post-independent India. He conducted remarkable fieldworks in Andaman

and Nicobar Islands during 1950s and wrote thought provoking theoretical articles in a bio-cultural framework (Guha, 2016).

2. There was no recorded information on the religious life of the aborigines of Little Andaman when Ganguly conducted this study. A.R. Radcliffe-Brown's study was on the communities of Great Andaman and there were marked differences between the tribes of Great and Little Andaman as regards religious beliefs and Ganguly mentioned this fact in the first paragraph of his article (Ganguly, 1961:243).
3. Three years later Ganguly published a 31-page detailed account on the vocabulary of the Onge in the *Bulletin of the Anthropological Survey of India* which revealed his deep acquaintance with the language and its grammatical structure (Ganguly, 1966:1-30).
4. Ganguly's bio-cultural perspective was his life-long pursuit. At the end of his career he published an article 'The incidence of Arcus Senilis in Nicobar islands and the Nicobarese food habits' which is an example of this pursuit (Ganguly, 1989: 163-167).
5. Under the section entitled 'Depopulation of the Little Andaman Island', Ganguly noted that there were only 121 Onge individuals in the Little Andaman Island in 1969.
6. Ganguly did not even exclude the sexual life of the tribe in his description. Thus, we find him depicting the Onge method of sexual intercourse which was different from the typical missionary posture. At the same time Ganguly also frankly admitted his own shortcomings whenever he failed to collect any ethnographic data.
7. Ganguly's comment in *Current Anthropology* on an article entitled 'Darwinian Psychological Anthropology: A Biosocial Approach' by Jerome H. Barkow may be recalled here. He commented 'I cannot wholly agree with the author's observation that the hominid trait of striving for prestige tends to increase social stability. Instances of destruction of lives and property for the sake of prestige are not rare; such actions tend to induce social disruption rather than social stability (Ganguly, 1973b:380).
8. Ganguly received three prestigious medals in the same year, viz., Sir Asutosh Mookerjee Gold Medal (1975), Bengal Immunity Research Prize and Gold Medal (1975) and Griffith Memorial Prize (1975) for his research on various topics in Anthropology (*Directory of Anthropologists in India,* 1981:110-111).
9. This paper was delivered as Presidential Address at the Anthropology and Archaeology Section of the 64th Indian Science Congress in Bhubaneswar held in 1977.
10. One should note that Ganguly used the term 'class' not 'caste' since his empirical findings revealed class differentiation within a caste was more important to understand the human biological variation in India—a point little recognized by the social anthropologists. It may be interesting to recall here Ganguly's comment published in *Current Anthropology* on Joan P. Mencher's famous article 'The caste system upside down or the not-so-

mysterious East' in 1974. I quote from Ganguly, 'From my field investigations in 12 districts of western Uttar Pradesh, I have gained the impression that the North Indian Brahamans are really no better-off than the low-ranked agricultural castes of that area' (Ganguly, 1974b:482).

11. After this statement Ganguly cited the case of the Juang population of Orissa and mentioned the findings of a biochemist, J.K. Roy of the Anthropological Survey of India who found that owing to severe malnutrition, the Juang population was decreasing for the last 25 years.
12. T.C. Das's lecture entitled 'Cultural Anthropology in the Service of the Individual and the Nation' and the title of S.S. Sarkar's lecture was 'The Place of Human Biology in Anthropology and its Utility in the Service of the Nation'. Das's lecture was published by the Indian Science Congress Association and the lecture of Sarkar was published in *Man in India* in 1951.

REFERENCES

Basu, A., Basu, M.P. and Adhikary, A.K. (Eds.) 1981. *Directory of Anthropologists in India*. Pranab Ganguly. 110-111. Calcutta: Anthropological Survey of India, Government of India.

Chaudhuri, Datta, S.S. & Ganguly, P. 1983. 'Fertility behaviour of female carriers of Haemophilia'. *Journal of the Indian Anthropological Society*. 18:51-54.

Das, T.C. 1941. "Cultural Anthropology in the Service of the Individual and the Nation". 1-29. *Presidential Address delivered in the Section of Anthropology in the Twenty-eighth Indian Science Congress*. Benares.

Dutta, P. & Ganguly, P. 1965. "Further observations on ear lobe attachment". *Acta Genetica et Statistica Medica*. 15 (1): 77-86.

Fisher, R.A. 1935. *The design of experiments.* Edinburgh: Oliver and Boyd.

Fox, R.1973. *Encounter with Anthropology*. New York: Harcourt, Brace Jovanovitch.

Ganguly, P. 1960. "Observations on the Teeth of Nicobar Islanders". *Bulletin of the Anthropological Survey of India*. IX (2): 43-50.

Ganguly, P. 1961a. "Religious beliefs of the Negritos of Little Andaman". *The Eastern Anthropologist*. 14(3):243-248.

Ganguly, P. 1961b. "The Car-Nicobarese Oil-press". *Anthropos*. 56(5-6):934-935.

Ganguly, P. & Pal, A.1961. "Morphology of Onge Foot". *Current Science* 30(8):300-301.

Ganguly, P. 1966. "Vocabulary of the Negritos of Little Andaman with grammatical notes and materials". *Bulletin of the Anthropological Survey of India*, 15(1-4):1-30.

Ganguly, P. 1973a. "The Nicobar islanders: a search for their ethnic identity" *Journal of the Gujrat Research Society*. 35:234-270.

Ganguly, P. 1973b. "Comment on Jerome H. Barkow". *Current Anthropology* 14(4): 380.

Ganguly, P. 1974a. "Variation in physique in North India in relation to urbanization and economic status". In: *Bulletins et Mémoires de la Société d'anthropologie de Paris*, XIII° Série, tome 1 fascicule 1, 1974. 3-43.

Ganguly, P. 1974b. "Comment on J.P. Mencher". *Current Anthropology*, 15(4): 482-483.

Ganguly, P. 1975. "The Negritos of Little Andaman Islands: a primitive people facing extinction". *Indian Museum Bulletin*. 10(1): 7-27.

Ganguly, P. 1976. *Physical anthropology of the Nicobarese*. Memoir No. 34. Calcutta: Anthropological Survey of India.

Ganguly, P. 1977. "The problem of human adaption: An overview". *Man in India*, 57(1): 1-22.

Ganguly, P. 1978. "The physique of Nicobar islanders: a study of sexual, populational, and spatial variation". *Indian Museum Bulletin*. 13: 7-21.

Ganguly, P. 1979. "Progressive decline in stature in India: a study of sixty population groups". 315-337. In *Physiological and morphological adaption and evolution*. Edited by William A. Stini. The Hague: Mouton Publishers.

Ganguly, P. 1983. "Account of a visit to Poland". *Human Science*, 32(1):13-32.

Ganguly, P. 1989. The incidence of Arcus Senilis in Nicobar islands and the Nicobarese food habits. *Journal of the Anthropological Society of India*. 24:163-167.

Ganguly, P. & Pal, A. 1960. "Some aspects of the judicial system in Chowra Island". *Folklore*. 2(3): 153-160.

Roy, B.C. & Ganguly, P. 1961. "Some Ceremonial Customs in Onge Life-cycle". *Folklore*, 2(6): 368-374.

Ganguly, P. & Pal, A. 1962. "Notes on the Material Culture of the Jarawa of Great Andaman: their Weapons and Implements". *Ethnos*. 27: 84-98.

Ganguly, P. & Pal, A. 1963a. Onge harpoon and spear. *Anthropos*, 58(3-4): 557-560.

Ganguly, P. & Pal, A. 1963b. "Distribution of Middle Phalangeal Hair among Chowra and Terressa Islanders". *The Eastern Anthropologist*. XVI (2): 122-132.

Ganguly, P. & Mukherjee, D.P. 1964. "Dermatoglyphics of the Shom-Pen of Great Nicobar". *Anthropos*. 59(5/6): 918-919.

Ganguly, P. & Pal, A.1974. "Secular trend in stature in India". 42-48. In *Indian Anthropology Today*. Edited by D. Sen. Calcutta: Department of Anthropology, Calcutta University.

Ganguly, P. & Bose, S. 1992. "Population trends in Midnapore district, West Bengal, 1872-1981". *Vidyasagar University Journal of Social Sciences*, Inaugural Number, pp. 1-13.

Guha, A. 2016. "Pranab Kumar Ganguly (In Memoriam)". *Anthropology News*. 57(7): e159-e160. (First Published online by The American Anthropological Association). http://www.anthropology-news.org/index.php/2016/07/25/pranab-kumar-ganguly.

Mandelbaum, D.G. 1949. *Selected Writings of Edward Sapir*. Cambridge: Cambridge University Press.

Mencher, J.P. 1974. "The caste system upside down or the not-so-mysterious East". *Current Anthropology*. 15(4):469-493.

Sarkar, S.S. 1951. "The place of human biology in anthropology and its utility in the service of the nation". *Man in India*. 31(1), 1-22.

Tax, S. 1971. "Urgent Anthropology: Associates' views on the definition of 'urgency'." *Current Anthropology*. 12(2):243-254.

7
The Master Theoretician
Gopala Sarana and His Contributions to Anthropology

Sumahan Bandyopadhyay

Background, Academic Life and Activities

Professor Gopala Sarana has earned a lot of respect and recognition in Indian Anthropology for his penchant for theoretical writings. However, he had some other unique qualities which placed him among some of the most accomplished anthropologists in India. His blend of anthropology signified an orientation towards the theory and holistic integration of the branches of anthropology within a theoretical construct. He was a man of achievements and followed many academic pursuits in life. Given the span of the active academic years spent by him in the Departments of Anthropology in the country and abroad, his writings may appear relatively few in number, but the worth of the publications outweighs their seemingly small number. He has mainly contributed to the methodological discourses in anthropology and made threadbare analysis of theories of functionalism, structural-functionalism and structuralism.

Gopala Sarana was born on 2nd January in 1935 at a village in the District of Balia in Uttar Pradesh in a family of traditional sweet makers. He passed B.A. and M.A. from Lucknow University and then worked in the Department of Anthropology, Lucknow University for a short period. In his academic orientation, he was influenced by Professor D.N. Majumdar who happened to be his teacher in Lucknow. The non-doctrinaire and holistic approach that characterises Professor Majumdar's work can also be discerned in Gopala Sarana's works. Sarana had such a profound respect for his illustrious teacher that he once remarked:

> *There have been, and currently are, great social anthropologists in Great Britain. But there is none like D.N. Majumdar there who has made significant contributions in his times to both social and physical anthropology"* (Sarana: 1983:48).

After working at Lucknow University for some time, he shifted to Punjab University for a brief stint of teaching before going to Harvard for doctoral research. Professor Alice Cora DuBois was his Ph.D. supervisor at Harvard. Sarana was awarded Ph.D. in 1966 for his thesis titled *Comparative Methods (Approaches) in Social-Cultural Anthropology: A Methodological Analysis* which was later published by Arizona University Press (Sarana,1975). He had a short teaching career at the University of California at St. Barbara in 1966, after which he returned to India and joined Karnataka University, Dharwad as a Reader. Here he continued till 1979 and then he joined the Department of Anthropology, Lucknow University from where he retired in 1995. Apart from being Professor and Head of the Department, he had to shoulder a number of administrative responsibilities in the University. Prof. Sarana became the Dean of Faculty of Arts for three times during 1981, 1984-87 and 1990 (Patel, 2011) and worked even as the Honorary Librarian of the Tagore Library (the Central Research Library of the University established in 1920) from 1988 to 1992. In 1988, he took charge of the Office of Controller of Examinations. Professor Sarana introduced the B.Sc. and M.Sc. degree courses in Anthropology, for which only B.A. and M.A. degrees were conferred by the Lucknow University till then. He visited Israel, Iran, Japan and the United States in connection with anthropologically related works. These visits did produce some works of anthropological significance like 'Some Reflections on Israel and India' (Sarana, 1993). Professor Sarana edited the Journal *The Eastern Anthropologist* from 1993 to 1996. The symposia organized by him on Radcliffe-Brown in 1981, on Malinowski in 1984 and on Levi-Strauss in 1990 were very illuminating. His interests in the works of these front ranking anthropologists were also reflected in his organizational activities.

It has already been mentioned that Professor Sarana did not write profusely, but whatever he contributed were substantial. Patel (2011) gave a list of about 90 articles, 10 books, 10 book reviews, and 2 obituaries penned by Sarana. Among his important books mention may be made of *Anthropological Method and Indian Anthropology* (1973), *The Methodology of Anthropological Comparison* (1973), *Introducing Anthropology* (1977), *Sociology and Anthropology and Other Essays*

(1983), *Explorations in Method and Theory in Anthropology* (2008). His articles reflected a wide range of interest and considerable depth of analysis. His academic worth was globally acclaimed as could be understood from his comments on Honigmann's paper 'Personal Approach in Cultural Anthropological Research' along with other papers in *Current Anthropology* (Sarana, 1975a, 1976a, 1976b).

A Synoptic View on His Contributions in the Academic Field

Professor Gopala Sarana made a lasting impression through his research in the less explored domain of theoretical anthropology in India. He was more interested in addressing the fundamental issues or the basic theoretical premises of anthropology. However, he did not lose sight of the fact that the knowledge and deliberations must find an easier communication to the younger scholars and students through technical know-how. For them he wrote many books both in English and vernacular Hindi. He wanted that the discipline should have more books in vernacular languages. With this intention in mind, he wrote *Pragitihas* (with Professor D.N. Majumdar), *Manav Vigyan : Ek Parichaya* and *Nri Vigyan ka Swarup aur Khsetra.* On his contribution, N. Subba Reddy wrote:

> *His writings cover a wide range of concepts and theories such as institutions, organization, functionalism, structuralism, semiotics, tenets of ethnography, rules of reinterpretation, criteria of scientific explanation, variability and universality of the nature of man and culture* (Reddy: 2011:143).

Patel (2011) made a more succinct note on the areas of work by Sarana. He was one who "...had great command over the areas of methodological issues, philosophical problems, epistemological queries, logical procedures, and scientific frames of analysis, applicable to anthropology and other social sciences."

In one of his papers written jointly with D.P. Sinha, he has given some sort of a justification of his own stand:

> *Although methodology has recently been discussed in several forums, interest in problems of general theory and methodology is not reflected in the writings of Indian anthropologists. In 1959 critical appraisals of Radcliffe-Brown's concepts, except those on kinship by Murdock, were*

> *rare, but in an article in 1959 G. Sarana showed how Radcliffe-Brown confused the distinction between social structure and social organization (42)." He further wrote on this theme in 1969 showing that Malinowskian functionalism was not "formless". He clarified the distinction between "functioning" and "having a function", pointing out its significance in understanding Malinowski's and Radcliffe-Brown's contributions to anthropology. In a paper presented at the American Anthropological Association meeting in 1965 in Denver, Colorado, Sarana made a critical appraisal of Levi-Strauss's concept of model and his procedure for the analysis of myth (43). He anticipated Leach's assessment of Levi-Strauss, which appeared several years later.*

Sarana's interest in anthropological methodology is a prolonged one. He has made a critical appraisal of the methodological premises of the German-Austrian historical school of ethnology and has demonstrated the importance of reinterpretation through the analysis of the Swazi data in his more recent essay on the anthropological procedures (44). But it is Sarana's contribution to the analysis of methods of comparison in social-cultural anthropology that is most noteworthy. In his 1975 book "The Methodology of Anthropological Comparisons", a systematic analysis of the comparative methods has been done from the point of view of the units, purposes, and techniques and methods of comparison (45). The three methods of comparison are: (a) illustrative comparison, (b) complete universe comparison, and (c) hologeistic sampled comparison. Sarana goes on to examine the relationship between ethnographic procedure, comparative methods, and explanation in social-cultural anthropology." (Sarana and Sinha, 1976: 223)

In fact, his writings on anthropological theories and methods are interwoven and interlinked in such a manner that it is hardly possible to distinctly separate them from one another. For example, his philosophical explorations are intricately linked to the methodology of anthropology and sciences. In spite of this inherent problem of categorization, let me try to discuss his views and contribution under the following sub-sections.

The Holistic Nature of Anthropology

Gopala Sarana was in favour of the holistic nature of anthropology. For him, anthropology is 'the only science of man which strives to understand man, his actions and his works in totality. It is the only subject which deals with what is biological in man and what is socio-cultural in his existence and how the two are interrelated (Sarana: 1977:1-2). In his small book, *Introducing Anthropology* (1977), he has briefly discussed the four branches of anthropology: Physical Anthropology, Social-Cultural Anthropology, Archaeological Anthropology and Linguistic Anthropology. In this connection, we may cite one important debate on the nature of anthropology, about whether it is science or humanities. Sarana holds the view that anthropology is a science, in support of which he has given the following arguments:

> *A discipline should be called a science if, as per the requirement of its subject matter, it evolves a suitable procedure. It should try to emphasize collecting data or information in an objective, dispassionate and detached manner* (Sarana, 1977:35).

He has questioned the applicability of the criteria of experimentation, verification, repetitiveness as the features of scientific disciplines by showing their limitations in case of some of the more accepted scientific disciplines in physical and biological sciences. Rather, he considers the objective and dispassionate enquiry to be a more important feature of science that anthropology has adopted. He concludes his discussion with the following words:

> *To narrow a definition of science will not do because in that case nothing except classical physics can be called scientific. Anthropology has a remarkable method of its own. It is not a social science of the usual kind* (Sarana, 1977:37).

The main attraction of anthropology, according to him, is its 'commitment to study all the manifold aspects of man and his works' (Sarana, 1983:12). He is of the opinion that the ultimate aim of anthropology is to become a 'coordinating science'(*ibid.*).

Sarana has made a very significant statement on the role of ethnographer in connection with anthropological inquiry. It runs:

> *...ethnographer takes cognizance of individuals as role-playing actors occupying socially approved positions. The description is couched in such terms that it is possible to rise from the particular and specific to the general. In this sense, the anthropological inquiry is multi-level* (Sarana, 2008:8).

Ethnography to him is:

> *...a first-hand account of the social life and culture of a particular human community or society obtained through the procedure of long-term and face-to-face fieldwork* (Sarana, 1983:28).

Though his view that social anthropology incorporates ethnography may be contested (Ingold, 2008), it does not seem incongruent with the idea of anthropology held by him as he considers it basically an observational rather than an experimental science. He has vouchsafed that the 'integrated knowledge about man' to be the main reason for the existence of anthropology. The understanding of the holistic nature of anthropology is reflected in his definition of social-cultural anthropology. It remains distinct from other disciplines of study which are only concerned with the 'segments' of society and 'culture', thus implying that the holistic approach remains specific to the social-cultural anthropology alone (Sarana,1983).

Anthropological Theories

Professor Gopala Sarana never gave any theory of his own; rather it is more prudent to say that he was a theoretician in his approach. With regard to theories, his major focus was on functionalism and structuralism. He had good personal relation with some of the towering figures of contemporary theoretical anthropology like Sir Edmund Leach, Raymond Firth, Leslie White. He received kudos for his theoretical critique of functionalism and structural-functionalism, though he did not hesitate to show the lacunae in Firth's ideas too. One such occasion was Firth's remark on Malinowski's functionalism which the former considered rather weak while dealing with the relationship between form and function. In the critique of Malinowski's concept of function, Firth said that function determined the form in case of material objects only; for non-material social and cultural realm its applicability was questionable. Sarana, though he made a severe critique of Malinowski, did not subscribe to this view of Raymond Firth. In refutation of Firth's view, he stated that Malinowski's concept of institution like any other non-material aspect of culture is structured and therefore, Firth's view was not tenable. However, Sarana, too, concluded that 'in Malinowski's brand of functionalism function and form were interrelated but not in all cases function determined form, at least not totally or mostly.' He said that Malinowski's main contribution lies in the recognition of discrete cultural wholes, even at the lowest levels.

He mainly dealt with the epistemological issues of functionalism and was not prepared to admit any logical positivist position for it as he thought that this position would led to the danger of falling into a kind of extreme reductionism. He questioned the nature of teleology of functionalism. For him, it is a bit different from the general teleological system like organism as the determinant of social system, which always continues to change keeping a basic form intact as change is inherent into the system itself. Sarana says that it is not possible to follow the deductive method of philosophy in social anthropology since the discipline has not formulated laws in the form of generalizations. Rather, it relies on explanation, one which he called 'contextual explanation'. He has also discussed the relationship between two frequently used words – 'cause' and 'function'. For him, cause and function are different. The function of a part is identified with a method called 'associative' by him instead of 'eliminative' as adopted in case of delineating a cause.

Sarana made a critique by raising the point whether the concept of social organization as stated by Firth is needed at all. For Firth, the social structure referred to the static aspect of social relations signifying stability and regularity. He presumed that there was no quotient of time to allow choice and decision making so as to account for the dynamism of the social structure. Therefore, he brought in social organization to accommodate this dynamic social entity. Sarana was of opinion that 'Firth's attempt to foist a separate concept of social organization to account for choice and decision is not needed at all.' He added that time cannot be 'squeezed' out of social structure since its rule-governing mechanism allows deviations and alternatives. In discussing the relation between structuralism and functionalism, he pointed out how Levi-Strauss made an incorrect statement on their relationship. Not only that, he tried to show how the concept of model as advocated by Levi-Strauss is not always tenable (Sarana, 2008). He is of the view that the so-called conscious home-made models as stated by Levi-Strauss are not models at all. The point Sarana raised in this regard was that the 'model is something that the investigator builds, not those whose behaviour he investigates' (*ibid.*). But at times his points of differences seem to have originated out of the differences in comprehension of the issue in question. For example, on the concept of social structure of Levi-Strauss, he observes that it was not clear to him how the social structure could simultaneously be a group of problems, a model and also a method. He advocates social structure as a concept and an analytical tool to describe, arrange and organize the data by the anthropologists (Sarana, 2008:119).

If it is so, then it is basically the same as what Levi-Strauss has said. The main issue here centres round problem formulation at the theoretical level and therefore conceptual in nature, as model is an analytical tool, and when it is used to describe and organize data then it relates to methodology.

On Methodological Grounds

It is clear that Gopala Sarana has made significant contribution to anthropological methodology, more particularly in the study of comparative method (CM). Comparative method is one of the unique features of anthropology. His study of comparative method revolves round three interrelated issues:

i. What anthropologists compare?
ii. Why do they compare?
iii. How do they compare?

By doing so, he has devised an approach which enables him to formulate the comparative method independent of any of the known theories like evolutionism, diffusionism etc. His approach is also distinctive from Harris' discussion of comparative method with regard to the grand anthropological theories of nineteenth or early twentieth century (Harris, 2001).

Sarana has mentioned that the main units of comparison are 'traits, institutions, aggregates or combination of categories, conceptual aggregates like totemism and cultural wholes.' The main goals of comparative method as stated by him are the following:

(a) The goal of CM is historical reconstruction;
(b) There is an attempt to formulate typologies; and
(c) There may also be a scope for arriving at some kind of generalization or understanding of a generalized process.

He most elaborately discussed how anthropologists compare and identify three main types of comparative method in this regard. The first one is illustrative comparison in which the comparison is done unsystematically or casually. It is generally applied to infer history, to validate concept and categories, to work out typologies and the like. The second type of comparative method is called controlled comparison after Fred Eggan (1954). In this method, the area or unit of observation is well delimited and defined. It is more of a conceptual rather than a geographic category. The third variety of comparative method is hologeistic or sampled comparison. It is also called the cross-cultural comparison. It is a systematic method covering the whole world.

Apart from this, he dealt with the methods of anthropological analysis. How anthropologists explain or interpret and what is the logical process of investigation followed by them come within its purview. Here, he examined the nature of ethnographic reinterpretation and how different concepts and categories like marriage, social structure, are defined and conceptualized. In this connection, his works such as analysis of Swazi 'rituals of rebellion', study of Leach and Gough's definitions of marriage deserve mention (Sarana, 2008). After a thorough scan of his writings, one must admit that the kind of engagement his works entailed is exemplary. He made critique of the towering figures of anthropology, some founding fathers of different schools of thought, for which he had to be highly cautious not to give any impression of misreading or misinterpretation on his part. This type of work necessitates a close reading of a vast collection of relevant literature. He himself admitted the amount of labour he had to give in connection with his study of Leach and Gough by way of making the following remark:

> *It was hard task to wade through facts and their interpretation presented by two ablest analysts of ethnographic material in twentieth century social anthropology* (Sarana, 2008: 14).

Sarana's paper on the contribution of Professor D.N. Majumdar to the study of Indian religion is an excellent example of a thorough academic appraisal of a scholar (Sarana,1961). Starting his paper with a biographical note and salient features of the academic distinctions of Professor Majumdar, he entered into the deliberations on religion as represented by Majumdar's work. Here, he compared Majumdar's position with the known concepts of functionalism, structural models (with reference to 'conscious model' and 'home-made model') and *gestalt* psychology. He rightly pointed out how Majumdar's *Bongaism* can be compared with Codrington's theory of *Manaism.* An interesting part of the paper is his attempt to place Majumdar's concepts among his Indian contemporaries.

Sarana got an opportunity to visit Israel, following which he compared the social situations of both the countries (Sarana,1993). He noted that there are differences between Indian and Israeli societies, but at the same time Israel is not the West. He felt that Israel was moving fast towards adopting the Western model of society with the fast declining influence of Kibbutz. It was said that the Kibbutz ideology would not be able to support large scale industrial progress and would suppress individual potential for entrepreneurship. Thus, attempts were now made to judge its utility in terms of economic benefits it could accrue. For Sarana, Kibbutz was a unique experiment of social reconstruction which translated 'a socialist utopia into a reality'. He judged it instead from an intrinsic value system that it fostered. Sarana wrote (1993:271):

> *That is why I look at the Kibbutz not in terms of its failure or success in economic sphere, though it ought not to be completely by-passed. The Kibbutz experiment has a tremendous value as it creates a social network of intimate (primary) relations – outside the family and kin groups – between its members. It thus provides a social cushion around the family which is conspicuous by its absence in the West.*

The paper indicated a kind of direction the Israeli society might have taken in its move towards the Western social system. In fact, his foresight proved to be true since the institution started facing a grave crisis for its survival. Notwithstanding this, Sarana (1993) was otherwise very much moved by the value-orientation of the Kibbutz. From the following sentences, we will be able to see how an anthropologist takes position on a subject of far-reaching consequences:

> *This is a warning not to fall in this kind of a social situation. Quite against this Israel has a system which one can be really proud of. It is in the interest of Israelis not only to let the Kibbutz continue, but to further the pioneering ideology of equality, fraternity and mutual cooperation. It is the duty of every right-thinking Israeli – not so much of the conservatives but especially of the most progressive amongst them – to strengthen the institution of Kibbutz which is their forefathers' unique contribution to the world* (Sarana, 1993:273).

Such a stand is usually unbecoming of an anthropologist unless he assumes a subjective stance. In this connection, I must add that although Sarana had a positivist leaning towards theoretical studies, yet he seemed so different at times. Probably, a scholar like Prof. Gopal Sarana cannot be assessed in stereotypic conventional terms.

Many of his articles collected in books were compilations of papers published earlier in different journals. For example, his papers like 'Rituals of Rebellion: The Swazi case Re-examined' and 'How Anthropologists Compare' which were included in *Explorations in Method and Theory in Anthropology* (2008) were published earlier in *The Eastern Anthropologist* in the years 1970 and 1971 respectively. The paper 'Structure and Function: Malinowski and Radcliffe-Brown Re-examined' published in *Man In India* in 1970 was included in the above-mentioned book. In fact, the same article was published in two books, namely, *Sociology and Anthropology and Other Essays* (1983) and *Explorations in Method and Theory in Anthropology* (2008). However, the article on Margaret Mead, which came out in *Man In India,* was not included in any of these books. The paper deals with the life and contributions of Margaret Mead (Sarana, 1991). The paper is interesting in the sense that he has narrated the life of the anthropologist in the backdrop of her academic activities. The rest of the paper focuses on two most important aspects of her career. Mead's most significant academic contribution was related to the domain of psychological anthropology. The development of Mead's academic works from a position of a broad-based theoretical inquiry into examining the roles of culture and biology in shaping a people's configuration has engaged Sarana's attention. Here, the guiding figure was Franz Boas, who was more concerned with applied issues of the psychological nature of culture. All these have been shown by Sarana in this section of the paper. The 'Mead-Freeman' controversy has been dealt with reference to a more fundamental question of the relationship between 'Anthropological fieldwork and issue of replicability', the moot point in anthropological research for a pretty long time. Sarana was rather critical of Freeman for dealing with the matter in a very discourteous and sweeping manner. He considered Freeman's mode of argument highly objectionable and termed it as a 'case of misapplication of Popperian logic of falsification'. I think by this he indicated the notion of demarcation as mentioned in Popperian methodology of falsification. In assessing Mead's work, one should not expect a replication as Sarana indicated. According to him, Freeman failed to understand this point in his hasty bid to 'unmasking' of an ethnographer.

In the paper on the status of social-cultural anthropology in India, authored jointly with D.P. Sinha in *Annual Review of Anthropology* (1976), he commented on the status of the discipline subjectively as well as objectively. The subjective position was apparent when they commented on the kind of study to be undertaken in the Indian context and wrote:

> *We must also devise special schemes for holistic description of different levels of organization, such as cities, regions, and the entire nation* (Sarana and Sinha, 1976 : 223).

The whole discussion has been divided into three sub-heads – 'Indian Anthropology in Focus', 'Spheres of Influences and emerging perspectives' and 'Continuing Interest and emerging trends'. Authors are of the opinion that anthropology in India emerged from a utilitarian demand of colonial administration and gradually shifted to academic fields of enquiry. In keeping with the shift in focus, the study of caste and village societies rather than remaining bogged down only with tribes would be a meaningful proposition. As the Indian situation was different from that of UK, for developing a holistic perspective to deal with diversities prevailing in India more and more anthropology departments should be opened in the Universities. After Independence, the need for social-cultural anthropology in India has been increasingly emphasized to carry out problem-oriented studies focusing on community development, education, tribal development, land alienation and some such issues. Of course, even after his plea for a change in focus, tribal ethnography continued to get attention from the Indian anthropologists. There could be a justification for that because some of the basic anthropological theories were developed from the study of tribal societies. Although Sarana and his co-author identified some new, emerging areas of anthropology, of which urban anthropology was one, they lamented that the Indian anthropologists had yet to develop a battery of their own theoretical tools to explain the Indian social situation. In his paper on the anthropological study of Indian civilization, Sarana made an attempt to illustrate how an insider would study the civilization going beyond the usual conventional way (Sarana, 1970).

Relation between Anthropology and Sociology: 'Sarana-Beteille Debate'

Gopala Sarana wrote a very lengthy article on the relations between sociology and social anthropology (Sarana, 1983). Sarana was convinced that social anthropology is distinct from sociology so far as their historical development, aims or objectives, methodology and philosophy of research are concerned. In this regard, he contradicts Professor Andre Beteille who 'advocates that sociology and social anthropology are identical.' Sarana goes on to show the self-contradictory statements made by Beteille in the following way:

> *In the light of his own admission, I am unable to understand Professor Beteille's argument that though 'sociology and social anthropology have similar or even identical aims' (Ibid., 4) and have 'the same approach to the study of social life, [and] that their methods are similar'* (Beteille, 1974 : 9) *and yet the two disciplines do 'very different kinds of work' (Ibid.,* p. 4). *How can this be possible?* (Sarana, 1983 : 20).

To substantiate his view, Sarana refers to Kroeber who once remarked that these two disciplines are temperamentally different and are almost antithetical in their motivations (*Ibid.*, p. 21). Sarana defines social anthropology as an 'empirical study of the real people and their daily life' (*Ibid.*, p. 28). On the other hand, he conceives that "the unifying theme of sociology in the areas of interest, research and theory is the consequence of its almost exclusive preoccupations with western society and its problems and issues" (*Ibid.*, p. 25).

Beteille (1974) mentions in his book the connotation 'Comparative Sociology' which sometimes carries the same meaning as social anthropology in Radcliffe-Brown's understanding. Sarana has shown how Radcliffe-Brown was not consistent with his use of the term comparative sociology. He derives four different positions of Radcliffe-Brown from the latter's writings on the topic. These meanings are: (i) Comparative Sociology originated from Social Anthropology; (ii) Social Anthropology and Sociology are identical; (iii) Social Anthropology is a branch of Comparative Sociology; and (iv) Comparative Sociology has not yet been established to stake a claim for formal acceptance. In this way, Sarana seems to have taken an opposite position to Beteille who has supported the view of Radcliffe-Brown that comparative sociology and social anthropology are the same. It is not always the fact that Sarana's discussion on the differences between sociology and social anthropology has been supported by factual evidences; he has only minced from Beteille's writings or sought confirmation from elsewhere. For example, Sarana writes that sociology has root in philosophy whereas the social anthropology does not have any such root (Sarana, 1983: 14). But Sarana's statement with regard to the philosophical roots of anthropology seems to be untenable since many authors have mentioned that anthropology too, was rooted in the philosophical traditions of the continent (Ghosh, 1994; Eriksen and Nilelsen, 2001). In spite of all these criticisms, we do not come across any counter-argument from Beteille in any of his writings which he had published in the subsequent years on similar issues. Not only that, we do not see any reference to Sarana's works on the comparative method in Beteille's article on the same topic which he wrote after Sarana's work was published.

Sarana has stated that anthropology developed earlier than sociology as a distinct discipline. It has also preceded sociology in the establishment of first University chair, starting of the first professional journal, and setting up of the first professional association of the practitioners of the discipline. Through museum, anthropology could earn recognition, which was beyond the scope of sociology. Apart from going into the historical realities to pin point differences between the two disciplines, Sarana was all along a strong advocate of social anthropology as distinct from sociology.

Conclusion

From the foregoing discussion, it is evident that Gopala Sarana left us a legacy of anthropology which has thrived in insightful thoughts and scholarly engagements. He was serious about his discipline and advocated a unified holistic anthropology distinct from sociology. Probably, he had some disquieting feeling over the wanton disciplinary swapping. He will be remembered for his meticulous theoretical exercises on the theories of functionalism, structural-functionalism and structuralism of Levi-Strauss. Moreover, he had raised some very pertinent questions on the basic premises of these theories and spotted conceptual limitations in them. His argumentative style of writing and eclectic ideas would remain an everlasting source of contemplation for posterity.

Acknowledgements

The author acknowledges Dr. Rahul Patel, Allahabad University and Dr. Nabakumar Duary, Anthropological Survey of India for providing some of the documents related to the preparation of this article.

REFERENCES

Bandyopadhyay, S. 2020. "Gopala Sarana (1935-2010)". In *Doyens of Indian Anthropology,* Part-2 Edited by A. Sarkar and S. Dasgupta, pp. 94-102. New Delhi: Agam Kala Prakashan.

Beteille, A. 1974. "Sociology and Social Anthropology". In *Six Essays in Comparative Sociology,* Edited by A. Beteille, pp. 1-20. Delhi: Oxford University Press.

Eggan, F. 1954. "Social Anthropology and the Method of Controlled Comparison". *American Anthropologist,* 56: 743-763.

Eriksen, T.H. and F.S. Nielsen, 2001. *A History of Anthropology.* London: Pluto Press.

Ghosh, A. 1994. *A Brief History of Anthropology from Philosophy to Anthropology.* Delhi: Arvind Publications.

Harris, M. 2001. *The Rise of Anthropological Theory.* Lanham: Altamira Press.

Ingold, T. 2008. "Anthropology is not Ethnography". *Proceedings of the British Academy,* 154: 69-92.

Madan, T.N. and Sarana, G. (Eds.) 1963. *Indian Anthropology – Essays in Memory of D.N. Majumdar,* Bombay: Asia Publishing House.

Mishra, P.K. 2004. "Gopala Sarana's Contribution to Anthropology". In *Studies in Indian Anthropology – Festschrift to Professor Gopala Sarana,* Edited by P.K. Mishra, pp. 1-14, Jaipur: Rawat Publications.

Patel, R. 2011. "Professor Gopala Sarana (Obituary)". *The Oriental Anthropologist* 11(1).

Reddy, N.S. 2011. "Professor Gopala Sarana (Obituary)". *The Eastern Anthropologist,* 64(1): 143-144.

Sarana, G. 1961. "Professor D.N. Majumdar and Anthropology of Indian Religion". In *Aspects of Religion in Indian Society,* Edited by L.P. Vidyarthi, pp. 1-12. Meerut: Kedar Nath Ram Nath.

_____. 1970. "Anthropology of Indian Civilization". *J. Indian Anthrop. Soc.,* 5: 31-39.

_____. 1973. *Anthropological Method and Indian Anthropology.* Madras: University of Madras.

_____. 1975. *The Methodology of Anthropological Comparison.* Tuscon: University of Arizona Press.

_____. 1975a. "Socio-archaeology [and Comments and Reply]". *Current Anthropology,* 16(3): 323-341.

_____. 1976a. "Studying Voluntary Associations as Adaptive Mechanisms: A Review of Anthropological Perspectives [and Comments and Reply]". *Current Anthropology,* 17(1): 23-47.

_____. 1976b. "The Personal Approach in Cultural Anthropological Research [and Comments and Reply]". *Current Anthropology,* 17(2): 243-261.

_____. 1977. *Introducing Anthropology.* Calcutta: The Indian Anthropological Society.

_____. 1983. *Sociology and Anthropology and Other Essays.* Calcutta: ISRAA.

_____. 1991. "Life and Work of Margaret Mead: A Brief Review". *Man in India,* 71 (2&3): 342-361.

_____. 1993. "Some Reflections on Israel and India, Part-II". *The Eastern Anthropologist,* 46(3): 249-276.

_____. 2008. *Explorations in Method and Theory in Anthropology.* Jaipur: Rawat Publication.

Sarana, G. and D.P. Sinha, 1976. "Status of Social-Cultural Anthropology in India". *Annual Review of Anthropology,* 5: 209-225.

8
Professor Deba Prasad Mukherjee and the Essence of Bio-cultural Approach in Anthropology in India

Bidhan Kanti Das

Initiation in Anthropology

Professor Deba Prasad Mukherjee's choice of pursuing a lesser-known subject like Anthropology at that time, rather than regular science subject, was very interesting. In the late 1940s and early 1950s, Bengal had witnessed communal riots and a huge influx of refugees from then East Pakistan (now Bangladesh). Against this backdrop, many relatives and well-wishers advised him that future prospects in the usual science subjects were rather dim. Ultimately, he discussed the matter with his childhood friend Pranab Ganguly, and both decided to venture into a field less crowded and carrying the possibility of exploring new areas. They found Anthropology to be a new science discipline, not very popular as an academic discipline in India. They went straight to Calcutta University and met Professor K.P. Chattopadhyay, then head of the department. Professor Mukherjee would later relate how, when the duo had informed Professor Chattopadhyay about their choice, the latter replied, "What you are likely to find after getting this degree is a solid wall and little chance of making any headway. So, do think twice." "But when we stuck to our decision, he took us to the library. I was charmed with the treasure of knowledge it boasted of", he said, and they decided to take up the subject. He successfully obtained his M.Sc. degree in Anthropology in 1951, along with Professor Ganguly.

Professionally, Professor Mukherjee was very active, dynamic and adventurist. The major part of his career was characterised by diverse academic assignments, at different places, at national and international institutions. All these assignments were primarily related to research and teaching. His professional career started as lecturer and head of the newly created Biology Department at Kandi Raj College, Murshidabad. Meanwhile, he accepted an offer to work at a UNESCO project on the effects of industrialisation under the then Planning Commission. His family's financial difficulties forced him to join Brahma Boys'School as Assistant Headmaster, as well as a part-time lecturer of Anthropology at Bangabasi College (Mukhopadhyay, 1997).

A new chapter began in the professional career of Professor Mukherjee in 1957, when he joined the Anthropological Survey of India (AnSI) as a research associate in Shillong, the AnSI's north-east regional headquarters. This provided him the opportunity to undertake extensive surveys among the tribals of the north-eastern regions, like the Khasis, the Nagas, the Manipuris and the Mizos, to collect anthropometric, dermatoglyphic, social and cultural information. The variation in dermatoglyphic patterns of palms and toes among the tribes he observed, provided him with a lasting interest and led him to explore the nature of variations, an important area in studying human variation in physical anthropology. In 1960, he was offered the role of research investigator for a survey among first generation Anglo-Indians, as a part of a project on race crossing under the leadership of Professor Ruggles Gates, a distinguished professor of human genetics. While working among the Anglo-Indians, he along with Professor Gates and Professor M.R. Chakrabarti became involved in an academic debate on whether the inheritance pattern of hypertrichosis (condition where a tuft of hair is present on the outer rim of external ear) is autosomal or Y-linked. One group led by Professor Curt Stern argued that the inheritance followed autosomal sex-linked. This was challenged by the group led by Professor Gates (Mukhopadhyay, 1997). It was not an easy task for the latter group to infer the inheritance pattern, as Professor Mukherjee shared with me during a conversation. He collected extensive pedigrees of families where this trait was observed. He analysed those lengthy pedigrees and came to a conclusion in favour of Y-linked inheritance. This article appeared in the prestigious *The American Journal of Human Genetics* in 1962. The title of the article is interesting – 'Final pedigrees of Y-chromosome inheritance'.

But Professor Mukherjee continued to take interest in dermatoglyphic research related to fingers, palms, toes and soles for ridge count, configuration of patterns and t-triradius. His initial work on dermatoglyphic characters and possible association with some diseases – that led to his admission in a doctoral programme – is worth mentioning. He undertook exhaustive studies on dermatoglyphic data of the Mahar caste of Maharashtra and developed methodological subtleties like measuring the position of t-triradius on hands.This led him to write a paper and send it to the *American Journal of Physical Anthropology* for publication. A copy of this paper was also sent to Professor L.S. Penrose, a distinguished scientist known for his study on association of elevated t-triradius and specific dermal patterns among some patients with mental disorders and diagnostic dermatoglyphic characteristics among the Down Syndrome patients. Professor Penrose was impressed with the data quality and the nature of its analysis, and thus invited Professor Mukherjee to England "for mutual benefit" (Mukhopadhyay, 1997). Though initially reluctant, he ultimately joined the Galton Laboratory as a Commonwealth scholar of Professor Penrose in 1964. He worked on dermatoglyphic data of Indian populations under the joint guidance of Professor Sarah B. Holt and Professor C.A.B. Smith, and completed his Ph.D. from the University of London in 1967, staying for another year as an MRC Fellow at Kennedy-Galton Centre. He returned to India in 1969 despite an offer to teach in England by Professor Penrose, due to his love for his motherland.

Professor Mukherjee always tried to explore new areas of research which are socially relevant. A new turn in research interest can be traced in his work after returning to India. His focus was on creating new departments or centres so that research can be concentrated on those issues. For example, after joining as Assistant Director at the National Institute of Family Planning (now re-designated as National Institute of Family Welfare), he founded a new division – Population Genetics and Human Development (Das, 2015). This had been created to study exclusively the different types of marriage patterns, family formation and their genetic implications. This new direction of research work was recognised in international fora. The World Health Organization (WHO) honoured Professor Mukherjee by appointing him as specialist in human genetics in 1971. He got an invitation to participate in the scientific group on genetic implications of family planning in Geneva, and presented a paper titled "*Patterns of marriage and family formation in Rural India and Genetical implication of family planning*". In that paper, he tried to present a new insight on long-term effect of national family planning on the micro-evolutionary process.

He was looking for opportunities to undertake further research in this direction. To pursue this, fresh and enthusiastic students with anthropological training at a university would be ideal, Professor

Mukherjee strongly believed. With this in mind, he joined as Reader and founding Head of a new Department of Anthropology and Sociology at Sri Venkateswara University, Tirupati in 1971 (Das, 2015). He established the department from scratch with all his experience, expertise and sincerity. His passion for research and ability of inculcating research interest among his pupils, inspired a lot of students from that institution to take research and teaching as their careers. Several students took up this issue of marriage patterns in their doctoral work later, enhancing the pool of knowledge related to genetic implications of marriage, and thereby established the importance of anthropological approach in human genetic research in India.

After spending the golden period of his career at the S.V. University, Professor Mukherjee joined ASI Kolkata as its Deputy Director in 1975, and founded the School of Anthropology there. In 1981, he joined the Department of Anthropology at Calcutta University as Professor of Physical Anthropology, and retired after more than 15 years of active academic tenure there. He guided a number of doctoral students under different universities, and also an MD dissertation. During this period, he was elected President for the Anthropology and Archaeology Section at the 84th session of the Indian Science Congress held at Delhi. He continued to teach in the Calcutta and Vidyasagar Universities as Guest Professor. He always cherished a dream of extending the knowledge he achieved beyond academic arena. To realize this dream, he engaged in genetic counselling and held awareness camps for doctors and health camps for medical screening and genetic study of hereditary diseases on out-door patients at R.G. Kar Medical College and Hospital.

As Teacher and Research Guide – My experiences

I will share my experiences and feelings about Professor Mukherjee as teacher and research guide, experiences which helped me immensely in improving my knowledge about anthropology as a discipline as well as in becoming a researcher on anthropological issues. Firstly, I had the opportunity to come in contact with Professor Mukherjee as a student of a postgraduate course in Anthropology. I can still remember his teaching on the papers 'Physical Anthropology and Human Genetics' in the first year and 'Population and Quantitative Genetics' in the second year. One topic continues to make me wonder: Why does variation occur? In other words, why are two people not alike? He had the rare quality to make us understand such complex topics in a lucid way. For him, the root cause of variation is the biological basis of inheritance. To make it simpler to us, he used to proceed step by step – from cell to chromosome to DNA to genetic code as the basis of inheritance, and showed the changes occurring at different stages causing variation. He always stressed on minute details and subtleties of each step and what happens when parts of chromosomes fail to recombine in ordered manner causing abnormalities. The way he presented the whole process of inheritance in the classroom was so vivid and clear that I can still visualize it after 34 years. Similar was the experience of him teaching us the scope and objectives of population genetics in the second year. He presented before us the importance of population research in human genetics and how anthropological research can thereby contribute towards understanding human genetic problems. He conceptualised the vast areas of study in population genetics in a distinct fashion according to objectives: (i) *population study of genetics*, which includes distribution, correlation, mutation, linkage etc.; (ii) *study of genetics of populations* to discern the factors of maintenance and change of genetic make-up of the populations; and (iii) the *genetic studies of population structure* which include genetic basis and consequences of the demographic aspects of populations (Mukherjee, 1972). That gave us a clear picture about the horizons of population genetics, which I can still remember. He always stressed on the core aspect of any topic and conceptual understanding of a topic or issue, not on how much techniques or tools one knows. According to Professor Mukherjee, DNA technology would not answer all questions in human genetics, rather new understanding and interpretation matters most. He always tried to clarify minute differences of various concepts, like pedigree *versus* genealogy, polygenic *versus* multi-allelic inheritance, or population structure *versus* population composition, by comparing real-world events. He did not need books or notes to conduct a class lecture. I enjoyed all of this a lot. In fact, it was his teaching technique, especially the way he made me understand the complexity of inheritance of traits and other human genetic problems in lucid manner, which helped to grow my interest in Biological Anthropology and finally made me choose Biological Anthropology as a special paper.

His clear understanding of population genetics, including demo-genetics and population structure, and, not least, his pleasing personality, attracted me to pursue doctoral thesis under his supervision. While working on my doctoral thesis, I interacted closely with him. He guided me in every stage of work, from data collection to analysis to interpretation of data with great care. He helped me learn how to systematically review a topic, what to extract from a paper and how to evaluate a paper in terms of strengths and weaknesses. It is Professor Mukherjee from whom I learnt which statistical methods are most suitable for getting the correct picture for particular research questions, and why. Though, I had a very tentative knowledge about statistical methods, Professor Mukherjee helped me become more comfortable with various statistical methods and techniques relevant for my research work, in a very lucid but sophisticated way. I learnt from him how to read data and how to make hair-splitting analyses of that data. I could appreciate the depth of his knowledge on anthropology and related areas, his analytical mind, and his extraordinary ability to read data, all too evident during his analysis and interpretation of my draft doctoral thesis. In fact, the draft chapters of my research which I still possess are full of underlines and scratches of red ink from his pen.

I can still recall the period when he was writing the presidential address for the Indian Science Congress session in 1996-97. His topic was 'Population structure as an emerging frontier of Anthropology and Human Development'. Whenever I met him at his residence during that period, he used to read whatever he had written and seek comments for every line, whether it was meaningful and sensible. Often, I would say, "Sir, it doesn't seem to be convincing. It may need to be rephrased." He always thought over it for a while and often gladly accepted my contentions. It was the rare quality of Professor Mukherjee as a researcher, teacher and scholar. He had the quality and capability of recognising other ideas, even from a student. He was a perfectionist when putting his ideas or contentions into writing, which compelled him to struggle with draft after draft till it became a detailed but dense, clear and focused work.

Contributions to Anthropological Research

If we look closely at his articles published at various peer-reviewed national and international journals, proceedings and edited volumes, Professor Mukherjee's research mainly concentrated on patterns and genetics of dermatoglyphic traits, quantitative genetics of continuous traits, and genetics of marriage patterns. But to my mind, his most important contribution to anthropology and human population genetics are inheritance pattern of dermatoglyphic and anthropometric traits and identification of nature of genes involved. To understand the complex inheritance patterns of human traits, he always strived to improve methodologies to overcome the problems of studying human beings. Here, I will discuss three major areas where he contributed most.

(a) Dermatoglyphics

Professor Mukherjee has an extensive body of work on the variation of finger and palm print patterns, as these characters are most useful in identifying genetic processes underlying quantitative variations. In the words of Professor Mukherjee, "they are not only the least modified by environment but they also provide the scope of observing varied expressions of same genotypes on several homologous parts – fingers, toes, palms and soles ... This facilitates the study of variations in the process of development of phenotypes from genes" (1996).

In the early 1960s, Professor Mukherjee collaborated with M.R. Chakraborti on a series of regional surveys on finger and palm print patterns in the tribes and castes of different Indian states – Assam, Meghalaya, Mizoram (1961); Nagaland, Manipur (1962); Kerala, Nilgiri Hills of Tamil Nadu (1961, 1964); Andhra Pradesh and Chotanagpur regions of Jharkhand. They also tried to throw light on the Mundari ethnic problem with dermatoglyphic traits (1964). They observed intra-population variations in those traits due to micro-evolutionary forces operating in the local populations. He also examined the dermatoglyphic patterns of Shompen of Anadaman Islands (Mukherjee and Ganguly, 1965).

The 1950s had one important research question: To what extent is the total pattern intensity on the ridged skin of an individual inherited? Ridge-count, which directly measures the pattern size, gives only an indirect indication of the type of patterns occurring on the fingers (Holt, 1961). Professor Mukherjee argued that the difficulty of finding all the triradii on a print, especially of the sole and the palm, may be overcome by using Penrose's formula. To study the number of triradii on fingers, palms and soles, he collected a sample of an endogamous caste – the Bengali Brahman of Calcutta and suburbs in 1964. In these exercises, he tried to propose absolute ridge-counts on fingers and toes, being the sum of newly defined ulnar loop ridge-count and radial loop ridge-count measuring on fingers, and fibular loop ridge-count, and tibial loop ridge count measuring on toes as combined measures of both pattern intensity and pattern size.

He and his associates richly contributed to dermatoglyphic genetics research. One of the contributions was heritability and modes of inheritance of dermatoglyphic traits. To clarify further on the process of inheritance and nature of genes involved, he and his students compared related individuals with different degrees of inbreeding through parental consanguinity among the local endogamous Telugu-speaking populations of Andhra Pradesh and Muslim populations of West Bengal (Mukherjee and Lakshmanudu, 1980, Mukherjee, *et al.*, 1990; Mukherjee, 1984, 1992; Mukherjee and Ghosh, 1983; A. Mukherjee, 1990). Those studies confirmed the suggestion of additive effects of a small number of autosomal genes for pattern intensity on finger and toes with the excess of whorls (or high ridge-counts) and arches (or low ridge-counts) on finger and toes (Mukherjee, 1998).

(b) Anthropological Genetics of Quantitative Variations

In human, genetics of quantitative traits primarily deals with the estimation of components of variation due to additive genes (heritability); non-additive genes and environmental influence, and identification of segregation of single loci, if possible (Mukherjee, 1984). In heritability studies, correlations are population-specific. Though there might be environmental factors for population differences, considerable genetic differences also occur between populations in traits like body proportions. Correlations depend on the degree of genetic heterogeneity and the structure of human populations. He cautioned against possible misuse of the measure of heritability. According to him, "it describes what proportion of the variation in a character like stature or ridge-count is the result of segregation of alleles". A population with more genetic variation would show more values of correlations, which can be shown in the studies on heritability in ridge-count on fingers (Mukherjee, 1996).

A high correlation only suggests strong genetic influence on a trait but it is not confirmatory. Professor Mukherjee and others argued that correlations may be affected by differences in genetic homogeneity, mating patterns and environmental variance (Mukherjee, 1966; Roberts, *et al.*, 1978). Relative values of correlations between the different types of relatives but of different degrees may suggest the mode of inheritance of a trait. But they fail to throw light on genotypes, specific effects of genes and interaction of loci (epistasis). Professor Mukherjee provided new lines of approach – examining inbreeding effects on metrical traits which can give better clarification on those aspects. He compared and analysed different anthropometric traits like stature, chest girth, sitting height and nasal height and breadth at different levels of inbreeding, in well-defined local endogamous populations of India. From the analyses, he concluded that inbreeding effects occur independently of hereditary and environmental differences in related and unrelated parents and their inbreeding level and assortative mating. Secondly, inbreeding effects indicate homozygosity of recessive genes with negative effects in the distribution of body size and of those with positive effects in the distribution of finger ridge-count, the multiplicity of recessive alleles being possible for a few traits. Thirdly, inbreeding effects represent not only a linear reduction with increasing F, but also an irregular non-linear deviation in anthropometric measurements which do not support non-additive epistasis between the involved loci. Fourthly, it displays clear segregation of a few additive genes on the two sides of an antimode, which marks the heterozygotes for stature, head length, cephalic index, ridge-counts, and provide evidence against the hypothesis of overdominance. The effect of a specific level of inbreeding on mean is correlated with the non-inbred mean, the change of variance and the difference between two modal frequencies in the inbred which are related to the frequency of genes and genotypes.

One of the Professor Mukherjee's important contributions is the study of frequency distribution for genetic analysis of quantitative traits in relation to inbreeding (1984). The influence of additive genes can easily be observed only in frequency distribution. He argued that the non-additive genes can be detected both in the change of means and in that of frequency distributions. The study of distribution thus may serve as a substitute for segregation analysis for some quantitative traits. This is demonstrated through the appearance of bimodality in the inbred distributions of a number of anthropometric traits, including menarcheal age, skin colour grade (Laksmanudu and Mukherjee, 1978). He further argued that the position of antimodes in the middle of the inbred distributions suggests equal frequencies of additive genes with positive and negative effects for anthropometric traits which are normally distributed in the non-inbred. But the antimode deviates towards the lower end of the asymmetrical distribution of the finger ridge-count and suggests higher frequency of positive additive alleles (Mukherjee, 1984).

(c) Methods for Studying Human Quantitative Traits

To Professor Mukherjee, proper research design and methods are extremely important to clarify the gene-environment causation of the complex phenotypes as these traits are "influenced by far more complex systems than molecular approaches are capable of characterising" (Vogler and Rao, 1993) and thus anthropological genetics is essential for analysing complex and quantitative variations. To understand the nature of inheritance and to identify nature of genes/alleles involved for variation of human quantitative traits, studying characters like stature, head shape or finger and palm print patterns is very useful. He stressed for proper interpretation of analysed data.

According to him, to study genetics of quantitative variations of anthropometric traits, which are useful in assessing population affinities, one has to examine the natural history and frequency distributions in defined genetic populations, in different environmental settings. After taking measurements, comparison of central values like means, mode and nature of distributions with degree and type of asymmetry is essential (Mukherjee, 1996). He further elaborated that mean value of a quantitative variation may be proportional to the concerned genes and genotypes, and also be influenced by the average amount of dominance of all those alleles. Moreover, "if in a population or a family, the heterozygotes express the dominant allele at one or more loci, the distribution of the quantitative values of the trait will become asymmetrical. The absence of dominance/recessivity of the alleles may make the distribution of the quantitative trait symmetrical" (1996). He further pointed out that "the direction in which the high frequency, that causes the asymmetry, occurs in the direction of the dominance effects. Thus, a negative skewness with a gentle slope on the left side of the distribution would indicate dominance of alleles giving positive or increasing effects of the trait. Conversely, an increased proportion of low values causing asymmetry would point to reducing (negative) effects of dominant alleles" (*Ibid.*). Hence, from the typical asymmetrical distributions of quantitative variations in skin ridge-patterns on hands and feet observed in different populations, one can infer, as argued by him, that there are only a few genes which control ridge-counts on fingers, number of triradii on fingers, palms, toes and soles and other variations.

According to him, dermatoglyphic patterns can be used as criterion for understanding affinities among the populations. In a study, he proposed a method of objective formulations of palmar and planter patterns. With this one can derive pattern intensity indices for palms and soles (Mukherjee, 1998). He argued that the number of palmar triradii was found to serve as an efficient independent criterion for studying ethnic affinities of north-east Indian populations (Mukherjee and Lakshmanudu, 1980). For him, modes and medians of distributions appeared to be more clearly indicative of ethno-historical backgrounds than means (Mukherjee, 1986).

Another important useful approach to study quantitative human genetics, according to him, is the study of inbreeding effects on the quantitative variation (Mukherjee, 1996). Inbreeding can be conceived as process through which individuals become homozygous for an increased number of ancestral genes (Das, 2001). To examine inbreeding effects, one has to compare a quantitative variation between individuals who are more closely inbred with those that are less closely inbred as all human beings have some homozygous loci. Marriage patterns like consanguineous marriage, assortative mating, local endogamy and small size mating group – all these enhance the degree of inbreeding in the offspring (Mukherjee, 1996). One can measure the degree of inbreeding directly through tracing pedigrees.

To him, proper study design is important to analyse a phenomenon. For example, some scholars have interpreted decrease in mean stature and chest girth in closely inbred individuals as an inbreeding effect.This, however, has been contested by others, who argue that high inbreeding occurs in poor and backward people; decrease in stature and chest girth is thus a reflection of poor nutrition rather than inbreeding. This problem can be rectified through improved design, as Professor Mukherjee argued: First, comparison of males or females with different degrees of inbreeding in the smallest reproductive isolate by tracing within same kindred or extended family, who have experienced similar socio-economic environment. Second, formulating design using finger, palm, toe and sole print patterns as these traits are unaffected by socio-economic conditions. Following this design, he "obtained consistent evidence of diminution of mean stature and ... elevation of mean in adult blood pressure, menarcheal age, and to slight extent of finger ridge count or triradii number" (1996). This observation verified the hypothesis that parents of the highly inbred have not differed from parents of low inbreds in the same way as their offspring (Mukherjee *et al.,* 1977, Mukherjee , 1984).

Professor Mukherjee and Biocultural Research in Anthropology in India

Since nature of man is a complex product of environmental conditions, genetic structures, physiological conditions, social norms and traditions, an integrative approach is essential for proper understanding of humankind. The bio-cultural analysis stresses on the interplay between the biological and cultural attributes. For example, marriage, a universal social institution, provides opportunity for the biological union of two individuals of opposite sexes leading to birth. Similarly, the food habits of any community, which are linked to eco-cultural factors, vary from one culture to another. The intake of food has an impact upon the physiological composition of the body, which leads to its overall growth as per nutrient requirement for the biological function of the human body and mind (Nandy, 1993). Thus, if we look deep into the human way of life, it is very difficult to disentangle the biological background from socio-cultural aspects.

Professor Mukherjee was a strong proponent of holistic, in-depth analysis of a particular problem in specific populations, for improvement of human conditions and the proper direction of human destiny. He devised a model to emphasize the 'wholism' that anthropology is the combination and interaction of human biology and culture. This idea was illustrated by an isosceles triangle with three vertices A, B and C to emphasize that Anthropology (A) has two interconnected components – Biology (B) and Culture (C). The height of Anthropology depends on the closeness of Biology and Culture. When B and C are the farthest apart, there will be no significance of A (Mukherjee, 1996). He extended further the idea for human development. Anthropology for human development has to consider ecological background (E) in addition to biology and culture, making it a quadrilateral ABEC (Mukherjee, 1997). According to him, molecular biology has been able to clarify the nature of genetic information and different mutant alleles of phenotypically similar genes for sickle cell, thalassemia or G6PD deficiency, and has allowed assessing paternal and maternal contributions to a gene pool (population) by probing Y-chromosome and mitochondrial DNA. But the meaning of that message depends on the decoding of DNA-protein synthesis, and that would be influenced by biochemical environment. Besides, there are unknown complexities between the new protein and the final shape and function of the individual, where anthropology and biology can contribute. Human variation shaped through development experience-environment and culture (Mukherjee, 1996). Also, its contribution to population ecology and adaptation remains to be clarified (Roberts, 1991). This necessitates bio-cultural investigation on human phenotypes. Anthropological knowledge in understanding complexity of social and genetical structure (Basu, *et al.*, 1993) and formulating genetic epidemiological question and collecting right kind of data (Mazumder and Rao, 1991) for analysis of genetic-environmental interaction and susceptivities are increasingly gaining attention among the scholars. Thus, a new paradigm evolved, popularly known as anthropological genetics. Professor Mukherjee argued, anthropologically relevant biological characters should be studied under bio-cultural framework, employing anthropological methods and fieldwork. Within anthropological genetics, it consider social grouping, patterns for family formation and relevant cultural practices within an ecological frame to clarify the gene-environment causation of complex phenotypic manifestation which are influenced by far more complex systems, may not possible through molecular approaches, he argued.

Professor Mukherjee in his presidential address at the Indian Science Congress emphasized population structure as a major frontier in anthropology and human development. It offers new opportunities of interaction and complementation between the framework of social structure and other concepts and methods developing in human biology, for further advancement of each specialization (1997). He argued that this conceptualisation provides a dynamic principle to hold the core of anthropology at a stable equilibrium, while its boundaries may remain undefined with horizons expanding for further exploration. According to him, human populations are structured in definite forms and also dynamic. The structure of a population is the way its component makes the whole greater than their sum. This is similar to social structure, defined as the "definite pattern in which the parts of a social system harmoniously work with the whole" (Mukherjee, 1993). Anthropological knowledge within bio-cultural framework can help to understand the intricacies of social and genetic structure (*Ibid.*). He undertook a series of research by identifying local endogamous populations. For him, "large samples required for obtaining significant effects of inbreeding are unrealistic due to aggregation of related marriages in a few kindred forming small circles within endogamous populations" (1997). The genetic effects of inbreeding have to be examined by controlling the genetic and environmental variances of the comparable groups, not possible in large samples. He and other scholars collected data on consanguineous marriage among small endogamous populations across India and showed an increase of congenital malformations, infant and child mortality and several recessive disorders and diseases with increase of inbreeding level that contradicts L.N. Sanghvi's suggestion of considerable decline of lethal recessive genes as a result of repeated inbreeding through hundreds of generations in Andhra Pradesh. Such results are not apparent only in large surveys without considering social structure or marriage isolation. In another study, Professor Mukherjee and others showed non-linear inbreeding effects on secondary sex ratio (1995). A consistent rise in male birth proportion in low inbreeding followed by its decline in high inbreeding level has been observed in endogamous populations. Further, there is a positive rather than negative correlation between paternal age and proportion of male births in younger paternal age in non-consanguineous marriage. It is suggested that the relation between father's age and birth order is sensitive to socio-cultural changes in the particular population under consideration (*Ibid.*).

Essence of Bio-cultural Perspectives in Anthropology

Amid persisting problem of malnutrition and infectious diseases, globalised capitalism triggers population displacement and environmental contaminations on a greater scale. Chronic diseases like diabetes, heart disease and obesity as well as new and re-emerging infectious diseases, also threaten human survival. Relevance of Anthropology lies on the ability to understand social, environmental and biological dimensions to these problems (Goodman and Leatherman, 1998). Ethnographic works and population descriptions are not sufficient to address these complex problems. Hence, there is an urgent need to understand local realities in global contexts. Bio-cultural synthesis has not been a central concern in anthropological theory for decades. Though practicing anthropologists have stressed on studying human beings from biological and social-cultural contexts, increased professionalism has resulted in increased specialisation into various subfields, threatening the integrative nature of the discipline itself (Guha *et al.,* 1989). Socio-cultural anthropologists have generally not concerned themselves with the biological consequences of changing cultures and environments. On the other hand, biological anthropologists have paid little attention to how broader politico-economic processes combine with local ecologies to shape biological traits.Yet, bio-cultural approach in Anthropology may help to address these complex challenges. Bio-cultural approaches are those that explicitly recognise the dynamic interactions between humans as biological beings and the social, cultural, and physical environments they inhabit. They focus on understanding variability in human biology as a function of responsiveness to the larger (social, cultural, and physical) environment (Dufour, 2006). Though the bio-cultural framework was considered a central concern in the initial period of Anthropology, it gradually lost significance.

A handful of anthropologists, however, have remained engaged in research through the bio-cultural approach. In a study conducted by us in the late 1980s to inquire how the problems of specialisation and integration are reflected in this discipline's different areas of discourse, it was observed that anthropologists have never been able to avoid the question of integrating the discipline around biological and socio-cultural aspects of humankind (Guha *et al.,* 1989). An analysis of articles published for four years in three international journals revealed that bio-cultural studies have gained importance, and show a steady and consistent growth over the years (*Ibid.*). A growing realization about the importance of social-cultural phenomena in interpreting biological facts and processes can be reflected in the writing of some social anthropologists in the mid-1970s. I will cite three prominent social anthropologists who argue for bio-cultural framework. For example, M.H. Fried in his article categorically stated that "no understanding of human social organization is possible without comprehension of sexual reproduction". As he further pointed out, "No culturally structured society can be adequately comprehended without the inclusion of such biological phenomena…" (1973). A similar perception of biological aspect in social anthropology, was expressed by another social anthropologist, Robin Fox, in his book "Biosocial Anthropology". He stated, "… But because sociology as a discipline has very little concern with evolution and man's physical nature while anthropology has always maintained an interest in these, I will use 'biosocial anthropology'." He continued, "using 'biosocial' I hope to stress that this approach is indeed concerned with social man and social behaviour, and is an injection of biological thinking into social anthropology" (1975).

In a major paradigm shift, Tim Ingold, British social anthropologist, wrote an edited book with Gisli Palsson, "Biosocial Becomings: Integrating Biological and Social Anthropology", where they tried to give a completely new approach to understanding the relationship between the biological and the social thinking of human life. For them, human life is a process of becoming, and focusing on *ontogenetic and developmental processes* as well as *social processes* (2013).They argued that a situation of reintegration of Biological and Social Anthropology is emerging as there is shifting paradigm in contemporary biology about organisms, largely not explainable by neo-Darwinian paradigm, which is similar to relational and processual thinking among contemporary social anthropology.

Recently in an interview on *Ways of Living: On Culture, Biology and Anthropological Task*, Professor Tim Ingold stated, "The interesting thing is that there are now substantial numbers of researchers even within the biological sciences who are calling for a radically new approach. People working in epigenetics, developmental systems theory and even in evolutionary theory are saying that with what we know now about organisms, the neo-Darwinian paradigm simply doesn't work. So, there's a huge paradigm shift going on in biology just now, and the interesting thing is that this paradigm shift brings us right into line with the most contemporary developments in social anthropology, with the kind of relational and processual thinking going on there too. So, the conditions for reuniting biological and social anthropology are better than they've ever been" (Fernandez, 2013).

He further clarified on shifting paradigm in contemporary biology. For him, "One of the most striking things about 20th century biology was the way in which a *strict separation* was set up between evolutionary processes, and developmental or ontogenetic processes; between the processes of evolution and the processes of growth. And one of the most important things happening in contemporary biology at the moment is that – from many different directions, adopting different ideas and frameworks – scholars are all arguing that we need a different way of understanding the relationship between ontogenetic and evolutionary processes."

While drawing attention to where the problem lies on integration, he further stated, "To my mind, the most important thing that is happening in biology at the moment is the reincorporation of our understandings of ontogenetic development into the heart of biological theory. It was only difficult because for so long biology meant evolutionary biology, which meant that if you were a social anthropologist and you wanted to link up with biology, then you had to be doing evolution, and doing evolution in a particular kind of way. But if we could say that to link up to biology means *focusing on development, on how people grow up and acquire skills, and become knowledgeable and practised in the things they do, and on how doing so entails certain kinds of engagement with materials in the environment*, then the connection would be obvious. Once this is understood, the task of synthesis becomes really very easy" (*Ibid.*).

So, integration of biology and culture in understanding human behaviour is gaining momentum and taking a concrete shape. From this perspective, Professor Mukherjee was clearly ahead of his time. In understanding bio-cultural interactions, he conceptualised health, for example, as central theme. In health studies, biocultural interactions can be explored in the process of ongoing evolution which can be used as criterion of adaptation of human groups to their environment, not only in terms of advantages that cultural behaviour gives to a population but also in terms of detrimental consequences (Lieben, 1973). On the other hand, mass scale use of antibiotics has led to increased virulence of infectious diseases. This is a field where biological and cultural interaction can be useful only with bio-cultural focus of medical anthropology (Nandy and Mukherjee, 1990). Culture may serve as the adaptive environment to which both biological and cultural responses interact in such a way that the two cannot be disentangled. He argued, for example, early marriage, its stability and joint family in rural India ensured high birth rates to balance the threats of famine and epidemics, but today a number of social practices, though not always beneficial, are tending to delay marriage and child birth (Mukherjee, 1971). Cultural and social changes which are related to social structure, are likely to affect the biological make up and functions of a population (Mukherjee, 1982). In an interesting paper, Professor Mukherjee and others tried quantitatively analysed demographic analysis of marriage patterns among the Muslims that have implications for social-cultural anthropology (1995). Quantitative data has not only helped to support to marriage related certain cultural norms but also reflect on the way to describe the degree of correspondence between ideal norms and actual practice, for example, widow remarriage among the Muslims. Study was also undertaken on the ways of family formed and the effect of various cultural determinants on fertility behaviour, age at marriage, marriage types and postpartum abstinence associated with child birth from the bio-cultural point of view (Mukherjee *et al.,* 1998).

An important challenge for anthropology, according to Professor Mukherjee, comes from practical point of view in terms of its social relevance and its importance in social development (Nandy and Mukherjee, 1990). Amitabha Basu, a distinguished anthropologist, used the same line of thinking to argue for constructing research problems which help to understand the social reality. In his article, "An Anthropologist in Search of Purpose: The Test Case of Pahira of Manbhum", he strongly pointed out that anthropologists should formulate socially relevant questions and try to solve them (1974). Studies should not be restricted to differences and similarities in terms of social or genetic markers, but should answer questions like 'Why the differences?', 'What is the role of other factors?' and 'What influence can policies or programmes have?'. For him, an anthropologist should not only engage in academic exercise, but strive to be an agent of change, bringing about improvements in living standards as a member of the society.

Under bio-cultural framework, anthropologists are better positioned with the framework's field and ethnographic methods to examine complex problems that are socially relevant, especially in developing countries like India where problems relating to the survival and well-being of human populations are manifold (Huss-Ashmore and Johnston, 1985; Basu, 1987). There are however efforts by anthropologists across the globe to solve the complexity of issues that hinder human development by collaborating with other disciplines.

In terms of engagement of anthropological studies in human welfare and solving the current problems in India, Professor Mukherjee's thinking about future directions seems to be pertinent. For example, in extending the study of population structure beyond theoretical research to understand variation and microevolution, he argued for study of plans and programmes for reduction of disease burden and promotion of health, social welfare and happiness. According to him, it is urgent to conduct detailed examinations of specific genetic populations, to locate different mutations in different populations, and to work out suitable strategies for managing or controlling diseases in specific environmental conditions in particular populations (Mukherjee, 1996). He provided directions about future research to make anthropological work useful for the welfare of the populations. He believed "anthropologists should conduct studies on all four dimensions of the population structure, collecting data on life ways, economy, nutrition and traditional methods of management of such diseases. This will enable health services to be equipped with necessary technology for diagnosis and management of specific genetic diseases in specific sections of the population in an area" (Mukherjee, 1997). He also strongly argued for anthropologists' engagement in genetic counselling. According to him, anthropologists can be engaged in screening programmes for locating carriers of such a gene, after the actual gene pool (genetic population) is identified. It would be easier for India as social structure is inherent in the population. The hospitals or health centres should have database about the structure of the population, specific genetic load in each of its units, and other relevant ecological, demographic and social data. Doctors with the help of anthropologists can reduce the burden of diseases like sickle-cell anaemia from a particular population through genetic counselling.

To make anthropology socially relevant, there is an urgent need to formulate research questions and answer those problems. Research has to be undertaken on subjects of policy relevance. While other disciplines can provide partial understanding about the complex problems due to their reductionist approach, anthropological study from bio-cultural perspective using participant observation methods has huge potential to demystify human problems and provide insights. Several scholars have identified issues of contemporary relevance for anthropological research using bio-cultural framework, like issues related health and disease stated earlier, and anthropology of food and nutrition, where studies are not to be restricted to measuring nutritional status but are to be integrated with the larger political economy and relevant policy. Studies can be extended to cultural and ideational systems and nutrition – aiming at understanding how particular beliefs relate to food selection, including food prescriptions and proscriptions (Ray, 2012). Research studies should be undertaken that have a considerable bearing on the survival and well-being of Indian peoples. Some areas can be identified for immediate attention. First is the anthropology of infectious disease – human beings are increasingly being exposed to a plethora of infectious diseases with changing environment. People's perception of what is happening in the environment is important. Building knowledge systems on infectious diseases with identification of factors involved, differences in perception and coping strategies and how this knowledge may affect social relationships and health, may provide useful insights. Anthropological data can contribute immensely towards understanding the impact of environmental change on social organisation and institutional responses to these changes over time. Secondly, fitness and health – one can explore the notion of 'fitness', influence of the market in 'construction' of fitness, strategies adopted in attaining fitness and its health implications. Thirdly, changing fertility status and role of policies and programmes – recent Census data shows two important observations: One is the sharper drop in fertility rate in rural Bengal compared to other parts of India, while the second is that fertility rate peaked in the age group of 20-24 years, while the figure is 25-29 nationally. Here, anthropological investigation can provide valuable insights into sudden drops in fertility rate and high fertility in certain age groups, which have tremendous policy implications. Fourthly, anthropology of hazards and disaster – How do people conceive risk and uncertainty in different conditions? How do disasters make people vulnerable? How do people cope with disaster? What is the role of indigenous knowledge in this resilience? Why and how are some people successful while others are not? How effective is scientific knowledge in mitigation? Fifthly, the anthropology of climate change – anthropological approach offers analytical and methodological tools to capture data on questions like: Who participates in the production of knowledge on global climate change? How do different groups receive and react to this knowledge? How does knowledge of climate change circulate? What kind of new political and economic opportunities and risks does climate change offer to different actors? How does it affect health and social networks? What are the pathways of mitigation in extreme environment? Societal dynamics, as drivers of change, always interact with climate change, an issue that needs recognition for successful public policies. Sixthly, anthropology of ignorance – one can explore knowledge-ignorance dynamics in various dimensions like health, nutrition, or infection. How does the state apparatus engage itself to make people ignorant during implementation of programmes and policies?These are some of the research issues where anthropologists can contribute immensely.

Concluding Remarks

Professor Mukherjee had astounding knowledge on every branch of anthropology and had the uncanny ability to pick up appropriate data from large datasets, interpret it accurately and present that data by skilful application of exact language. He had the rare quality of having extensive knowledge and interest on other branches of anthropology, and possessed quality of observing real life events, a mind to imagine and skill to innovate new ideas. He was a magnificent thinker and a great source of inspiration to his colleagues and students. To me, Professor Mukherjee was one of the most imaginative and thought-provoking anthropologists of his generation,with a penchant for creative work. His research in examining and explaining the process of human variation and conceptualisation of population structure as future directions in anthropological research and human development under bio-cultural framework, should be considered as a milestone in Anthropology in India, as bio-cultural approaches are today gaining momentum globally. He was a strong supporter of cultural diversity unique to India, and believed that anthropology can retain its uniqueness among the disciplines if researchers undertake studies under bio-cultural framework on socially relevant issues that threaten human survival. Above all, he always adhered to a realization that anthropology is well-positioned in understanding human beings at cross-cultural level.

REFERENCES

Basu, A. 1987. "Human Biology in India: Its possible role in a Third World society under rapid transformation". *Coll. Anthrop.*, 11: 233-250.

Basu, A. 1974. "An Anthropologist in search of a purpose: The test case of the Pahira of Manbhum". *The Indian Museum Bulletin,* vol. 9, No. 2, July 1974.

Basu, A., R. Gupta, R.E. Ferrell, R.C. Elston, D.F. Roberts and D.P. Mukherjee. 1993. "Panel discussion on genes, environment and disease". In: *Human Population Genetics*. Edited by P.P. Mazumder. New York: Plenum Press. pp. 315-330.

Chakravartti, M.R. and D.P. Mukherjee. 1961. "Dermatoglyphic study of the tribes and castes of Nilgiri hills". *Current Science,* 30:461-464.

Chakravartti, M.R. and D.P. Mukherjee, 1961. "Dermatoglyphic study of the tribes and castes of the state of Assam". *Science and Culture,* 27 : 584-585.

Das, B.K. 2015. "Obituary: Professor D.P. Mukherjee". *The Eastern Anthropologist,* 68 (2 & 3): 411.

Dufour, D.L. 2006. "Biocultural approaches in human biology". *Am Jr Hum. Biol.,* 18:1-9.

Ferrández, L.F.A. 2013. *Ways of living: Tim Ingold on culture, biology and the anthropological task.* Revista de Antropología Iberoamericana www.aibr.org Vol. 8. No 3. Septiembre-Diciembre 2013, pp. 285-302, DOI: 10.11156/aibr.080302e

Fox, R. 1975. "Introduction". In: *Biosocial Anthropology.* Edited by R. Fox, London: Malaby Press.

Fried, M.H. 1973. "The concept of culture and the science of man". In : *Explorations in Anthropology.* Edited by M.H. Fried, New York: Thomas Y. Crowell Company.

Goodman, A.H. and Leatherman, T.L. 1998. "Traversing the Chasm between Biology and Culture: An Introduction", In: *Building a New Biocultural Synthesis: Political-Economic Perspectives on Human Biology,* Edited by A.H. Goodman, and T.L. Leatherman, Ann Arbor: University of Michigan Press: 3-42.

Guha, A., B.K. Das, S. Ghosh and H. Pradhan. 1988. "Bio-cultural studies in Anthropology: A preliminary review", *Jr of the Indian Anthrop. Society,* 23: 214-222.

Holt, S. 1961. "Inheritance in dermal ridge patterns". In: *Recent advances in Human Genetics.* Edited by L.S. Penrose, London: J.A. Churchill Ltd., p. 101.

Huss-Ashmore, R. and Johnston, F.E. 1985. "Bio-anthropological research in developing countries". *Ann. Rev. Anthrop.,* 14: 475-528.

Ingold, T. and G. Palsson (eds.). 2013. *Biosocial Becomings: Biological and Social Anthropology* , Cambridge: Cambridge University Press.

Lieben. 1973. Cited in Nandy and Mukherjee, 1990.

Lakhsmanudu, M. and D.P. Mukherjee, 1978. "Inbreeding effects on head size and shape". Abstract. *Proc. X Inter. Cong. Anthrop. Ethnol. Sci.,* New Delhi.

Mazumder, P.P. and D.C. Rao. 1991. "Genetic epidemiology and its relevance in Physical Anthropology". *Jr of the Indian Anthropological Society.* 26: 51-62.

Mukherjee, A. 1990. "Inbreeding effects on bilateral asymmetry of dermatoglyphic patterns." *Am. J Phys. Anthrop.* 81: 77-89.

Mukherjee, D.P. 1971. "Patterns of marriage and family formation in rural India and genetical implications of family formations". WHO Sc. Group. Geneva, pp.1-13. Reprinted in *Jr of the Indian Anthrop. Soc.,* 8: 131-145.

Mukherjee, D.P. 1972. "Some recent trends in population genetics in India". In : *Genetics and Our Health,* Technical Report Series 20, Indian Council of Medical Research, pp. 234-242.

Mukherjee, D.P., P.C. Reddy and M. Lakshmanudu. 1980. "Dermatoglyphic effects of inbreeding". *Jr of Indian Anthrop. Soc.,* 15: 67-69.

Mukherjee, D.P. 1965. "Anthropological observations on toe print patterns among the hill tribes of North-east India". *Z Morph Anthrop.,* 56, pp. 217-231.

Mukherjee, D.P. 1966. "Inheritance of total triradii on fingers, palms and soles". *Ann Hum Genet.,* 29:349-353.

Mukherjee, D.P. 1984. "Inbreeding and genetics of quantitative traits in man". In: *Human Genetics and Adaptation,* Volume 1. Edited by K.C. Malhotra and A. Basu. Indian Statistical Institute Golden Jubilee International Conference, 1982, pp: 533-561.

Mukherjee, D.P. 1982. "Some biological dimensions of tribal economy in India". In: *Economics of the Tribes and their transformation*. Edited by K.S. Singh. New Delhi: Concept Publishing Company.

Mukherjee, D.P. 1992. "Consanguineous marriages and their genetical consequences in some Indian populations". In: *Isolation, Migration and Health*, edited by D.F. Roberts, N. Fuzuki and K. Torizuka, Cambridge: Cambridge University Press.

Mukherjee, D.P. 1993. "Chairman's address. Part III of panel discussion on genes, environment and disease". In: *Human Population Genetics*. Edited by P.P. Mazumder. New York: Plenum Press, pp. 323-330.

Mukherjee, D.P. 1995. "Some sources of biological anthropology in ancient India". *Jr of the Asiatic Society*, 37, pp: 43-66.

Mukherjee, D.P. 1996. "Anthropological Genetics of Quantitative Variations." *Jr of Indian Anthrop. Soc.,* 31:217-224.

Mukherjee, D.P. 1997. *Population structure as an emerging frontier of Anthropology and Human development*. Presidential Address in Anthropology and Archaeology Section, 84th Session, New Delhi, Indian Science Congress Association.

Mukherjee, D.P. 1998. "The tradition in Indian Anthropology with special reference to Biological Anthropology." *Jr of Indian Anthrop. Soc.* 33: 145-180.

Mukherjee, D.P., B.K. Das and A. Guha. 1995. "Nonlinear inbreeding effects on secondary sex ratio in relation to birth order and parental age." *Vidyasagar University Jr of Biological Sciences,* 1 : 32-41.

Mukherjee D.P. and G.C. Ghosh. 1983. "Pattern intensity index for palms and soles." *Jr. of the Indian Anthrop. Soc.,* 20: 71-76.

Mukherjee, D.P., P. Guha, B.K. Das and A. Guha. 1995. "Patterns of marriage among the Muslims of a Calcutta slum: A quantitative approach." *J. Indian Anthrop. Soc.*, 30:153-160.

Mukherjee, D.P., P. Guha., B.K. Das and A. Guha. 1998. "Family formation among Muslims in a Calcutta slum." *Jr of Family Welfare*, 44(4): 36-44.

Mukherjee, D.P. and M.R. Chakravartti, 1964. "A dermatoglyphic approach to the Mundari ethnic problem." *Z Morph Anthrop.,* 55, p. 32.

Mukherjee, D.P. and M.R. Chakravartti, 1964. "Dermatoglyphic affinities of the tribes and castes of Nilgiri Hills (India)." *Jr Morph Anthrop.* 55: 335-356.

Mukherjee, D.P. and P. Ganguly, 1965. "Dermatoglyphics of the Shom-Pen of Great Nicobar." *Anthropos,* 65 : 918-19.

Mukherjee, D.P., P. Mandal and D. Mukherji. 1990. "A test for X-linked influence on the dermatoglyphic traits in pedigrees of deficient colour vision". *Abstract.*

Proc. Internat. Conf. on Progress and trends in Dermatoglyphic research, Calcutta.

Mukherjee, D.P., S. Bhaskar and M. Lakshmanudu. 1977. "Studies on inbreeding and its effects in some endogamous populations of Chittoor district, Andhra Pradesh". *Bul. Anthrop. Surv. India,* 26:10-22.

Mukherjee, D.P., R.R. Gates and M.R. Chakravartti. 1962. "Final pedigrees of Y-chromosome inheritance". *American Jr of Human Genetics,* 14: 363-375.

Mukherjee D.P. and M. Lakhsmanudu. 1980. "Effects of inbreeding on polygenic traits". *Proce. with annual conf. Indian Soc. Hum. Genet.,* Hyderabad.

Mukhopadhyay, D. 1997. *Profile of an Anthropologist: Professor D. P. Mukherjee.* Calcutta.

Nandy, S. 1993. "Biocultual Approach in Anthropological Study: A Preliminary Observation". *Man in India,* 73(3): 289-294.

Nandy, S. and D.P. Mukherjee, 1990. "The nature and scope of medical anthropological research with reference to India". *Jr of Anthropo. Survey of India,* 39:90-99.

Ray, S. 2012. "Anthropology Today: Addressing the need of the hour". *The Eastern Anthropologist,* 65: 3-4, pp. 289-304.

Roberts, D.F., W.Z. Billewicz and I.A. McGregor. 1978. "Heritability of stature in a West African population". *Ann. Hum,Genet.*, 42 : 15-24.

Roberts, D.F. 1991. "Trends in biological anthropology: the wheel turns full circle?" *Jr of the Indian Anthrop Soc.*, 26: 1-8.

Vogler, G.P. and D.C. Rao. 1993. "Path analysis in genetic epidemiology: theory and applications". In: *Human population genetics: A centennial tribute to JBS Haldane.* Edited by P.P. Mazumder, pp. 291-304. New York: Plenum Press.

9

Remembering Sri Biswanath Banerjee and His Teaching of Anthropology

A Tribute

Sekh Rahim Mondal

Introduction

Sri Biswanath Banerjee (BNB), popularly known as '*Biswanth Babu*', was a legendary teacher of the Department of Anthropology, University of Calcutta. He was known to his students for his unique style of teaching anthropology and doing research. He was a good fieldworker and an excellent research supervisor. His anthropological journey started from the stage of making a meticulous study of all branches of anthropology followed by the field-based study of folk communities of North East India and other parts of the country. Biswanath Banerjee possessed a rich knowledge on tribes, peasants, castes and other communities of hills and plains distributed all-over rural and urban areas. Moreover, he nurtured inclusive ideas about Indian societies, cultures and civilization, which made him somewhat different from other anthropologists of his time.

This chapter is an attempt to highlight the life and works of BNB Sir in brief, more as a tribute to him on the memorable occasion of hundred years of teaching and research in Anthropology in India. It has been prepared based on the information obtained from different published and unpublished sources and on my own memories and personal experience as one of his close students for over four decades. For the preparation of this chapter other necessary information were also gathered from some of his many students, friends, colleagues and others with whom he used to maintain a very close relation.

Early Life and Education

Sri Biswanath Banerjee was born on May 8, 1932 in Gauhati, Assam and breathed his last on 26th January, 2009 in Kolkata. He was the third child and only son of Sri Kamaksha Prashad Banerjee and Smt. Champaklota Banerjee. He was born and brought up in a joint family, which helped him to inculcate the habit of sharing, caring and sacrificing. His family members used to call him '*Khokan*'. At the age of 22 years, he lost his father and subsequently grew up under the guidance of his father's elder brother (*Jathamahashaya*) and mother (*Maa*). The situation made him mentally prepared to shoulder family responsibilities since his young age.

BNB's family members trace their ancestry from the sister's side of Maharaja Krishna Chandra Roy of Navadweep, Nadia in West Bengal. His family history suggests that BNB's grandfather Sri Surendra Nath Banerjee along with his brother Sri Nonigopal Banerjee moved to Gauhati (Assam) from Bengal for establishing their constructional business and later settled near the famous Jubilee Park of the city. BNB's family was a very well known one in the locality. Since childhood, BNB was known for his simplicity and kindness. His humility and meritocracy attracted the attention of his relatives as well as neighbours and made him very popular in his locality. It may be noted here that the famous Assamese Singer Sarboshree Dr. Bhupen Chandro Hazarika was BNB's childhood friend and the relationship between the members of their two families was very cordial.

BNB was meritorious and equally studious since his childhood days. He was a serious learner and listener but his listening and learning habit was not only confined to class-room based studies but extended to other fields like singing, dancing, craft making and so on. He had his basic education in Gauhati, wherefrom he passed the Matriculation from the Bengali High School in 1948 securing first division with letter marks. He obtained his I. Sc. degree from the famous Gauhati Cotton College (now Cotton University) in 1950 with anthropology as one of his major papers and was graduated (B.Sc.) from the same college with Honours in Anthropology in 1952. At the final year B.Sc. practical examination, he came in contact with Prof. K.P. Chattopadhyay, who happened to be his external examiner. Prof. Chattopadhyay was very much impressed with the performance of BNB in the practical examination and motivated him to go for higher education in anthropology from the University of Calcutta. He moved to Calcutta and took admission in P.G. Course of Anthropology under the University of Calcutta. BNB got the M.Sc. degree in

Anthropology from the said university in 1954 with the specialization in Social-Cultural Anthropology. He considered it his good fortune to get the opportunity of being taught by luminaries like Prof. K.P. Chattopadhyay, Prof. T.C. Das, S.S. Sarkar, Prof. M.N. Basu, Prof. D. Sen, Prof. G.S. Roy, Prof. J.K. Bose, Prof. T.C. Roychowdhury and many others which had enriched him theoretically and made him a sincere fieldworker. Another mentor of BNB was Prof. N.K. Bose from whom he derived the real interest of teaching Anthropology. As a student he also came in deep contact with Prof. S.C. Sinha and was considerably influenced by his personality and academic excellence. BNB learned the art of fieldwork from Prof. T.C. Das, Prof. N.K. Bose, Prof. D. Sen, Prof. G.S. Roy, Prof. J.K. Bose and Prof. S.C. Sinha and later proved himself as an excellent fieldworker. He was widely known for his anthropological fieldworks among the indigenous communities at various parts of N.E. India, Bihar, West Bengal and some other states. His anthropological studies on the city of Calcutta (Kolkata), Varanasi and the town of Navadweep deserve special mention.

As a Teacher in Anthropology

BNB started his professional career as a teacher after completing the M.Sc. degree in Anthropology. He joined as a Lecturer in Dinabandhu Mahavidyalaya, at Bongaon of North 24 Parganas (W.B.) in 1956, at the age of only 24 years. He left the said college and joined as a Lecturer in the Department of Anthropology of Sri Chaitanya College of Habra of North 24 Parganas (W.B.) in 1958. He used to teach courses covering all the three major branches of anthropology and even accompany the students for field training at various places of the country. BNB joined the Department of Anthropology of the University of Calcutta on 20th February in 1963 as a Lecturer and he retired from the said Department as Reader on 5th April in 1994. He served for more than three decades in the said Department as a very popular teacher. It is necessary to mention here that BNB acted as a centrifugal force to attract the students of not only anthropology but also of many other disciplines in the Ballygunge Science College of the University of Calcutta. This was primarily due to his versatile knowledge, both in academic fields and performing arts (drama, dance and music) as well as in games and sports. He possessed a vast knowledge on Vedanta and Hindu views of life and had a very deep knowledge on original Indian philosophy and Indian civilization. Tagore's thoughts as reflected in his writings on society and civilization created a lasting impression on BNB's mind.

In the Calcutta University P.G. Department of Anthropology, BNB was primarily engaged in teaching courses in social-cultural anthropology. The courses on which he had a strong command were social structure, social organization, culture, civilization, research methods and above all the thoughts and theories of anthropology. Among the courses taught by him, his teachings on family, marriage, kinship and the history of growth and development of anthropology in India left a deep imprint on the students' mind. In addition to class room-based teaching, BNB felt more at ease in teaching students in his departmental chamber or in his own rented home through informal ways. Students liked him for his ability to explain tough subjects in a very lucid manner. His teaching was almost like reenacting the ancient "*Guru-Shishya*" tradition. He established himself as a teacher methodologically well equipped and a teacher par excellence. For reasons unknown BNB was never actively associated with any professional association of anthropology as a formal member. But though he was not directly associated with any professional association, he joined his classmate A.R. Banerjee, Gaurango Chattopadhyay, Suhas K. Biswas, Biman Dasgupta, Bikash Roychoudhury in the formation of the Indian Anthropological Society at its initial stage from the earlier 'Anthropological Club' (1921) of the University of Calcutta under the active leadership of Dr. S.S. Sarkar.

Academic Connections and Activities Connected with Academic Administration

BNB was a popular teacher, for which he was known to many veteran anthropologists, sociologists and scholars belonging to other disciplines. Among Indian anthropologists he had close relations with Prof. N.K. Bose, Prof. Madhab K. Goswami, Prof. S.C. Sinha, Prof. A. Betteille, Prof. L.K. Mahapatra, Prof. I.P. Singh, Prof. B.K. Roy Burman, Prof. R.K. Mukherjee, Prof. Sachidananda, Prof. L.P . Vidyarthi, Prof. S .N. Ratha, Prof. B.N. Saraswati, Dr. A.K. Das, Dr. Sudhendu Mukherjee, Prof. B.M. Das, Prof. A. Bhagobati, Prof. Usha Deka, Prof. Manish Chakraborty, Prof. Gopala Sarana, Prof. Y. Singh, Prof. N.C. Chaudhury, Mr. H.N. Rakshit, Prof. A.K. Danda, Prof. Suhas Biswas, Prof. Amitava Basu, Prof. Aloke Ghosh and many others. He also maintained an amicable relation with his departmental colleagues in spite of differences of opinion with some of them. BNB was familiar with some research scholars and their supervisors from Great Britain, USA, France and Japan working in the field of anthropology. Actually, relations with BNB developed from the end of those scholars who sought his help and academic support to study the folk and village communities of India in the capacity of their local (Indian) supervisor. It may be worth mentioning here that one of his Japanese students Dr. Swatoo got an important position in anthropology in Japan. This is also true for some other foreign scholars with whom he was closely associated. As far I know, BNB got many opportunities to visit foreign Universities as a visiting teacher. But he never showed any interest to accept those invitations. This proves that he was not among those to whom career comes first.

BNB was meticulous in organizing several academic programmes; among them the important ones were organizing field-works, examination related works, many other academic curricula for U.G., P.G. and Research studies. His colleagues and students stated that he was very active in performing his duties as a Chairman of Board of Research Studies in Anthropology of C.U. during his tenure. It was his habit to call the members personally by making phone calls or contact them by sending messengers to make the meeting successful. In this way, he helped many students in their Ph.D. registration and submission of thesis on time. For ill health, familial responsibilities (looking after the old mother) and religious as well as spiritual commitments, BNB had not shown any interest in time bound administrative works. Several times, he declined the departmental Headship. Only once for a short period he worked as a HOD, but could not continue and complete the full term because of acute illness. To him, co-operation, initiating dialogues, frank exchange of views and working out a consensus opinion are important for gaining success in administration. With this approach in mind, he used to perform the academic works related to administration assigned to him as a teacher in the Department of Anthropology of the University of Calcutta.

Personality and Identity

BNB was a man of unique personality. He himself was a typical example of modernization of tradition appearing as a man of saintly appearance dressed in a typical manner in his own inimitable style. White *dhoti* and light saffron *kurta* (Panjabi) with gold button up to neck, a cotton side bag (*jhola*) and a simple cane stick umbrella was his most common trademark. The unique of all was his footwear, which was always an English boot of chocolate colour. A small leather wallet (*batua*) and a German made pilot fountain pen in the chest pocket were something very special to him. His casually shaved, smiling and charming face attracted the attention of many. He was a man of very simple character but at the same time a very tough decision maker. The blending of these two distinct characteristics made him a man of a unique personality. He was very open-minded, at times outspoken and never compromised with any bad behaviour or any immoral act. A tough fighter against all odds, he saved the students of his Department many times from the clutches of powerful lobbies.

BNB was a highly religious and spiritual man and at the same time very secular by heart and mind. He was always helpful and would be ever ready to extend his helpful hand to others. Outwardly, he wore a traditional look, but in his action he was highly rational, logical and liberal. The way he could maintain a balance between professional engagements on the one hand and social life on the other was exemplary. He always stood by his students and close ones, relatives and non-relatives. I feel it necessary to mention here that he had denoted all of his last life savings to a non-kin member who was a child and whose parents were very close to him during his last days. BNB was neither a rightist nor a leftist but a true humanist. He had constructed his own personality and an identity not just as a scholar but as a devoted teacher and a mentor. That is the reason why his students considered him as a true '*guru*' (*mastermosai*).

Contributions to Anthropology

BNB was a person who commanded a wide knowledge in various fields ranging from socio-cultural existence of man to music, dance, drama, drawing, and even performing fine arts. He was a man whose daily schedule was divided into two separate domains, viz., material and pragmatic, religious and spiritual. In the professional field he established himself as a teacher of anthropology specializing himself in the field of socio-cultural anthropology. He had also a versatile knowledge of Indian rural and urban societies. The courses on Indian tribes, castes and other village communities he used to teach in such a simple but lucid way that these had attracted the attention of the students and motivated them to do research in those areas.

At the theoretical level, BNB came under the influence of both historical and functional schools of thought. Theories of evolutionism, diffusionism, structure-functionalism and even structuralism he used to explain to his students with such clarity that very soon these became interesting topics to them. He was also very much aware of critical anthropological theories and reflexive methodologies. Incidentally, his most favourite topic of discussion was "culture", which he would explain from various perspectives of anthropology supported by ground level examples. The major concepts and theories of culture and its dynamic processes were his special interest areas of discussion and interpretation.

His deliberations and meaningful expositions directed students towards social-cultural anthropology and do research in this field. While discussing the issues confronting the society he would start from explaining the structure of society, its institutions, functions, organization and change. Even when there was some hesitancy in using the term "social-cultural anthropology" to cover both social and cultural anthropology, BNB was clear about it and used it freely without keeping any doubt in his mind. He strongly believed that both are interrelated and are inseparable. The cultural theory of Malinowski, social relational theory of Radcliffe Brown and social organizational theory of Raymond Firth impressed him, which also enabled him to think positively in terms of studying the structure and change of society and culture in the Indian context. Similarly, he was motivated by Redfield's ideas of peasant community and his theory of folk-urban continuum as well as by Sinha's ideas of tribe-caste-peasant continuum, which he used in different ways for examining the continuity and change in Indian societies. Above all, his idea of Indian civilization had grown from the thoughts of many Indian social thinkers including his mentors N.K. Bose and S.C. Sinha.

He strongly advocated that anthropology is not simply a discipline for tribal studies alone; it is the discipline of the study of all human beings, all human societies and cultures and above all, the entire humanity. The study of structure, change and continuity with respect to all societies and cultures were his special focus of anthropological interest. His approach was primarily that of a structural functionalist but he did not quite ignore the historical perspectives and processes involved. In his thoughts and works, he gave equal importance to British, American and French anthropologists directing him to go through almost all major classical anthropological monographs produced by them. Many of those classics he used to refer to his students for thorough reading. However, though he commanded a vast knowledge of the Western anthropological thoughts and traditions, personally he was in search of an Indian perspective to study societies and communities. He developed this interest after coming in contact with his mentors and friends like T.C. Das, N.K. Bose, S.C. Sinha, B.N. Saraswati, N.K. Behura, A.C. Bhagoboti and others.

BNB had a thorough knowledge about *Varna-Jati* concepts and relations between them including the caste systems of India, which he acquired by reading classical texts and by closely observing the caste communities in empirical contexts. He himself did some excellent works on some caste groups of Assam and Bengal from the perspective of

Indian civilization, of which the most important was his work on the potters. While it may be possible to examine *Varna* from the texts and text-book sources, he thought it is necessary to examine the functional caste system at the empirical level through field studies. Students of BNB remember him for his almost total dedication to the cause of Indian civilization, which he thought should be the guiding principle of Indian anthropology. At the same time, he was highly motivated by the ideas of civilization as proposed and developed by Robert Redfield, B.S. Cohn, Milton Singer, N.K. Bose and S.C. Sinha. In addition to Chicago and Indian Schools of thought, he came under the strong influence of the thoughts of Tagore, Gandhi and some other liberal Indian thinkers. Exposure to different and varied sources helped him build up a comprehensive knowledge about Indian civilization.

His vision of a hierarchical model of caste system in India is much closer to the views of Louis Dumont. However, I am inclined to believe that he had independently developed the model based on his own understanding and knowledge. According to BNB, '*dharma*' and '*karma*' as well as purity and pollution are the key beliefs and attributes working behind the Hindu caste hierarchy. He was of the opinion that the ideas surrounding the *Varna* system is grossly oversimplified and the real basis of the caste system lies in the concept of *Jati*. For BNB, the caste system today represents much more closely to the *Jati* system rather than *Varna*, which has a political overtone. Accordingly, castes in modern India reflect more clearly the identity issues developed in the political life rather than functioning as a structural principle of social life as was strongly prevalent in early days.

BNB used to believe that India was a land of biological and cultural diversity within a composite and inclusive civilizational whole. Peoples living in this vast country have different ethnic and social backgrounds, different cultural moorings and ways of life. However, these diverse groups interact with each other in their day-to-day life and thereby share some common elements and traits of each other's culture unconsciously or consciously. To him, the different social and cultural groups of this vast country represent something like a garden of different flowering plants of varied colour and fragrance and together they give it a distinctive character. This could be one of the simplistic ways of looking at societies and cultures in the context of the grand civilization of this vast country. Hence, the role of anthropology is to explore, examine and interpret the social-cultural mosaic of India, Trusteeship, cooperation, inter-dependence, fellow-feeling, sharing of selective cultural elements from each other are some of the fundamental attributes of the ways of life of the peoples of this country. These bound them together and played a great role in creating the grand civilization of this country. As said very often, India is a land of different groups of human population with varieties of cultures, but somewhere they could strike a common chord. As a result, both cohesive and contradictory forces have worked upon them. Coexistence, cooperation and occasional conflicts among different social groups in India are a social reality. In India, various peoples have been living together for centuries catering to each other's needs and necessities. All these seem to be BNB's prime consideration in undertaking anthropological studies. To him, peoples, societies and cultures in India are like the ingredients of a "salad bowl", which means he was not in favour of a "melting pot" theory.

BNB is well known for continuing the legacy of anthropological fieldwork tradition of C.U. Being a teacher of anthropology, BNB was also known for his unique strategy of doing fieldwork. He was a total and methodical fieldworker who brought realism to fieldwork, where his humanitarian approach to impression creation and rapport establishment with the people in the field proved to be of tremendous advantage. Very often, he would tell his students that for doing fieldwork and to equip one for fieldwork reading books or attending classes was not enough; one had to live with the people and learn in the process. So fieldwork to him is a form of practical learning from the common people, for which "listening to people's voices and observing people's activities" are the most important.

BNB himself did many fieldworks for his own purpose and for his teachers and friends of repute. His major fieldworks were among the Daflas, Garos and many other ethnic communities of N.E. India. His study of the potters of Assam and many other tribal groups of the then Bihar and West Bengal are important contributions. In addition to tribal groups, BNB also did several important fieldworks among non-tribal caste groups and other communities of rural and urban Bengal and of other parts of India. His studies of towns and cities like Nabadwip, Varanasi, Haldia and Calcutta (now Kolkata) could open a new dimension of anthropological research. Particular mention may be made of his study of *Sarbojonin Durgotsab* of Calcutta, which is a significant contribution to anthropology's expanding domain. He had a special inclination towards intensive fieldwork, following comparative method and multisited ethnography and was in favour of adopting multidisciplinary approaches in anthropological research.

BNB had no hesitation to include quantitative method in anthropological works, more so in data analysis, which makes it imperative for the collection of quantitative or quantifiable data. His interest in using statistics or quantitative data developed out of his interactions with Prof. Ramakrishna Mukherjee and his classmates Prof. Suhas Biswas and Prof. Kumar Chattopadhyay of the Indian Statistical Institute.

The two most important lessons given by BNB in his fieldwork training was drawing a genealogy and meticulous use of kinship data in the study of research problems related to social-cultural anthropology. He himself would indulge in drawing several extensive genealogies while he was studying and doing fieldworks. Needless to say that the art of drawing exhaustive genealogy he had learned from his teachers Prof. K.P. Chattopadhyay, Prof. T.C. Das and Prof. J.K. Bose. The present author also learned the method of preparing a long genealogy from him and used it effectively in his field studies on the Muslims and their kinship systems in Bengal as his M.Sc. dissertation work. BNB used to give a special emphasis on keeping and maintaining the field diary at the time of fieldwork. To him, keeping field diary containing all the details of diary keeper's interaction with the people, the events he or she comes across in course of fieldwork is a prerequisite for an anthropologist.

A Teacher and a Mentor

BNB devoted his entire life to teaching and supervision of students and in the process was able to produce several scholars as well as teachers of repute. If not for any other reason, he would only be remembered for his unique teaching style and research guidance. By arranging open-air classes, initiating debates and discourses and discussing the points of agreement and disagreement on emerging social and cultural issues he was able to create a place for himself among students. He was a strong believer of "lab to land" and "land to lab" approaches to cultivate true anthropological knowledge and its application. About fifteen scholars did Ph.D. under his active supervision. One interesting point is most of his Ph.D. scholars did their researches on unconventional research problems, beyond known anthropological stereotypes. They indicated a shift from studies of agriculture to industry, tribal to non-tribal communities, rural to urban societies, Hindus to Muslims, fine arts to performing arts, sacred to secular activities, and from fixed structural stereotypes to extending network of social relations. He was highly concerned about the plight of marginal sections of Indian society and was very vocal about the social (human) responsibilities of the human or social scientists including anthropologists. He repeatedly pointed out that the role of anthropologists is not simply to know the peoples but also to save them from social and political ostracities. He was one among those who was in search of relevance and representation of anthropology.

Personally, BNB did not do much research and wrote much on anthropological issues, but all the time he was highly engaged with research works of his students and also of his own teachers and friends. At the initial stage of his academic life, he was deeply involved in associating himself with the research projects of his teachers of the Department, among whom mention may be made of Prof. K.P. Chattopadhayay, Prof. T.C. Das, Prof. M.N. Basu, Prof. D. Sen, Prof. G.S. Ray, Prof. J.K. Bose, Prof. N.K. Bose Prof. S.C. Sinha and Prof. Suhas Biswas.

He spent almost his entire life for the success of research of his students. He used to tell them that anthropological research is nothing but a curiosity to know the social and cultural (even biological) facts in depth. He had the ability to master the art of questioning for the quest of knowledge. To him, the ability to see beyond the immediate indicates the success of a researcher. He taught his students to frame questions in mind at the time of doing research. Questions like what is there to know about, why should one know, how to know, what is the purpose of knowing are related with the domains of ontology, epistemology, methodology and ethics, which also equally apply to anthropology. He had the idea that the research requires a proper frame of mind to be able to go deeper and deeper to know the unknown. The motivating factor in anthropological research in his view was raising the level of observation to knowledge seeking. It is not enough simply to know about change; more important perhaps is to know how and why the changes are taking place and that too in a specific direction. BNB was a unique personality who was able to blend his scientific mind with the spiritual mind for understanding man and his life, i.e. human nature and culture. He raised and tried to explain the most fundamental questions of anthropology like: (i) how man (humanity) came? Why they came? Why do they live in society? He taught his students how to keep themselves logically equipped to be able to disagree on conventional ideas and issues when required. This in a way could contribute to the growth of new knowledge system.

One of his close friends Kumar Chattopadhyay remarked that once Prof. N.K. Bose told him that "Biswanath is a wonderful fieldworker". And he went on further, "I was totally astonished by his imaginative understanding of the area of study and possible result predicted" (Chattopadhyay, 2012).

Lessons Left

The most important lesson that BNB has left to us is to cultivate one's own creative mind. His main motive was to train the students not simply as a scholar but as a true human being. Honesty, morality and dedication held special meaning in his life. Throughout his entire life, he never thought for himself but for his students, kin members, neighbours, friends and society at large. Studying, listening, learning, disseminating knowledge and motivating others were his main interest areas. He left behind a rich tradition of teaching and supervision of research. He had the notion that ethnography is like true story-telling based on facts as gathered by the ethnographer who is also a story-teller. BNB's anthropological ideas and thoughts had grown out of his meticulous studies of the works of British, American, French, German and Indian Anthropologists and Sociologists. In addition, he was much influenced by social thinkers of India like Tagore, Gandhi, Ramakrishna Paramhansa, Swami Vivekananda, Pandit Nehru. He had a vast knowledge of literary works and Bengali literature, particularly of Rabindranath Tagore and Sarat Chandra Chattopadhyay. BNB was a follower of Pandit Gopinath Kabiraj and his views and philosophy on the social life of India had a profound effect on him. He was also much influenced by the classical spiritual traditions of Kashi and Varanasi. All these together shaped the anthropological mind of BNB. He dwelt at length about "diversity and unity", "sacred and secular", "differences and uniformities", "boundaries and their flexibilities", "tradition and modernity", and "continuity and change". To him, all these are at the very core of Indian societies and cultures, which have shaped the Indian civilization, the way we know about it.

BNB left behind a legacy of teaching, thinking and research for the students. He taught his students to think and to do fieldwork and then to write on them. His main aim was to produce students and to groom them on their own merit. According to BNB, the peoples and societies of India need to be studied from 'environmental', 'historical', 'social-cultural' and 'civilizational' perspectives and here anthropology's participation was significant. To him, space, time, people and ethics (morality) were equally important for anthropological understanding of all social events and problems developed. 'Time-space' framework which he proposed for studying "structure and organization" of a society has great anthropological relevance. He was a great story-teller and story-maker and his stories were mostly based on empirical evidences.

He was very much critical of the concept of "development" with respect to the study of social transformation in India. Development, he thought, should ensure freedom, democracy, achievements and attainments in life and these need to be expressed by the concerned groups of people rather than by the power groups and agencies.

Acknowledgements

For preparation of this write up, the author received tremendous helps and encouragements from many of BNB's students, friends and colleagues and most important of them are Sri Dipak Piplai, Dr. Amitabha Sarkar, Dr. Sankha Priya Guha, Dr. Naba Kumar Duary, Sri Kamal Krishna Dey and Prof. Ranjana Ray. I am thankful and indebted to all of them.

REFERENCES

Banerjee Biswanath, 1965, "An Outline of the Background, Theory and Methods of Social Cultural Anthropology". *Bulletin of Cultural Research Institute,* Vol. 4, 1965.

Banerjee Biswanath, 1968, "The Habitat and Culture of Primitive Hill People of India", In *The Proceedings of the 21st International Geographical Congress,* Kolkata, India

Banerjee Biswanath, 1973, "Sarbojonin Durgotsab in Calcutta: A Preliminary Report of the Pujas in 1969", *Folklore,* September, pp. 347-353. [Also published in *Mastermasai, The Teacher*: the commemorative volume of the Teacher – Biswanath Banerjee, 2012, Edited by D. Piplai, Kolkata: Prof. Biswanath Bandhopadhyaya Smriti Raksha Samiti].

Banerjee, Biswanath and Amitabha Sarkar, 1996, *Fundamentals of Social-Cultural Anthropology*, Calcutta: Farma KLM Pvt. Ltd.

Beteille-Andre, 2012, "Biswanath Banerjee as I known him", In *Mastermasai – The Teacher,* Edited by D. Piplai, Kolkata: Professor Biswanath Bandhopadhyay Smriti Raksha Samiti, pp. 1-15.

Chattopadhyay, Kumar, 2012, "Prof. Biswanath Banerjee: A Tribute", In *Mastermasai – The Teacher,* Edited by D. Piplai, Kolkata: Professor Biswanath Bandhopadhyay Smriti Raksha Samiti.

Indian Anthropological Society, 1963, "A Brief History of the Indian Anthropological Society", In *Souvenir* on the occasion of Silver Juvilee (1957-1982), December 6-9, 1963, Calcutta.

Piplai Dipak (Ed.), 2012, *Mastermasai : The Teacher* [Commemorative volume of the Teacher – Biawanath Banerjee] Kolkata: Professor Biswanath Bandhopadhyay Smriti Raksha Samiti, Kolkata.

Guha, Sankha Priya, 2012, "Biswanath Babu: The Teacher of My Life", In *Mastermasai – The Teacher,* Edited by D. Piplai, Kolkata: Professor Biswanath Bandhopadhyay Smriti Raksha Samiti.

Mandal, Sekh Rahim and Amitabha Sarkar, 2019, *Biswanath Banerjee* (1933-2009), In *Doyens of Indian Anthropology,* edited by Amitabha Sarkar and Samiran Dasgupta, Delhi: Agam Kala Publication, pp. 177-181.

10
In the Memory of Professor Dibyendu Kanti Bhattacharya

Avick Biswas and *Rupendra Kumar Chattopadhyay*

As we sit down to write about Prof. D.K. Bhattacharya, memories flush back in our mind. We are filled with cherished memories of our mentor Prof. Dibyendu Kanti Bhattacharya. While Prof. Bhattacharya commanded a towering professional stature, he was well appreciated globally and his writings were well received all around; yet for us, he was much more than an academic person. Rather, he was a father figure to us who would always even without a second thought render all possible help and assistance to those who were really in need of. There were nonetheless many other qualities that Prof. Bhattacharya possessed which always kept us in awe. We marvelled at the depth of his academic endeavours, his professional behaviour and conduct, and most importantly, his profound philosophy of life.There was something special in him, a magical spell that he could weave around his students, inspiring the most ordinary of minds to do something extraordinary.

Furthermore, in academic terms too, Prof. Bhattacharya's tremendous intellectual acumen has often spilled over into the lives of his students. For instance, we have pursued our basic research in prehistoric archaeology, the main foundations of knowledge of which came from our close association with our great teacher. For the second author (Chattopadhyay) also it was hard to forget the close academic association he had with Prof. Bhattacharya from August 1981 to November 2000. These two decades had gone a long way in shaping him what he is today, both professionally and at the personal level.

Having said that, we must confess that we are certainly aware of our limitations and somewhat lack of competence to write on someone as eminent a scholar as Prof. Bhattacharya is. This particularly applies to the field of anthropological archaeology, of which he was a master. We were fortunate to have close connections with him and whenever we are reminded of Prof. Bhattacharya, we tend to feel highly nostalgic and reminiscent, particularly of those good old days that we had spent in Prof. Bhattacharya's company. We are very much aware of the fact that we are prone to turn sentimental on such occasions, and hence deem it necessary to add a caveat right at the outset that our words apart from highlighting Prof. Bhattacharya's brilliant academic accomplishments would also focus on our personal vibes with him for a rather prolonged stretch of time. Even though Prof. Bhattacharya's role in making us what we are today is something we can never deny, yet we find ourselves seriously with a strange paucity of words to actually explain the tremendous influence he always had on us, not merely as an academic but also as a human being.

The second author still remembers vividly the day of 29th July, some four decades back, in 1981 to be precise, when he was a scared little creature, walking up to meet Prof. Bhattacharya at his residence at 10, Tagore Park in the company of Prof. Dilip K. Chakrabarti, another perennial academic mentor of him. Sitting in front of two of the greatest names in their respective fields, in that July morning he felt quite nervous. Just a University pass out, he could little understand the significance of such an academic rendezvous. For a novice as he was at that time, he was rather dragged into the field of prehistoric archaeology and what a spark it ignited within him. Coming out of Prof. Bhattacharya's house, he was a different man, injected with boosted confidence, cultivated interest and a readiness to academically explore the field of prehistoric archaeology. That was a different day for him because that marked the beginning of a perpetual teaching learning process with Prof. Bhattacharya. It was under him that he could launch himself into the academic world of prehistoric archaeology. On a quotidian basis he would instruct and enlighten him in the fields of tool type technology, lithic object analyses and so on. For him it is rather difficult to deny Prof. Bhattacharya's role in giving him such an academic exposure in such a short time. If one takes the pain of having a perusal of the Man and Environment and *puratattva* related issues during that period, one cannot but encounter publications of DKB, DKC, and RKC at regular intervals.

After the first author completed his Masters, he requested Prof. Bhattacharya for supervising his Ph.D. work in the field of Prehistoric archaeology. As Prof. Bhattacharya had already retired from service, he immediately contacted his student Prof. R.K. Chattopadhyay (the second author) to take the responsibility of supervision. So, eventually Prof. Chattopadhyay became his official supervisor with Prof. Bhattacharya as the unofficial supervisor. Prof. Bhattacharya was invited on several occasions at the 'Centre for Archaeological Studies and Training in Eastern India' (henceforth CASTEI) by the first author to deliver lectures on Prehistory courses. He had never declined requests for giving lectures on his favourite topics despite his busy schedule. Whenever he visited Kolkata, he told the first author 'to be kind and sympathetic to students'. Prof. Bhattacharya was much concerned about what the students might be facing outside the classroom and that's why they should be properly equipped. In November 2017, Prof. Bhattacharya arrived at Kolkata Airport by wheelchair as he was unable to walk properly. But he accepted the invitation by CASTEI and for him delivering lecture was as much a service to students as it was to the subject he loved so much. The only tonic he needed was remaining engrossed with his study area and sharing knowledge with young students. He refused to accept the honorarium that the institutions offered him and instead donated it to libraries.

So many eminent academicians we have encountered over the years, all of them profoundly erudite and intellectually gifted. However, there is hardly any hesitation for us to say that Prof. Bhattacharya's love for his subject was something very unique, if not extraordinary. Prof. Bhattacharya is known even among his adversaries as a 'lover of anthropology', as 'he loves anthropology more than his life'. All these years anthropology was uppermost in his mind. Any topic, no matter how pedantic, no matter how monotonous and mundane it seemed to be, Prof. Bhattacharya had the potential to perceive it through an anthropological prism and make it relevant and worth pursuing; the latent idea being that each modicum of behaviour, no matter how petty or dizzy, how trivial or frivolous, is always an evocative entity and hence must be explained.

As a teacher too, Prof. Bhattacharya's dedication and sincerity were astonishing, for so tirelessly would he serve his students and the discipline that these would leave a lasting impression on his followers. There was something unique about his approach. He was never a promoter of his subject. He would never tell anybody to study anthropology or archaeology, nor would he ever explain the benefits of studying it. Yet the passion with which he taught would automatically kindle a strange curiosity in the hearts of his students that they would feel immensely inquisitive to know more about it.

Prof. Bhattacharya had that rare quality of being able to escape all sorts of academic snobbery. He was highly accessible, always available to his students. A man of gravity, but otherwise there was not a moment when his students would hesitate to knock at the doors of his cabin. He would always be there making himself available to his students. As a teacher, he had lived his life to the brim. Always surrounded by his students, so many minds he had nurtured and inspired over the years that one almost looses count. Much of his time was spent in his laboratory and study room, sometimes carrying out experiments, sometimes doing sketches, all for his students. All his students knew, no matter what the problem they were confronted with, that 'Sir' would always be there by their side. Not only would students approach him for discussing their problems in understanding prehistory which was a new subject to them, who had joined anthropology after their graduation in natural and biological sciences. They would also seek Prof. Bhattacharya's guidance on personal matters and he would readily extend a helping hand to them in terms of offering his counsel and providing financial support.

To make a meaningful sense out of Prof. Bhattacharya's academic life and contributions, we have a strong predilection to classify it as:

a. a physical anthropologist,
b. a lifelong learner and explorer of prehistory, and
c. a great contributor to the field of anthropological archaeology.

Prof. Bhattacharya's introduction to the anthropological world had been more as a physical anthropologist, having done his Ph.D. under Prof. P.C. Biswas on blood group analyses. However, there was from the very beginning a strong inclination on his part to explore the dark domains of prehistory, which was further honed once he reached up to Prof. H.D. Sankalia at the Deccan College. It was after his close association with Sankalia that his knowledge of archaeology, ethnology and palaeo-anthropology got a boost.

Here began Bhattacharya's interminable interest in the fields of lithic cultures and object analysis of associated objects along with tool type technology. Bhattacharya moved to Europe and deluged himself in the world of prehistory, making diligent attempts to understand prehistoric Europe with particular reference to all the tool vestiges that could be discovered. Sitting in Germany, he wrote *Palaeolithic Europe*, a true testament of his immense academic potential. However, while doing all these, Bhattacharya's inquisitiveness about Indian prehistory remained as strong as ever. He was disheartened with the Indian academic outlook in this context, and in fact found it locked in the Kuhnian 'pre-paradigmatic stage'. Even though archaeologists continuously exhumed prehistoric artifacts, Bhattacharya considered Indian archaeology as almost dead.

However, with the positive outlook Prof. Bhattacharya epitomizes, he now meticulously and diligently strived to explain transformation in Indian prehistory, particularly in geo-climatic terms. While explaining the Neolithic, he threw light on the absence of discussions and took upon himself the task of introducing the causative approach, i.e. how the cause of a change of one kind occurring at one place and absence of similar change in another place was a valid enough proposition in Indian prehistory.

In doing all these, Bhattacharya's interest and commitment towards archaeology increased further. And thus, particularly in his post retirement years, he delved deep into the field of anthropological archaeology. His brand of archaeology was deeply rooted in the theoretical columns of cultural analysis, neo-evolutionism, symbolism, hermeneutics, phenomenological interpretation, and ecological anthropology. His efforts to place anthropology at the centre of archaeology provoked him to explore models of social and physical anthropology, precisely through the lens of archaeology.

Prof. Bhattacharya was particularly worried about the descriptive nature of Indian archaeology and longed for its analytical phase to develop fast. For understanding the Palaeolithic India better, he relied to a great extent on models of technological analyses and evolutionary processes. He in fact used archaeological evidences to demonstrate ancient India as an active corridor for human migration. Despite Indian archaeology's steady progress, much to the liking of Prof. Bhattacharya, he was nonetheless worried about its obsession with the Lubbockian Geo-Zoological methodology, which he reckoned was a major impediment in successfully reconstructing the socio-cultural traits of any region at any time.

Synoptically speaking, if we are to assess Prof. Bhattacharya's academic outlook, we must understand that his primary academic objective was to cultivate within his students a strong desire to study prehistory, both fieldwork based and laboratory-oriented. Particularly remarkable has been his untiring effort throughout his life to bring students within the fold of prehistoric investigations covering geo-archaeology/contextual archaeology, palaeo-environmental study and various other findings related to lithic assemblages with a specific focus on reconstructing the survival strategies of prehistoric man. He made a concerted effort to inculcate a scientific perspective among his students.

Furthermore, Prof. Bhattacharya throughout his life behaved as a student of prehistoric study. There were essentially two perspectives through which he perceived the prehistoric world. Initially, he started working on tool types. As a result, his initial publications attempted to standardize the typo-technological aspects of prehistoric findings, like palaeoliths, mesoliths/microliths and neoliths. During later stages, he was frustrated with the typo-technological studies or simple 'prehistoric discoveries' and his later works reflect a synergy, a harmony between theoretical and practical observations regarding the prehistoric research of Indian subcontinent. Some of the major writings during this period include, "Is Prehistory Dead in India?", "Interpretation in Indian Stone Age Archaeology: A Reappraisal", "Out of Africa: Revisited within the Framework of Indian Prehistory", "Palaeolithic India and Human Dispersal", "Revisiting Issues of Transformation in Indian Prehistory".

For a man of his stature, awards and rewards were bound to come. Prof. Bhattacharya was no exception to this and he too had a highly prolific professional career. Recipient of the Dharani Dhar memorial plaque awarded by the University of Calcutta, he had also delivered the 1993 Panchanan Mitra Memorial Lecture at Calcutta's Asiatic Society. He had also delivered the D.N. Majumdar Memorial Lecture and was elected the President of the Anthropology and Archaeology section of the 86th Indian History Congress. His global recognitions were not few either. As a Member of Japan's Anthropological Society of Nippon, he had traversed the world, teaching and learning. In the calendar year 2003, for instance, within a span of few months he had travelled to USA, Germany and Czech Republic, all as a part of the Millennium Ecosystem Assessment programme.

However, he was never overwhelmed by the glitz and glamour of his academic career. Rather, a humble man that he was, he would feel as happy in Delhi as he was in Frankfurt, as energetic in Calcutta as in Prague. So often he was seen taking notes and writing papers silently even amidst all the clamor and clatter of the class rooms. There was hardly anything that could deter him. While travelling in train, particularly in field trips, so often would he sit alone, silently reading and writing amidst all that hustle and bustle around him.

But then all of what we have said about Prof. Bhattacharya is not mere eulogy. We have not written any panegyric. Rather, the statements about him are so true. They are exactly what we have seen him doing everyday, day and night. Enthralled by his personality, we feel no hesitancy in confessing that we have over the years not merely dreamt of being a scholar like him but also dreamt of being a teacher like him. There are indeed very few teachers in the real sense of the term and Prof. Bhattacharya was certainly one of them, whose classes students would rarely miss. He was a teacher par excellence, a great human being and a legendary figure in the field of Archaeology and Anthropology. His energy in taking classes amazed us all. His passion and love for the subject and students can hardly be matched. In his classes and in his room academic activities went on uninterrupted, without any break. As students and learners we will always miss him and his every beat of teaching we received so far and the wonderful time spent with him will remain with us for ever throughout our life.

Prof. Bhattacharya, the superbly dexterous and versatile academic that he was, had indeed thought much about archaeology and anthropology. In a befitting tribute to our great Indian anthropologist, it now stands as a cherished responsibility of ours to take up his unfulfilled dream and try to give some shape to it. In writing about our Prof. Bhattacharya, we are indeed tempted to quote Trenfor's famous lines, for these so well define him: "A good teacher is he who shows you where to look at but does not tell you what to see." Prof. Bhattacharya gave his students that all important freedom to see for themselves without being fixed to any pre-conceived notion of what to see.

REFERENCES

A Bibliography of Professor D.K. Bhattacharya

Books

Bhattacharya, D.K. 1972, 1990. *Prehistoric Archaeology: A Comparative Study of Human Succession.* Delhi: Hindustan Publishing Co.

Bhattacharya, D.K. 1977. *Palaeolithic Europe: A Summary of Some Important Finds with Special Reference to Central Europe.* Atlantic Highlands, N.J.: The Humanities Press and Oosterhaut, Netherlands: Anthropological Publications.

Bhattacharya, D.K. (ed.). 1978. *Anthropologists in India* (Revised Directory of Professional Anthropologists). Delhi: Indian Anthropological Association.

Bhattacharya, D.K. 1978. *The Emergence of Culture in Europe*: Delhi: B.R. Publishing Co.

Bhattacharya, D.K. 1979. *Old Stone Age Tools: A Manual of Laboratory Techniques of Analysis.* Calcutta: K.P. Bagchi & Co.

Bhattacharya, D.K. 1984. *Archaeology and Social Formation*. Delhi: Spectra of Anthropological Progress.

Bhattacharya, D.K. 1989, 1999, 2003. *An Outline of Indian Prehistory* (12th Reprint Edition). Delhi: Palaka Prakashan.

Bhattacharya, D.K. 1990. *Ecology and Social Formation in Ancient History*. Calcutta: K.P. Bagchi & Co.

Bhattacharya, D.K. 1994. *Steps to Indian Prehistory, Step 1*. Delhi: Arvind Publications.

Kalla, A.K. and D.K. Bhattacharya. 2003 (Eds). *Understanding People of India: Anthropological Insight*. Delhi: Department of Anthropology, University of Delhi, India.

Malik, S.L. and D.K. Bhattacharya. 1986. *Aspects of Human Ecology: A Dynamic Inter-Relation between Man and Environment*. New Delhi: Northern Book Centre.

Paper Published

Bhattacharya, D.K. 1962. "Betanin Excretion in Urine: A Preliminary Study among Three Indian Communities". *The Eastern Anthropologist*, 15(3): 50-54.

Bhattacharya, D.K. 1963. "Vital Capacity of the Jar Males of Punjab: A Modification of the Formulae Existing for its Computation". *Indian Journal of Medical Research*, 51(2).

Biswas, P.C. and D.K. Bhattacharya. 1963. "A Somatometric Study of the Bhil (Males) of Rajasthan". *The Anthropologist*, 11(1/2).

Bhattacharya, D.K. 1964. "The Palmar Dermatoglyphics of the Anglo-Indians of India". *Zeitschrift fur Morphologie und Anthropologie*, 55(3): 357-367.

Bhattacharya, D.K. 1964. "Tasting of P.T.C. among the Anglo-Indians of India". *Acta Geneticae Medicae et Gemellologiae* (Roma), 13(2): 159-166.

Biswas, P.C. and D.K. Bhattacharya. 1964. "An Anthropometric Study of the Juvenile Delinquents of India". *The Anthropologist*, 11(1 and 2): 25-34.

Bhattacharya, D.K. 1964. "Finger Dermatoglyphic Study of the Anglo-Indians of India". *Zeitschrift for Morphologie und Anthropologie*, 54(3): 346-354.

Bhattacharya, D.K. 1966. "Deviation Quotient of Digital Triradii: A New Dimension in Metric Variability of Palmar Dermatoglyphics". *Zeitschrift for Morphologie und Anthropologie,* 57(2): 199-206.

Bhattacharya, D.K. 1966. "Frequency of Colour Blindness among the Anglo-Indians of India". *Journal dr Genetique Humaine*, 15(1/2): 1-6.

Biswas, P.C. and D.K. Bhattacharya 1966. "Deviation Quotient of Digital Triradii: A New Variable in Palmar Dermatoglyphics." In *Proceedings Volume of International Symposium on Dermatoglyphics*. Edited by P.C. Biswas and A. Sharma, Delhi: Department of Anthropology, pp. 19-22, 317.

Bhattacharya, D.K. 1966. "A Note on the a-b Ridge-Count of the Anglo-Indians of India". In *Proceedings Volume of International Symposium on Dermatoglyphics*. Edited by P.C. Biswas and A. Sharma, Delhi: Department of Anthropology, pp. 251-253 and 330.

Biswas, P.C. and D.K. Bhattacharya. 1966. "Growth Trends in Northern Indian Population – Variation of Four Anthropometric Traits from Birth to Maturity (Cross-Sectional)". In *The Proceedings of the Symposium on Human Adaptability to Environments and Physical Fitness*. Edited by M. S. Malhotra, Madras: Defence Institute of Physiology and Allied Sciences, pp. 270-280.

Bhattacharya, D.K. 1968. "A Somatometric Study of the Anglo-Indians of India". Zinruigaku-Zassi: *The Journal of the Anthropological Society of Nippon*, 76(759): 21-30.

Bhattacharya, D.K. 1968-69. "The Anglo-Indians in Bombay: An Introduction to their Socio-Economic and Cultural Life". *Race: A Journal of Race and Group Relations*, 10: 163-172.

Bhattacharya, D.K. 1969. "Anthropometry of a Negro Population in India – Siddis of Gujarat". *Zinruigaku-Zassi: The Journal of the Anthropological Society of Nippon*, 77(5/6): 254-259.

Bhattacharya, D.K. 1969. "Comment to Trade and Culture Process in European Prehistory, by Colin Renfrew". *Current Anthropology*, 10(2-3): 162.

Bhattacharya, D.K. 1969, "A Study of RH-HR and MN Blood Groups of the Anglo-Indians of India". *Human Biology*, 41(1): 115-124.

Bhattacharya, D.K. 1970. "Indians of African Origin". *Cahiers D'Etudes Africaines*, 10(4): 579-582.

Bhattacharya, D.K. 1971. "Comments to Infectious Diseases in Ancient Populations", by T. Aidan Cockburn. *Current Anthropology*, 12(1): 54-55.

Bhattacharya, D.K. 1971. "Evolution of Man". *Science Reporter*, 6(8): 282-284.

Bhattacharya, D.K. 1971. "Variation of C-Line Terminations in the Palmar Dermatoglyphics: Three Co-ordinates as Possible Method of Population Discrimination ". *The Anthropologist*, 18(1 and 2): 41-44.

Bhattacharya, D.K. 1971. "Zum Problem der trager des Palaiolithikums in Indian and Ihrer Herkunft. Ethnologie." *Archaeologie, Zeitschrift*, 12(4): 487-493.

Bansal, I. J. S. and D.K. Bhattacharya, 1972. "Inheritance of C-Line Termination Types in Palmar Dermatoglyphics." *Zeitschrift for Morphologie und Anthropologie*, 63(3): 385-390.

Bhattacharya, D.K. 1972. "A_1A_2BO Blood Groups and Color Blindness among the Koyas of Kavartty Islands (Laccadive, Amindive and Minicoy Islands, India)". *The Eastern Anthropologist*, 25(1): 39-50.

Bhattacharya, D.K. 1972. *Prehistoric Archaeology: A Comparative Study of Human Succession*. Delhi: Hindustan Publishing Corporation.

Bhattacharya, D.K. 1973. "A Note on Authority and Leadership in a Matrilineal Society". *The Eastern Anthropologist*, 26(1): 95-99.

Bhattacharya, D.K. 1975. "Social Status of Anglo-Indians Women". *Social Work Forum*, 13(3): 17-22.

Bhattacharya, D.K. 1976. "Review to an Evolutionary Approach to the South-East Asian Cultural Sequence". *Current Anthropology*, 17(2): 229-301.

Bhattacharya, D.K. and P.K. Tewari 1977. "A late Palaeolithic Industry from Mirzapur". *The Eastern Anthropologist*, 31(2): 197-202.

Bhattacharya, D.K. 1977. *Palaeolithic Europe: A Summary of some Important Finds with Special Reference to Central Europe*. Netherlands: Humanities Press.

Bhattacharya, D.K. 1979. "Identity Crisis in Anthropology". *Spectra of Anthropological Progress*, 2:27-29.

Bhattacharya, D.K. 1979. "Typology of Culture: An Indian Example Discussed". *Man and Environment*, 2:93-98.

Chakraborti, Dilip K., D.K. Bhattacharya and R.K. Chattopadhyay. 1979-80. "Lithic Industries of Bankura". *Puratattva: Bulletin of the Indian Archaeological Society*, 11: 39-48.

Bhattacharya, D.K. and Dilip K. Chakraborti. 1981. "Three Soanian Implements from Dehra Gopipur, Kangra". *Indian Anthropologist*, 11(2): 163-164.

Bhattacharya, D.K. 1981. "Pragaitihasik Puratattva (in Hindi)". In *Prachin Bharat Ka Itihas*. Edited by D.N. Jha and K.M. Shrimali, Delhi: Hindi Madhyam Karanvay Nideshalay, University of Delhi, pp. 31-73.

Bhattacharya, D.K. and Sruti Kona Dey. 1982. "Microliths from Srirampur near Diamabad in Maharashtra". *Indian Anthropologist*, 12(2): 175-180.

Bhattacharya, D.K. 1982. "Early Man around Narmada". *Bionature*, 2:37-40.

Bhattacharya, D.K. 1983. "Conditions of the Emergence of Agriculture". *Man and Life: A Journal of the Institute of Social Research and Applied Anthropology*, 9(3 and 4): 169-179.

Banerjee, Saria and D.K. Bhattacharya. 1983. "A Note on the Discovery of Some Proto-Historic Mounds from Amritsar". *Indian Anthropologist*, 13(1): 51-53.

Joshi, P.C. and D.K. Bhattacharya. 1985. "Palaeoliths of Delhi". *The Eastern Anthropologist*, 38(4): 341-345.

Bhattacharya, D.K. 1986. "Palaeoanthroology: A Neglected Field of Indian Anthropology". *Indian Journal of Physical Anthropology and Human Genetics*, 12(1): 85-88.

Bhattacharya, D.K. 1987. "Conditions of Emergence of Agriculture". In *Archaeology and History: Essays in Memory of Shri A. Ghosh,* Volume 1. Edited by B.M. Pande and B.D. Chattopadhyay, New Delhi: Agam Kala Prakashan, pp. 11-17.

Ratha, S.N. and D.K. Bhattacharya. 1988. "Lower palaeoliths from Kuchinda (Orissa)". *Man and Environment*, 12: 23-27.

Bhattacharya, D.K. 1989. "The Deccan Neolithic (Chalcolithic). An Anthropological Explanation". In *Anthropology in Indian Context*. Edited by I.J.S. Bansal, New Delhi: Today and Tomorrow's Printers and Publishers, pp. 65-70.

Bhattacharya, D.K. and Arun Sonakia. 1989. "Cultural Remains from the Earliest Hominid Site on Narmada". In *Changing Perspectives of Anthropology in India*. Edited by S.C. Tiwari, New Delhi: Today and Tomorrow's Printers and Publishers, pp. 313-320.

Bhattacharya, D.K. 1989. "The Philosophy of Survival and the Choice of Technology for India Today". In *Changing Perspectives of Anthropology in India*. Edited by S.C. Tiwari, New Delhi: Today and Tomorrow's Printers and Publishers, pp. 351-361.

Bhattacharya, D.K. 1989. "Terracotta Worship in Fringe Bengal". In *The Meaning of Things. Material Culture and Symbolic Expression (One World Archaeology 6)*.Edited by Ian Hodder. London: Unwin Hyman, pp. 12-22.

Bhattacharya, D.K. 1991-1992. "Emergence of Neolithic in South Bihar: A Case of Stress Theory". *Journal of the Bihar Puravid Parishad*, 15 & 16: 31-47.

Bhattacharya, D.K. and Abhik Ghosh. 1992. "Ecology, Hypocrisy and Human Survival". *Indian Anthropologist*, 22(1):75-84.

Bhattacharya, D.K. 1992. "Punctuation Model in Culture Change: A Case of Mesolithic". *Journal of Indian Anthropological Society*, 27(3): 201-207.

Bhattacharya, D.K. 1993. "Is Prehistory Dead in India?" *Journal of the Asiatic Society*, 35(3): 52-73. (Read in 1992 under Panchanan Mitra Lecture Series).

Bhattacharya, D.K. 1994. *Provincial Museums and their Role in Rural Education*. Culture, Collection and Preservation, Calcutta.

Bhattacharya, D.K. 1995. "Origin of Family Re-Examined". *Trends in Social Science Research*, 11(1).

Bhattacharya, D.K. and Rahul Sen. 1995. "Issues in Social Structure: The Economy and Polity of Indus Valley Civilization". In *India at Dawn of History*. Edited by Ashok Datta, Ashok. K. Ghosh and C. Margabandhu, Delhi: Agam Kala Prakashan, pp. 175-195.

Bhattacharya, D.K. 1996. "Ecology and Human Destiny". In *Eco-Philosophy and Eco-Dharam*. Edited by P.R. Trivedi and Henrye Skotimovski, New Delhi: International Center for Eco-Philosophy and Indian Institute of Ecology and Environment, pp. 84-98.

Bhattacharya, D.K. 1996. "Towards a Regional Archaeology in India". In *Indian Archaeology Since Independence*. Edited by K.M. Shrimali, Delhi: Association for the Study of History and Archaeology, pp. 85-94.

Bhattacharya, D.K. and Rahul Sen. 1996. "Early Holocene Adaptation in India: An Anthropological Perspective". In *Exploration in Art and Archaeology of South Asia – Essays Dedicated to N.G. Majumdar*. Edited by Debela Mitra, Calcutta: Directorate of Archaeology and Museums, Government of West Bengal, Calcutta, pp. 97-113.

Bhattacharya, D.K. 1997. "History in Folk Culture". *Trends in Social Science Research*, 4(1).

Bhattacharya, D.K. and Manoj Kumar Singh. 1997-98. "The Palaeolithic Evidence from Pathalgarwa in Bihar". *Puratattva*, 28:12-25.

Bhattacharya, D.K. and Manoj Kumar Singh. 1997. "Shidihwa: A Late Palaeolithic Site from Kharagpur Valley of Bihar". *Indian Anthropologist*, 27(1): 29-55.

Bhattacharya, D.K. 1997. "Interpretative Archaeology for India". *The Eastern Anthropologist*, 50(3-4): 369-380.

Bhattacharya, D.K. 1998. "Ecology and Development". In *Contemporary Studies in Human Ecology: Human Factor, Resource, Management and Development*. Edited by M.K. Bhasin and S.L. Malik, Delhi: Kamla-Raj Enterprises, pp. 1-9.

Bhattacharya, D.K. and Manoj Kumar Singh. 1998. "Jurpaniya: The Epi-Palaeolithic Tradition of Kharagpur Valley in Chotanagpur Plateau". *Man in India*, 78 (3 and 4): 189-204.

Bhattacharya, D.K. 1998-1999. *Prehistory in India: An Urgent Need for Change*. Presidential Address read out at the 86th Science Congress.

Bhattacharya, D.K. 1999. "Prehistory in India: An Urgent Need for Change". *Man in India*, 79(1-2): 1-20.

Bhattacharya, D.K. 2000. "History of Hunger and Rise of Farming in South Bihar". *Man in India*, 80(1-2): 107-119.

Bhattacharya, D.K. 2000. "The Warning of Nature We Missed". In *Man-Environment Relationship*. Edited by M.K. Bhasin and Veena Bhasin, Delhi: Kamla-Raj Enterprises, pp. 309-313.

Bhattacharya, D.K. 2000. "Rethinking in Indian Anthropology". *The Anthropologist*, 2(1): 1-5.

Bhattacharya, D.K. 2000. "Indian Anthropology in Next Century". In *Anthropology at the Turn of the Century*. Edited by R.N. Vasiṣhat, B.G. Banerjee, R.K. Pathak and C.J. Edwin. Chandigarh: Department of Anthropology, Punjab University, pp. 1-8.

Bhattacharya, D.K. 2000. "Future Prospects of Human Evolutionary Studies". *The Anthropologist*, 2(2): 107-111.

Bhattacharya, D.K. 2000. "Anthropological Probing in Indian Mesolithic". In *Felicitation Volume in Honor of Prof. Gopala Sarana*. P. K. Mishra, Mysore.

Bhattacharya, D.K. and Manoj Kumar Singh. 2000. "Bharatiya Puratattva Vigyan Ke Naye Dristikone (in Hindi)". *Gyan Garima Sindhu*, 2-3: 30-36.

Bhattacharya, D.K. and Manoj Kumar Singh. 2000-2001. "Adhwariya: A New Palaeolithic Site from Kharagpur Hills, South Bihar". *Puratattva*, 31:16-24.

Bhattacharya, D.K. 2001. "Vision of Anthropology and Archaeology in India in the Twenty First Century". Dibrugarh: Bulletin of the Department of Anthropology, Dibrugarh University, 29:1-6.

Bhattacharya, D.K. 2001. "Old Age in Prehistory". *Journal of Human Ecology*, 12(4): 301-305.

Bhattacharya, D.K. 2001. "Anthropology and Social Health". *The Anthropologist*, 3(3): 195-199.

Bhattacharya, D.K. 2001. "Comment on the Bronze Age: Unique Instance of a Pre-industrial World System by Shereen Ratnagar". *Current Anthropology* 42(3): 366.

Bhattacharya, D.K. 2002. "Mesolithic in India: An Anthropological View". *The Eastern Anthropologist*, 55(1): 57-70.

Bhattacharya, D.K. and Deepra Bhattacharya. 2002. "Agro-Pastoralism in Contemporary Ethnography: Its Relevance in Explanation of Archaeological Material in India". In *Indian Archaeology in Retrospect Volume III*. S. Setter and Ravi Korisetter, New Delhi: ICHR and Manohar, pp. 155-168.

Bhattacharya, D.K. 2004. "Prehistory of India Revisited". *The Eastern Anthropologist*, 57(1): 29-44.

Bhattacharya, D.K. 2004. "Prehistoric Sequence Dating: A Review". In *Science in Archaeology and Archaeo-Materials*. Edited by Arun Kumar Biswas, pp. 37-46. New Delhi: D.K. Printworld (Pvt.) Ltd.

Bhattacharya, D.K. 2006. "Interpretation in Indian Stone Age Archaeology: A Reappraisal". *Puratattva*. 36: 12-23.

Bhattacharya, D.K. 2008. "Out of Africa: Revisited within the Framework of Indian Prehistory". *Puratattva*. 38: 16-23.

Bhattacharya, D.K. 2011. "Palaeolithic India and Human Dispersal". *Ancient India*. 1: 69-86.

Bhattacharya, D.K. 2017. "Revisiting Issues of Transformation in Indian Prehistory". *Man and Environment*. Vol. 40 (1): 1-10.

11
Professor Amitabha Basu, Indian Statistical Institute and Our Research

Susmita Mukhopadhyay

Let me first of all pay homage through this article to my teacher, Professor Amitabha Basu, and then highlight personal, professional and academic domains of his life based on his field of research and our experiences as well as involvement in a process initiated by him. I have no hesitation to say that by being a part of it, I could proceed towards building my research career on the one hand and get a feel of humanistic anthropology on the other. Professor Basu (our beloved *Amit-da)* was otherwise known as an internationally reputed anthropologist, an excellent teacher, a conscientious scientist and a great human being. Since he breathed his last on 12 December, 2009, we, his students, have been grappling with the stupendous task to imbibe his academic philosophy and fulfil his dream of consolidating academic anthropology at ISI.

Prof. Subho Ray, Prof. Basu's youngest doctoral student, has already provided a portrayal of life and works of Amitabha Basu, in the form of his own tribute to him through a skillfully written article published in 'Architects of Anthropology in India' edited by Prof. Sarthak Sengupta. He dealt at length with Prof. Basu's life events and his academic achievements citing examples of his leading papers and research projects. Of course, he mentioned about other anecdotes of his life, especially about his philosophy of life which is also reflected in his works (Roy, 2021). Besides, Prof. Mukhopadhyay presented a synoptic portrayal of Prof. Basu's personal and academic life in his passionately written obituary (Mukhopadhyay, 2011).

Here in my article I have chosen to give an account of his life stories centring mainly around his academic life at ISI and seeking reflection and continuity of his academic philosophy in our research.

I

Professor Amitabha Basu was born on 6th January, 1938 in his maternal grandfather's residence located in a village in East Bengal (now in Bangladesh). He hails from a very respectable family. His parental home is in Subhasgram in the district of South 24 Parganas. Professor Basu's father Parbati Shankar Basu was a lawyer by profession. Unfortunately, he lost his mother when he was a two-and-a-half-year-old child and he was brought up under the loving care of his aunt (father's sister). His paternal home was located in 2, Circus Avenue in Beckbagan area of Kolkata. He used to take pride in this house where he stayed for a long time and where he got the warmth of his family elders being the eldest son in his generation. Affection from his father and aunts was something which had given him mental strength and solace. Being a member of a traditional joint family, throughout his life he had to shoulder many family responsibilities remaining solidly behind the family in the hours of need, especially after his father's demise. The elder sister's family members, especially the nephew and nieces were his very dear ones. The last decade of his life was spent in his 55/A, Mahanirban Road (in south Kolkata) residence. Prof. Basu's personal life revolved around his family members comprising kin, both immediate and extended, who included father, elder sister, brother-in-law, nephew, nieces, cousins, uncle and aunt. He didn't enter into wedlock and considered his students to be the members of his own family.

II

Professor Basu's schooling was in a south Kolkata school, Tirthapati Institution, which carries a long tradition in the history of education. After the completion of school education in 1954, he joined Moulana Azad College (then named as Central Calcutta College) for his graduation in science stream and did his Honours classes in Anthropology in the post-graduate Department of Anthropology, Calcutta University located at the Ballygunge Science College (now named as Taraknath Palit Shiksha Prangan). His post-graduation years ranged between1958-1960. He stood first in M.Sc. in Anthropology and was a gold medalist. Having passed M.Sc. in 1960, Basu decided to go ahead with pursuing Ph.D. in Anthropology with specialization in Physical Anthropology (now it is called as Biological Anthropology) in the University of Calcutta under the supervision of Dr. Sasanka Sekhar Sarkar, the doyen of Physical Anthropology. Prof. Basu undertook a population genetic study among the Pahiras, a small sized tribal community inhabiting Ayodhya and Dalma Hills of the Purulia district of West Bengal, for his doctoral research. This study proved to be a novel one because of the fact that his analysis of demographic and biological data among the studied population could reveal distinct population level differentiation in terms of geographical and other biological factors. The results were published in the *American Journal of Physical Anthropology* (Basu, A., 1969). By virtue of this seminal work Prof. Basu obtained D.Sc. instead of Ph.D. degree, for which he initially worked, from CU. The Examiner of the thesis was none other than Prof. Curt Stern, who was a renowned human geneticist.

Dr. S.S. Sarkar, who was very often remembered by Basu, was popularly known in the Department of Anthropology of Calcutta University as '*Sarkar Mosai*' and certainly he was a very popular teacher. To his students he was 'Sir' and each one of them became very close to his heart. We have heard many stories about the relationship between Dr. Sarkar and his students generating much affection and love. I'm tempted to quote few lines from the introductory Chapter of the book "Physical Anthropology and its Extending Horizons", S.S. Sarkar Memorial Volume, edited by A. Basu, A.K. Ghosh, S.K. Biswas and R. Ghosh in 1972. They write, "For us he was much more than a mere teacher within the narrow limits of a specific academic discipline. He was our preceptor in life in a wide context, where the boundaries of specific academic disciplines fade out and become integrated in a wide world of reality, awareness and conscious human action. He has been for us a symbol of uprightness, wisdom, fearless zeal and undaunted optimism and of an analytical, holistic and action-oriented attitude towards life. It is in the upholding of these qualities and values that the memory of Sarkar will continue to be with us. What a student could acquire from him was not only a set of concepts and techniques—which are decidedly useful as methodological tools but are not ends in themselves—but a mental orientation which demands looking at Man not as a *thing* but in terms of a *process*, and a continuum of change, set in the perspective of the total physico-bio-psycho-social milieu".The paragraph above is a testimony to the feeling of depth in relationship between a teacher and his students.The foundation of Prof. Basu's anthropological career, as indicated by him in his lifetime through his accounts and statements, was solidly based on the academic inspiration derived from his teacher Dr. Sarkar. From all indications, it appears that Prof. Basu was in favour of accepting the holistic paradigm of academic anthropology encompassing its social relevance. To us, those who were Prof. Basu's students, the genesis of his holistic mentorship and its proper value was a late realization.

III

In 1967, Prof. Basu got an opportunity to join the Indian Statistical Institute, Kolkata founded by Professor P.C. Mahalanobis (PCM), who himself took an avid interest in bio-anthropological research. In a project initiated by PCM in collaboration with H.L. Shapiro on the measurement of urban stress in the slum dwellers of Calcutta, Prof. Basu had the opportunity to contribute his bit at the academic level. This also gave him the chance of interacting with PCM. However, his association with this project discontinued following his obtaining Fulbright fellowship during 1967-69.

After joining the Department of Anthropology, University of North Carolina at the Chapel Hill as a Post-doctoral Fellow, he had the opportunity to work in Haiti on demographic-genetic aspects of Haitian population. At Chapel Hill, his mentor was Professor William Sprott Pollitzer whose inspiration and academic depth touched Prof. Basu and which remained as a benchmark almost throughout his lifetime. The experiences at Chapel Hill and the nature of relationship with Professor Pollitzer and family have come up for a special mention by Prof. Basu in Prof. Pollitzer's obituary written by him (Basu, 2002).

Prof. Basu rejoined ISI after the completion of Fulbright Fellowship and continued his research activities for a while. In 1974, however, he left for the UK to join the Department of Human Genetics, University of New Castle upon Tyne, as a visiting Fellow. During this visit to UK, his academic interaction with Prof. Derek Roberts provided him with the opportunity to be trained in laboratory techniques on chromosome studies. Upon his return to India at ISI, in the capacity of a Senior Lecturer, he established a Chromosome Research Laboratory and started working on chromosomal abnormalities.

It remains clear that with the call of time and prioritizing his own career interest and full time involvement, he did superb and ahead of time population genetic and human chromosomal studies among the Pahiras, Haitian populations and so on. But then, during 1970s, his concerns in the paradigm of social relevance of anthropological studies got reflected in his undertaking of further studies as a Faculty of ISI. Basu preferred to shift to human population biological studies under the rubric of Human Adaptability Studies.

During that time, international research programmes, viz. International Biological Programme (IBP, 1964-1974), sponsored by International Union of Biological Sciences (IUBS), Man and Biosphere (MAB), and by UNESCO (in 1971) became real motivational instruments to change scientists' line of thinking and orientation all-over the world, prompting them to undertake researches on human communities inhabiting a wide variety of ecological settings for evaluation and estimation of their biological and health profiles in relation to genetic and environmental factor complexes under the Human Adaptability Section of IBP. For quite some time, Prof. Amitabha Basu became an indispensable part of it.

During early 1976, Prof. Basu developed a research programme namely 'Human Adaptability Programme' (HAP) in the then Anthropometry and Human Genetics Unit of ISI. HAP has been a multidisciplinary programme of ISI based on inter-Unit collaboration conducted since 1976 following the recommendations of the International Biological Programme of UNESCO mainly aimed at evaluating the health status of various human communities of eastern India in relation to their physical, biological and socio-cultural environments. Appropriate anthropological, clinical/medical and statistical tools were used to analyse the variety of data generated for implementing the projects under this programme. It was envisaged that the projects under this research programme would be able to help the cause of social welfare and national development, which is one of the objectives of ISI. Attainment of such an objective was also possible in due course by initially providing systematic information and advice for conducting further research and/or formulating realistic rural health programmes. Several types of data were collected for this purpose, viz. socio-economic condition, demography, adult body size, child growth, haematology, intestinal parasitic infestation, general physical (medical) characteristics, dietary status and blood genetic polymorphisms, from a number of populations inhabiting contrasting physical environmental zones covering deltaic and hill mountain regions. Within each zone, data were collected from different ethnic/linguistic/religious groups and within some of the groups from their socio-economic sub-groups. The strategy for data collection from groups and sub-groups was made with a view to examine not only the individual effects of the causative factors but also of the relative effects of the different sets of causative factors on the health measures considered appropriate. The other expectation was to develop suitable statistical tools in collaboration with the statisticians of ISI for measuring the relative effects of the sets of factors considered.

Under HAP, the following specific projects were undertaken:

Impact of altitude on human populations to evaluate altitude related physical environmental stresses on human biological traits

The objective of this project was to examine the effects of altitude on biology and health of the Sherpas of the Eastern Himalaya. Sherpas of Solu, a village in Upper-Khumbu, Nepal with an altitude of >10,000 ft. and Kalimpong with an altitude of <5000 ft. were compared in respect of demographic, anthropometric, haematological, dietary and medical traits. Indeed, altitude effect was discernible in some traits. Furthermore, this study considered comparison of low altitude Sherpas with low altitude Lepchas, the former being migrant and later indigenous adapted to low altitude. The study pointed out that apart from high altitude stress, characterized by hypoxic hypoxia and other environmental stresses, socio-economic and cultural factors do matter in the manifestation of health status of communities. Prof. Basu's first Ph.D. student Ranjan Gupta did this study and became an established scholar in high altitude studies in India. This landmark project under HAP of high altitude studies was possible because he was in ISI, which he himself admitted. Prof. Charles Weitz of Temple University, USA also contributed much in the high altitude studies in Nepal did have continuous academic interactions with Prof. Basu.

Apart from the above-mentioned high altitude study, his other projects were on:

(i) Migration and Health Status: conducted by Chumki Piplai among Oraon tea-garden labourers in Jalpaiguri.
(ii) Socio-economic Condition, Nutrition and Health Status: conducted by Premananda Bharati among Mahishyas of rural Howrah.
(iii) Socio-cultural Profiles and Health Status: conducted by Barun Mukhopadhyay among the Lepchas of Kalimpong areas.
(iv) Labour Productivity and Health Status: conducted by Subrata K. Roy among Oraon tea-garden labourers in Jalpaiguri district.
(v) Working Status, Stress and Health of Working and Non-Working Mothers: conducted by me among groups of women in Kolkata city.
(vi) Dietary Practices, Food Sharing and Health Status: conducted by Mita Chakraborty in rural south 24-Parganas.
(vii) Aging and Health Status: conducted by Mitali Das among the elderly population in Kolkata city.

(viii) Poverty, Impoverishments and Health Status: conducted by Subho Ray among populations inhabiting squatters of Kolkata city.

In addition to the projects mentioned above, Prof. Basu's other projects of significance were:

(a) A study on health and biological profile of the Portuguese descendants as against the neighbouring Hindu caste groups. The project was based on Mirpur near Geonkhali area of Purba Medinipur. It was an interesting place for study, initially meant for population genetics and thereafter for demographic and other related studies. All the male students of Prof. Basu, till mid-1980s, had the opportunity to conduct demographic and interrelated studies in Mirpur and surrounding villages. This was practically the site for learning data collection methods, especially that of demography, anthropometry and related fields. Actually rigor in fieldwork was learnt from here in order to be able to move to other places for Ph.D. work.
(b) A study on evaluation of elderly health and nutritional status in old-age homes of Kolkata. It was based on dietary intake pattern, body composition, intestinal parasitic load and other health indicators among the inmates of two old-age homes in Calcutta city.
(c) A study on the spatial and temporal distribution of intestinal parasites among several social groups in West Bengal focusing particularly on the distribution pattern of intestinal parasites in culturally distinguishable communities of West Bengal.

Prof. Basu produced nine Ph.Ds. in all, who worked under his supervision to answer research questions pertaining to a variety of aspects of health of a number of communities inhabiting diverse ecological settings in the State of West Bengal, and also in Nepal, as mentioned earlier. Prof. Basu was too firm about the rigors of fieldwork. He didn't ever compromise on field training and was staunchly against any short-cut method to be followed in field-work.

Other than supervising nine Ph.D. works, he produced dissertations, many standard publications which appeared in national/international journals. Of course, we, the students of Prof. Basu, got the opportunity to develop ourselves and built our professional career by trying to follow his line of approach and paradigm of work set by him. Both harder and softer sides of his personality had had some influence on us and made us anthropologists, who are still in the making if we go by his standard.

ISI, during 1970s, 1980s and partly in 1990s was a flourishing institution that offered both resources and freedom to its scientists pursuing research in which application of Statistics was a must. Research on Human Adaptability conducted by Prof. Basu continued till he retired in January 1998. For this ISI funding was made available, besides other sources of finance.

After his retirement, he continued to think a lot on his type of anthropology, and concentrated on publishing, giving some expression of his thoughts. However, I am not going into the details of such publications to avoid repetition [glimpses of which are available in Roy, 2021].

Apart from his Ph.D. supervision in which he had excelled, he was considered to be a very popular teacher of anthropology for B-Stat. students of ISI. Prof. Basu was also an able academic administrator. He served as Head, Anthropometry & Human Genetics Unit as well as Professor-in-Charge, Biological Sciences Division of ISI. He served in many administrative and review committees in ISI and elsewhere. He was a person who genuinely believed in the philosophy behind ISI's formation and was proud of being a part of it. His contribution towards ISI administration covering different aspects is noteworthy. I did observe his nature of interaction with many of his ISI colleagues across divisional boundaries and could hardly remember any occasion when his acceptability was questioned. He was also popular among ISI workers of different categories.

Prof. Basu and Prof. K.C. Malhotra, who now can be considered as a living legend in the field of biological anthropology and human ecology, were equally responsible for earning ISI a great name in both national and international arenas of anthropology. We consider ourselves fortunate to have been part of their academic tutelage.

Prof. Basu and late Prof. Alok Ghosh (our beloved *Alok-da*) of NEHU were students of Dr. Sarkar and were very close friends. Both were bachelors and both left us untimely depriving us of their much-needed guidance. Prof. Ghosh's academic sojourn at ISI was no less educative for us. It also gives me the opportunity to put on record substantial contributions made by Prof. Ranajit Chakraborty and Prof. Partha Majumder, both ISI students and stalwarts in the field of Statistics and Genetics, to the cause of Biological Anthropology. Unfortunately, we have lost Prof. Chakraborty a few years back.

During his ISI days, we were fortunate enough to be able to academically interact with Professors Derek Roberts, Geoffrey Harrison, Edward Clegg, Pavao Rudan, Igor DeGarine, Henrik Forsius, who visited ISI on Prof. Basu's invitation. The person who put indelible mark on his academic life was Prof. Paul Baker of Penn State University (and his wife Mrs. Thelma Baker). Prof. Baker and one of his students Prof. Charles Weitz remained very close to Prof. Basu till his retirement and visited ISI more than once.

IV

It goes without saying that Prof. Basu was respected, loved and adored by members of the larger anthropology fraternity in India. To his contemporaries, his colleagues, both elder and younger, Prof. Basu was held in high esteem. He was linked with PG education in Anthropology in various capacities. His association with different Universities in India in respect of fixing assignments on anthropological education, his fruitful participation in matters of organization of professional bodies of Anthropology has left an indelible mark in the process of growth of Anthropology in India. He was associated with the Vidyasagar University, Midnapur in the formative years of its Department of Anthropology in working out the strategy for formulation of the syllabi and course content. Not only that, he also played his part in encouraging the young faculty of the Department to begin their teaching career in right earnest. As a teacher in the Department of Anthropology of Calcutta University [between 1972 and 1974], Prof. Basu could leave a lasting impression among his students. Prof. Basu took active part in the functioning of several professional bodies of Anthropology,in India and abroad (see Mukhopadhyay, 2011 for details) and attended many International/National Conferences, Workshops in various capacities. Simultaneously, he encouraged his research students like us to be involved in the activities of the professional bodies of Anthropology and wanted us to actively participate in national and even international conferences and seminars.

Prof. Basu was an ethicist par excellence. From our research experience we could observe that he never dreamt of being unethical in his deeds and actions. When he collected his data set for research or even when we collected our doctoral research data, we didn't have to face ethics committees because through his teachings, formal or informal, we tried to remain ethical all the time. On his instructions, we took verbally informed consent from our study participants. As a matter of fact, our interest, in research ethics predates his teachings on ethics for both research and all aspects of life.

I have found him avoiding self-publicity of his achievements. Self-praise or appreciation was something he would carefully avoid. He discouraged us once to bring out a 'Felicitation Volume' in his honour. However, because of other reasons we had to drop the idea midway through.

Basu was an ardent follower of Leftist ideology and his erudition on Marxist literature is noteworthy. *Che Guevara* was his hero, as we have often been told. He wholeheartedly supported Leftist movement in the 1970s in Bengal and remained pro-poor all throughout his life and used to provide monetary help, on a monthly basis, to many poor persons till his death.

V

Since 1976 to 1990s, nine of us, enrolled as his Ph.D. students, were fortunate enough to receive fatherly affection and guidance from him. He continued his teacher's (Dr. S.S. Sarkar) tradition in maintaining '*Guru-Sishya parampara*' (continuity) and we, on our part, have tried our best to follow him in maintaining that tradition.

In the concluding part of this presentation, while expressing my gratitude to him as my teacher, I would like to say that those of us who became faculty members at ISI and elsewhere have been trying our best to continue the tradition of bio-cultural anthropological research established by him at ISI. In fact, each one of us, in our own modest way, have tried to further that tradition with available resources, while keeping in mind the continuous development of research areas in terms of both theoretical and methodological inputs of research replete with new research questions.Thus, the type of bio-cultural anthropology followed by us has to put emphasis on trans-disciplinary approach, social relevance and human welfare, all of which could be attributed to him either directly or indirectly.

To be more specific,

(i) Prof. Ranjan Gupta continued till his retirement in 2013 to answer questions on the health changes of migrant high altitude Tibetans in urban environments of low altitude;

(ii) Prof. Premananda Bharati till his superannuation in 2016 examined how over time socio-economic condition changes with its imminent health impacts in rural communities;

(iii) Prof. Barun Mukhopadhyay, till his superannuation in 2019 examined geographical variation *vis-à-vis* cultural variation of the health status of the Lepchas and Bhutias of Darjeeling and Sikkim Himalayas as well as carried out a number of investigations on several bio-cultural dimensions of aging;

(iv) Prof. Subrata Roy continued measuring the influence of labour productivity on health across different occupational groups in Jalpaiguri ranging from tea garden to agricultural labourers; and

(v) I had chosen to examine health of women in their life course, i.e. adolescence, middle-aged and elderly living in affluence as well as in relatively resource poor settings in the city of Kolkata.

Needless to say, five of us who have got the opportunity to serve in ISI as faculty and the rest (4 others) attached with other Institutions have contributed as per their research interests and priorities. The common theme on which all of us have endeavoured to pursue our research revolves round his chosen path of answering pertinent questions on human adaptability or more specifically, bio-cultural adaptation.

VI

A towering anthropological personality in the name of Amitabha Basu was an asset to Indian Anthropology and was undoubtedly one of the best in his generation of anthropologists. Indian anthropological fraternity will remember him and implore the new generation anthropologists to emulate his example.

As students we have shared his joys and sorrows. We became co-sharers of his anxieties, worries, successes and even failures because he used to consider us part of his life. Prof. Basu was truly our friend, philosopher and guide and would remain so as long as we remain alive. There is an apprehension that in ISI after 2022 none will be there to pursue anthropological research, as it stands today. That will be a sad commentary on a rich tradition set up by visionaries like Prof. Amitabha Basu. We can only hope that our students will continue to pursue bio-cultural research in anthropology that they have learnt from ISI, their institution of work. And thus, Prof. Basu's cherished research tradition can continue even if with a changing direction and hopefully in a new set up.

Acknowledgements

I owe a debt of gratitude to all the students of Prof. Basu from whom, I had the opportunity to come to know many things of him in addition to my own observations.

I am thankful to Madhusree Gupta, Prof. Basu's elder niece for providing some information about Prof. Basu which I was not aware of.

REFERENCES

Basu, A., Ghosh, A.K., Biswas, S.K. and Ghosh, R. Eds. 1971. "Introduction" In: *Physical Anthropology and Its Extending Horizons.* Orient Longman, Calcutta. pp. 1-15.

Basu, A. 2002. "Obituary: William Sprott Pollitzer". *Journal of the Indian Anthropological Society*, 37: 295-296.

Basu, A. 1969. "Pahira: A population genetical study". *American Journal of Physical Anthropology,* 31: 399-416.

Mukhopadhyay, B. 2011. "Obituary: Amitabha Basu". *Journal of the Indian Anthropological Society,* 46: 119-122. "Works of Amitabha Basu". In: *Architects of Anthropology in India,* Volume I. Edited by S. Sengupta. Gyan Publishing House, New Delhi, pp. 251-268.

Roy, S. 2021. "Life and Works of Amitabha Basu: A Tribute". In: *Architects of Anthropology in India,* Volume I. Edited by S. Sengupta. Gyan Publishing House, New Delhi, pp. 251-268.

Index

Abject poverty and social neglect, 42
Action Research Unit, 61
Anglo-Indians, 99
Anthropological Survey of India, 17
Anthropology and sociology, relation between, 94
Anthropology, essence of bio-cultural perspectives in, 111
Article 38(2), 7
Article 38, 7
Ascetics of Kashi, 23
Assam Census, 2
Association for Anthropological Diplomacy, Politics and Society, 67
Association of Third World Anthropology, 67
Autonomous Councils, 8, 9

Banaras (Varanasi), 17, 18
Banerjee, Biswanath,
  a teacher and a mentor, 130
  academic connections and activities connected with academic administration, 124
  as a teacher in anthropology, 123
  contributions to anthropology, 126
  early life and education, 122
  lessons left, 132
  personality and identity, 125
  remembering his teaching of anthropology, 121-134
Basu, Amitabha (Professor), Indian Statistical Institute and our research, 148-159
Bhattacharya, Dibyendu Kanti, in the memory of, 135-147
Bhowmick, Prabodh Kumar (Professor),
  a brief life sketch, 39
  an action-*cum*- development anthropologist of India, 39-54
  Bidisa –the dream project of, 46
  contributions beyond anthropology, 50
  doctoral work, 41
  international exposure, 50
  major contributions in Indian anthropology of, 47
  post-retirement activities and supervision of Ph.D. works, 51
  seminal contributions to anthropology, 44
'Bhutan Mela', 3
Biological Anthropology, 150
Biswanath Banerjee (BNB), 121, 123
British Empire, 15
Buddhist neophyte, 18

Centre for Archaeological Studies and Training in Eastern India, 137
Chenchus, 48
Chin Hills Regulation, 1896, 8
Collective marginalization, 6
Comparative method, 90
Constitution of India, 5
Council of the Indian Anthropological Society, xii
Criminal tribe, 43
Cultural anthropology, 71

Deka, Usha (Professor),
  a humanist to the core, 32-38
  Recorder of Anthropology and Archaeology
DNA technology, 102
Down Syndrome patients, 100

Ethnography, 74, 88

Father of Indian Ethnology, 56

Ganguly, Pranab,
  a rare kind of anthropologist, 69-82
  story of human adaptation, 75

Hindu civilization, 57
History, down the Boulevard of, 14
Human Adaptability Programme, 152
Human rights, 2

ILO Conventions, 12
Impact of altitude on human populations to evaluate altitude related physical environmental stresses on human biological traits, 153
Indian Anthropology Association, 33
Indian anthropology, 56
Indian civilization, 14, 22
Indian Cultural Tradition, 24
Indian Science Congress, 103, 110
Indianness, 62
Institute of Social Research and Applied Anthropology, 46
Integrated Tribal Development Project (ITDP), 61
International Congress of Anthropological and Ethnological Sciences (ICAES), 66
International Union of Anthropological and Ethnological Sciences (IUAES), 66
International Union of Biological Sciences (IUBS), 152

Kibbutz, 92

Laukik tradition, 18, 19
Liberation of the self and liberation of the community, 5
Linguistic anthropology, 60
Little and Great Traditions, 19

Man and Biosphere (MAB), 152
Man and Life, 45
Model Ashram hostel, 46
Mukherjee, Deba Prasad (Professor),
  and biocultural research in anthropology in India, 108
  and the essence of bio-cultural approach in anthropology in India, 98-120
  as teacher and research guide, 101

contributions to anthropological research, 103
on anthropological genetics of quantitative variations, 105
on dermatoglyphics, 104
on methods for studying human quantitative traits, 106
initiation in Anthropology of, 98

N.K. Bose Memorial Foundation, 16
Naxalite movement, 52
NEFA, 33
North East India, 1, 6, 8
North-East India: Ethno-Cultural Perspectives and Process, 4

Onge, policy issues around the, 73
Oral Cultural Tradition (OCT), 18, 24

Particularly Vulnerable Tribal Groups, 45, 47

Reality Myth, 21
Report of the North-East Frontier (Assam) Tribal and Excluded Areas Subcommittee (Bordoloi Committee), 1
Roy Burman, B.K., 1
an expert in North East Indian tribal affairs, 2
North East India holds a special place of importance in study of, 1-13

Sacred Complex, 58
Sarana, Gopala,
and his contributions to anthropology, 83-97
anthropological theories, 88
background, academic life and activities, 83
holistic nature of anthropology, 86
on methodological grounds, 90
synoptic view on his contributions in the academic field, 85
Sarana-Beteille Debate, 94
Saraswati, Baidyanath,
a life's journey from Mithila to Varanasi via Gaya and Calcutta, 16
mythologising the reality, 21
UNESCO Professor, 16
walking with on the road to Indian civilization, 14-31
Scheduled Tribes, 5, 6
Seventy-third (73rd) Amendment of the Constitution,7
Sixth Schedule to the Constitution (Amendment) Act, 1995, 8
Social Cultural Profile of Kashi, 19
South-east Asia, 15
Swadeshi movement, 15

Task Force on the Development of Tribal Areas of Planning Commission, 61
Textual Cultural Tradition (TCT), 18
The Eastern Anthropologist, 70
Timelessness, 21
Tradition(s), 26
Transcendental Cultural Tradition (Trans-CT), 18
Tribes of North East India, 11

UNESCO project, 99
UNWGIP's Draft Declaration 1993, 12

Vidyarthi, Lalita Prasad,
action and applied anthropology: welfare and development, 60
an anthropologist with a difference, 55-68
and Department of Anthropology in Ranchi, 65
expansion of the discipline of anthropology, 64
grooming the students, 63
in 1960s, 57
in search of Indianness, 62
initiation into anthropology, 56
President of the IUAES, 66
seminars and conferences, 65
understanding Indian civilization, 58
understanding the processes of urbanization and industrialization, 59

Village Studies' programme, 3

World Anthropology series, 75

interest in research ethics predates his teaching [illegible] ethics for both research and all aspects of life.

I have found him avoiding self-publicity of his achievements. Self-praise or appreciation was something he would carefully avoid. He discouraged us once to bring out a 'Felicitation Volume' in his honour. However, because of other reasons we [illegible] enough.

Basu was an ardent [illegible] literature is noteworthy. The Gu[illegible] as we have been told. He wholeheartedly supported [illegible] movement in the [illegible] in Bengal and [illegible] all through his life and used [illegible]

[illegible] 1970 to 1990 [illegible]

[illegible]